CW00926770

THE NEW INSTITUTIONAL ARCHITECTURE OF EASTERN EUROPE

The New Institutional Architecture of Eastern Europe

Edited by

Stephen Whitefield
Lecturer in Russian and East European Studies
School of Slavonic and East European Studies
University of London

St. Martin's Press

First published in Great Britain 1993 by
THE MACMILLAN PRESS LTD
Houndmills, Basingstoke, Hampshire RG21 2XS
and London
Companies and representatives
throughout the world

This book is published in Macmillan's *Studies in Russia and East Europe*
Chairman of the Editorial Board: M. A. Branch, Director, School of Slavonic
and East European Studies

A catalogue record for this book is available from the British Library.

ISBN 0–333–55039–0

Printed in Great Britain by
Ipswich Book Co Ltd, Ipswich, Suffolk

First published in the United States of America 1993 by
Scholarly and Reference Division,
ST. MARTIN'S PRESS, INC.,
175 Fifth Avenue,
New York, N.Y. 10010

ISBN 0–312–10289–5

Library of Congress Cataloging-in-Publication Data
The new institutional architecture of Eastern Europe / edited by
Stephen Whitefield
p.   cm.
Includes index.
ISBN 0–312–10289–5
1. Europe, Eastern—Politics and government—1989–
2. Associations, institutions, etc.—Europe, Eastern.   3. Post
–communism—Europe, Eastern.   I. Whitefield, Stephen.
JN96.A2N492   1993
947'.0009'049—dc20
                                    93–22155
                                    CIP

Contents

List of Tables

Preface

Since 1989 there have been dramatic transformations in the political institutions of Eastern Europe. From the relative convergence in the region on the classic Soviet model of the one-party state, countries now exhibit divergent tendencies – in some cases resulting in the break-up of old states themselves. In all countries, however, the legacy of the communist past on society, parties, and the state continues to shape political structures today.

This book presents an analytical guide to the institutional architecture of Eastern Europe in transition. In two comparative chapters Gordon Smith and George Schopflin discuss the dilemmas of reform from communism to liberal democracy. The remainder of the book deals with the specific constellation of institutional power emerging in countries in the area. Among the main issues discussed are the constitutional debates, the relationship between parliament and executive, and the new party systems and elections.

The book began as a series of seminars in the winter of 1991 at the School of Slavonic and East European Studies in London. Since then, the process of institutionalisation and, in some case, institutional collapse, has continued at pace. I am very grateful to all the contributors for agreeing more than once to update their chapters to take account of events, as I am to Radojka Miljevic at SSEES and Tim Farmiloe for their patience. Before this book is published, no doubt, further change will have taken place, but I am confident that the book will both illuminate and anticipate developments to come.

STEPHEN WHITEFIELD

Notes on the Contributors

Judy Batt is a Lecturer in Soviet and East European Politics, Centre for Russian and East European Studies, University of Birmingham, and the author of *East Central Europe from Reform to Transformation* (London, 1991).

Richard Crampton is a University Lecturer in East European History at Oxford University, and Fellow of St Edmund Hall. He is the author of *A Short Histort of Modern Bulgaria* (Cambridge University Press, 1987).

David Dyker is a Senior Fellow at the Science Policy Research Unit, University of Sussex. He edited and contributed to *National Economies of Europe* (Longman, 1993).

Jonathan Eyal is the Director of Studies at the Royal United Services Institute and the editor of *The Warsaw Pact and the Balkans* (Macmillan, 1989).

Karen Henderson is a Lecturer in East European Politics at the University of Leicester and author of 'East German Politicians in the New Federal Republic' in J. Osmond (ed.), *German Re-unification: A Reference Guide and Commentary* (Longman, 1992).

George Kolankiewicz is the Co-ordinator of the Economic and Social Research Council East-West Programme and the author (with Paul Lewis) of *Poland: Politics, Economics, and Society* (1988).

Bill Lomax is a Lecturer in Sociology at the School of Social Studies, University of Nottingham, and the author of 'The Rise and Fall of the Hungarian Working Class', *The Journal of Communist Studies*, No. 2, 1990.

George Schopflin is a Lecturer in East European Political Institutions (jointly at the London School of Economics and Political Science and the School of Slavonic and East European Studies, University of London) and a contributor and editor (with Nancy Wood) of *In Search of Central Europe* (Polity, 1989).

Gordon Smith is Professor Emeritus at the University of London and the author of *Politics in Western Europe* (Dartmouth, 1989).

Stephen Whitefield is a Lecturer in Russian and East European Politics, School of Slavonic and East European Studies, University of London, and the author of *Industrial Power and the Soviet State* (Oxford University Press, 1993).

1 Transitions to Liberal Democracy

Gordon Smith

THE PROBLEM OF TRANSITION

One result of the upheavals in Eastern Europe over recent years is that we can now describe most of these countries as being strung out 'somewhere on the road' to liberal democracy. This rendering of where they now stand – and where they are heading – is vague, and it may be preferable to turn to the more exact terminology of political science. Yet not too much help should be expected, as becomes apparent in referring to the two terms that are particularly appropriate in discussing current changes – 'transition' and 'consolidation'.

Both convey the idea that discrete stages are involved and that each has a set of well-defined features. However, neither can be used in a precise way; so much is evident in seeking answers to questions that inevitably arise in analysing changes in Eastern Europe from one form of regime to another as well as in examining developments within a regime. When did a transition begin and how long is it likely to last? What are the different phases to be expected within a stage of transition? Are any to be counted as critical in affecting the future course of events? How can the decisive move from transition to consolidation be determined? Problems of clear demarcation abound: the beginnings of a transition may well, for instance, be located within the former regime, and so, too, can traces of transition persist even after a new regime has become consolidated.

Care has to be taken in applying ready-made labels, since the processes involved are not always self-evident, and no country will follow precisely the same course. At best we can say that during a transition the situation is still open-ended: there are several feasible outcomes, a partial reversion is one possibility, and only one route of several may lead to the consolidation of a liberal-democratic regime.

EASTERN EUROPE AS AN 'AREA'

Little assistance is to be found in the broad literature on comparative politics in studying actual transitions beyond assembling useful pointers as to how a framework for analysis should be constructed.[1] That is understandable considering the difficulties in trying to generalise about countries with vastly different historical experiences and problems. Not so long ago 'area specialists' were regarded as somewhat parochial in their endeavours by the 'true', generalising comparativists. Times have changed, and many would argue that it is only in comparing transitions in political systems which have several characteristics in common that comparative politics is on sure ground. If it is the case that within-area comparisons have the greatest validity, then it follows that across-area comparisons are likely to be of limited use. The experience of transition in Latin America, say, will not have many lessons for Eastern Europe.

Yet what constitutes an 'area'? Precise delimitation of an area presents problems and is bound to involve some arbitrary judgements. The division of Europe into East and West was a product of political developments after 1945; yet, despite the sharpness of the rupture, neither Eastern nor Western Europe is entirely homogeneous, and now, with the disintegration of the communist world, the idea of Mitteleuropa has again become significant. We should not expect to find a complete conformity among the countries in Eastern Europe, although there are three principal defining features: the impress of communist political rule, similarities in socio-economic structure, and the close correspondence in the timing of the transitions. The experience of a uniform type of regime is a leading criterion, and Eastern Europe stands out in this respect in contrast to other areas – Western Europe after all included countries which for a long period were decidedly not liberal democracies. Communist rule entailed the general imposition of a particular type of planned economy as well as a fundamental restructuring of society. The third feature – the fact that the communist regimes all began to crumble at around the same time – is especially important, since it allows direct comparisons to be made without having to take into account intervening changes in external circumstances.[2]

TRANSITION – TO WHAT?

The concept of transition does not prejudge the final direction a political system will take – or at least ideally it should not do so. However, the end-result is often assumed or made explicit, just as the title of this chapter points to liberal democracy as the eventual outcome. There are usually good reasons for favouring one line of development rather than another, such as recognising the force of popular demands and expectations, as well as the intentions of those holding power. But the dangers are evident: concentrating on one 'preferred' line of development leads to a neglect of other possibilities, so that departures from the main line are too readily treated as temporary aberrations. The problem is not peculiar to transition: the literature on 'development' carries the message of 'modernisation', a process which is often assumed to lead to a form similar to that of the already advanced and developed societies.

The classic European case of a transition to liberal democracy which failed is the Weimar Republic (1919–33). In the event it proved to be a transition to an entirely different kind of regime, totalitarianism. Despite the provisions of its constitution and the imposing set of democratic institutions, the republic soon succumbed under the weight of economic collapse and social tension. There were several special reasons for the failure of the Weimar Republic, but its fate serves as a general warning against assuming that a liberal democracy, once set up, will probably survive. This pessimistic view is reinforced in recalling the downfall of democratic regimes throughout Europe in the inter-war years.[3]

What are the arguments that the present transitions in Eastern Europe will lead to a consolidation of liberal democracy? The evidence thus far is impressive enough. The starting-point was the initial weakening of communist power: a decline of authority and confidence, a delegitimation in popular perceptions, and then a loss of control. Subsequently there has been swift progress in instituting democratic reform: the free formation of political parties has resulted in flourishing multi-party systems, and genuinely competitive elections have been held – all supported by the open expression of opinion and opposition.[4] For the most part, too, the governments formed have been an accurate reflection of majority opinion.

These are all requirements of a functioning democratic system, but the concept of liberal democracy sets other demands which go beyond the provision of institutional arrangements that are designed to articulate and aggregate social demands and to form representative governments. In the early stages the quality of the 'liberal' element is difficult to judge, since it depends on a gradual build-up of mutual confidence and restraint. The extent to which minority dissent is tolerated, the upholding of individual rights, the absence of discrimination, the freedom of the press, the independence of the judiciary, and the effectiveness of its control over the executive – these attributes of liberal democracy develop more slowly, and may be completely integrated only after several crises have been resolved.

One expression for these more elusive components of liberal democracy is the doctrine of constitutionalism, and they are implied as well in the idea of 'limited government'. Constitutionalism has been described as 'a practical modification of democracy'; and the checks and balances that develop within a liberal democracy express the Western tradition that majority rule should be ringed round by constraints. For Eastern Europe it is too early to decide whether these 'liberal' elements are being successfully incorporated into the working democratic systems. Indeed, once they had been, the new democracies would already have become consolidated.

THE ECONOMIC IMPERATIVE

Liberal democracy is closely associated with the operation of a market system, that is, with the free interplay of market forces: freedom of choice in the political arena is matched by related freedoms in the market-place, including those of private property. Although the possibility cannot be dismissed, it is difficult to envisage a functioning liberal democracy in a completely planned economic system, just as it is to imagine a completely unfettered market economy in the absence of political choice. Historically, the questions of timing and the causal relationship between the economic and political spheres has been important, but for Eastern Europe there is no time to wait for a slow evolution: the market and liberal democracy have to be anchored both quickly and in tandem if the stage of transition is to be successful.

Throughout Eastern Europe the inefficiency of the socialist economic system made it utterly discredited; instead, the market order holds out the promise of achieving prosperity, and with the example of the level of affluence attained by their capitalist neighbours, it is no wonder that Western Europe has become the major point of reference. The problem is that, although the initial commitment to basic change was not difficult to make, the high hopes of rapid progress could soon be dashed. If so, economic disappointments and frustration will throw an increased burden on to the political institutions.

Much will depend on how the switch to a market system is made and what type of balance is maintained between the public and private sectors. There is no single model of how the market should be allowed to operate, and in Western Europe there is a diversity of approaches.

Undoubtedly the idealised version of Thatcher's Britain seems attractive for those who are intent on destroying the all-embracing state sector. Yet the social and economic dislocation likely to result could lead to a radical political reaction. The range of possible options from Western Europe, in style and structure, is wide – for instance, neo-corporatism in Austria, the social-market economy in Germany, the dominant public sector in Sweden allied with comprehensive social engineering. No one model is readily applicable to Eastern Europe and various strategies will be adopted, but there are political penalties to be paid for failed and half-hearted experiments.

THE ROLE OF THE EUROPEAN COMMUNITY

In making their choices the countries of Eastern Europe will not be entirely free agents, because the West, and Western Europe in particular,[5] is bound to exert pressure. Substantial aid and private investment will be forthcoming only to the extent that market freedom is encouraged – and in the context of democratic stability.[6] The twin pressures, economic and political, will be made evident in the strategic position of the European Community. For the new democracies the EC offers the best chance of securing market outlets and economic support, so that gaining membership of the EC is a high priority. With so many potential applicants – essentially in competition with one another – the EC has a power of economic and political leverage pushing them to conform with its norms and practices.

How the European Community can act as a controlling mechanism is shown by the experience of the former Mediterranean dictatorships – Greece, Portugal and Spain – with obvious application to Eastern Europe. The Portuguese dictatorship (1932–74) and the Spanish (1939–74), were of much longer duration than that of the Greek military junta (1969–74), but they did not have to wait for very long before becoming full members of the EC. Despite opposition to joining expressed by several parties (most notably Pasok in Greece), for the governments concerned the economic benefits expected were of critical importance – their relatively backward economies would be pulled up to the EC-level. Once the major political condition had been met – the promise of stable democratic government – their admission soon followed: Greece in 1981, Portugal and Spain both in 1986. Their entry can be taken to signify that the transition had been accomplished, alternatively that bringing them into the Community was a means of ensuring consolidation. Either way, none of the three countries now shows signs of slipping away from the West European mainstream.

What was true of these examples does not necessarily apply to the future. The European Community is unlikely to welcome an indefinite enlargement, and although loose forms of association will be offered, they will not have decisive political and economic consequences. This reservation draws attention to the likelihood that Western Europe will not be so supportive towards Eastern Europe as is often assumed. The EC, intent on achieving closer integration and in strengthening its own position in the world, could well become less outward-looking and more reluctant to assume new obligations. Nor can the possibility of prolonged economic difficulties in the West be ignored. It is not only the direct economic factors – trade policies, aid, investment – that may be adversely affected. Also of importance are related matters such as those involving the labour market and immigration policy. If, say, restrictive immigration policies are not counterbalanced by large inward investment, then large-scale unemployment could result. The shake-out of excess labour caused by the switch to a market economy can be mitigated by capital investment or by the safety-valve of emigration, and the movement of people from east to west is likely to be a mounting pressure on Western Europe.[7] This prospect of a flood of immigrants may lead to tight controls, but if governments do follow a liberal course, they can expect to encounter a political backlash in their own countries.

It would be unwise to assume that the economic drives of the market system, the affluence of Western Europe, and the integrative role of the European Community will inevitably smooth the transition to liberal democracy. At all events, the rapid absorption of the German Democratic Republic into the Federal Republic only provides a distant parallel for the future integration of Eastern and Western Europe. In the GDR the popular demands for 'unity and freedom' (together with the Deutschmark) led to the West German 'takeover', in economic and institutional terms, so that liberal democracy was the inescapable consequence.[8] The case of East Germany is exceptional, but the negative effects, now evident, of the precipitate rush to a market economy will be a warning to other countries.

TRAJECTORIES OF TRANSITION

Liberal democratic institutions need backing at a popular level if a stable political system is to develop. A key question facing East European democracies is the extent to which their political culture – political values and attitudes towards political institutions – will help to buttress the new regimes. A supportive political culture cannot be stamped

out of the ground, and popular enthusiasm at the outset need not lead
to a long-lasting attachment. The decisive factor is the performance
of the system over time: legitimacy depends on effectiveness. It takes
time to build up reserves of goodwill, trust and loyalty which can
be called upon in periods of crisis. In the early phases of transition
a 'negative reinforcement' for the new system is an invaluable asset,
albeit a wasting one. Thus, whatever their present shortcomings, the East
European democracies can be favourably contrasted with their previous
communist regimes. However, if early hopes are disappointed, aspects
of the old order will appear better in retrospect. How, say, will personal freedom plus unemployment be balanced against security plus
repression?

It is instructive to look at some examples of transition in Europe
after 1945 in order to appreciate how long it took for some democracies to become firmly established and how slowly a supportive political culture developed. There is a significant contrast to be made with
the much briefer transitions of the newer West European democracies.
West Germany is a good example of a slow but unimpeded growth in
support for liberal democracy. After 1945 democratic institutions were
soon put in place, and the presence of the Western allies guaranteed
stability and security. The negative reinforcements were powerful: the
experience of the Nazi dictatorship together with the grim picture of
communist rule in East Germany. At first regard for democracy was
passive and instrumental; moreover, the Federal Republic, with Germany
divided, lacked the focus for loyalty of a normal nation state. What
helped to secure democracy was the sustained economic recovery from
the 1950s onwards; without it, political stability might have quickly
evaporated.

The steady build-up of support in Germany was not matched by two
other countries, France and Italy. Depending on the criteria used, the
transition in post-1945 France was both long and uncertain. Indeed, the
whole of the Fourth Republic can be regarded as a transitional regime.
Only after the founding of the Fifth Republic in 1958, and with the
surmounting of the crisis of May 1968,[9] were the endemic divisions in
French society gradually overcome, thanks at least in part to a re-casting
of political institutions and the introduction of a presidential system. In
Italy an ever-present sense of crisis pervaded the political system, and
yet fragile as it was, the republic survived. The instability was masked
by the long-term dominance of the Christian Democrats in government,
although it was also precisely their hold on power which fed disaffection.
The slow process of stabilisation – as well as the avoidance of collapse

– is traceable to the disjunction between the low regard for government and the political system on the one hand, and the underlying stability of Italian society on the other. Forecasts of imminent disaster proved wrong, and with the gradual erosion of Christian Democratic hegemony, a stable relationship has come about between the political system and society at large.

These three cases of regime discontinuity show 'trajectories of stabilisation' quite different from that of the new Mediterranean democracies – they have rapidly become stable liberal democracies.[10] All three show special features. In Spain, the central role taken by the restored monarchy provided a unifying influence during the transition which the parties by themselves could not have supplied. The failure of the Armed Forces Movement in Portugal to carry through its social revolution in the wake of the dictatorship left the way clear for undisputed civilian rule. The Greek situation was more complex: on one level the abolition of the monarchy after the ending of military rule in 1974 enabled the parties to build up popular support free from interference and constraints; on another level the whole period after 1947 (the end of the Civil War) can be regarded as an extended transition.

How are the differences between the earlier and later transitions to be explained, and is there any applicability to Eastern Europe? One reason for the later transitions being completed relatively quickly is that, despite the dictatorial form of government, social changes had not been blocked. In the economic sphere, industry and commerce developed in much the same way as for the rest of Western Europe and with a similar unimpeded growth in managerial and business élites. It was chiefly in a political sense that they were isolated from the West European mainstream, and once the political changes came about the transition was speedily completed.

For Eastern Europe it is be questionable whether a remotely similar basis for social and economic pluralism is available.[11] The trajectories they follow are likely to resemble one or other of the early post-1945 cases. Social change has been massive, but it was directed towards securing social uniformity. Elite-formation was controlled, and the leading professional and managerial groups were incorporated into party-élites or state-élites. Over the next few years substantially the same personnel has to become the new managerial/business élite, capable of making a rapid transfer to the requirements of the market system. This demand may be more difficult to meet than the parallel ones for a new political élite. Can, for instance, the 'barons of state corporations' make the change to become successful 'captains of industry'?

PARTIES AND ELECTORATES

There is now so little in common between the social structures of Eastern and Western Europe that it is difficult to draw parallels in forecasting how the new party systems will develop. Much of the argument for the stability of Western European democracies is based on the extent of social pluralism – competing and co-existing social groups and interests – which is reflected in the variety of parties and political traditions. Even where social differences in the past were strong and gave rise to class-based and other cleavages, they were often cross-cutting so as to modify their polarising effects. In whatever way the present era of stability is best explained, it was not an overnight acquisition; it would be wrong to expect stable democracies to emerge in Eastern Europe through following the same evolutionary path.

Throughout Western Europe there is evidence of a long-term electoral dealignment at work, that is, voters are becoming less tied to individual parties and are increasingly volatile in the support they give. Superficially there may be some resemblance to the new democracies, since loyalty to any one of the rash of new parties can scarcely be strong. Yet there is all the difference between an electorate that is on the way to becoming destructured and one that is still *un*structured.[12] In Western Europe the four major political traditions – Conservatism, Christian Democracy, Liberalism and Social Democracy – have permanently shaped party systems and electoral behaviour. Despite electoral change, the structuring of party competition has altered very little, and the major parties based on the established political traditions can still rely on a substantial 'core' vote.[13]

The fundamental uncertainty facing the East European democracies is the basis on which political competition will come to be structured. There are two possible kinds of lead from Western Europe. One is the emergence of so-called 'catch-all' parties, ones which in being ideologically bland are able to win support from all sections the electorate; these 'people's parties', pragmatic and moderate, can achieve a dominant position, and they are kept on a moderate course through the compromises they have to make to keep the party and its support intact. This possibility for Eastern Europe is attractive, since – it may be assumed – the 'unstructured' electorate will have no fixed political commitments, and there is no real basis for, say, strong class-based cleavages. The problem with applying this model is that it requires making an 'evolutionary leap', leaving out the fact that the catch-all parties developed from the pre-existing parties and still embodied their traditions. More significantly, they first developed within a period of increasing affluence and were in part a product of decreasing social tension.

To the extent that similar parties develop in Eastern Europe, they are likely to be far less stable.

A second kind of lead from Western Europe for the structuring of party competition points in a different direction – towards the distinction between 'left' and 'right' on which West European party systems still depend. Imprecise as this terminology is, there are several points of relevance for Eastern Europe on a socio-economic level. The four major bases of party differentiation on a left-right axis can be summarised as follows:[14]

1.   Governmental vs. private ownership of the means of production;
2.   A strong vs. a weak governmental role in economic planning;
3.   Support of vs. opposition to the redistribution of wealth from the rich to the poor;
4.   The expansion of vs. resistance to governmental social welfare programmes.

All four are highly relevant to policy options in Eastern Europe, and all four will affect the future pattern of party competition, although parties need not take a uniform place on the 'left' side or 'right' side. The role of governments in the economy may be a leading source of conflict, rather than the redistributive and social welfare aspects which one would expect to develop later as important issues. However, even though the left-right axis appears to offer a promising basis for inter-party competition, what is unclear is the extent of electoral underpinning that their kinds of party positioning would attract. The problem here is quite different from the electoral base of the catch-all party, since the latter makes its appeal precisely because there are a few marked social differences, whereas the left-right nature of the party competition requires them in order to maintain stable support.

A further form of electoral stabilisation may promote political destabilisation: sub-national/ethnic parties can threaten the integrity of the existing 'nation state'. Even though they need not be aiming at outright separatism, the point is that such parties attract an over-riding loyalty from their adherents so that the stabilising effects of cross-cutting cleavages are not operative. Western Europe has largely been spared sub-national tensions, and in the post-1945 era they have been largely restricted to relatively small minorities (the Basques in Spain, Northern Ireland, the Italian South Tyrol, and Corsica). Belgium is the exception: the near parity of Flemish and French-speaking population led to a complete fragmentation of the party system and to a radical restructuring of the unitary state. In several East European countries even more intense pressures are building up, and they, unlike Belgium, do not start with the benefits of reasonable affluence and a political system that over the years has facilitated negotiation and compromise.

The lesson may be that extensive measures of decentralisation and the granting of regional autonomy should be implemented before the pressures on the fragile democratic systems become too strong. Yet this kind of foresight is not likely to prevail just at the time when countries are facing crushing economic problems which require clear overall strategies and firm central guidance. Nor, too, just when states have recovered their sovereignty are they disposed to allow it to be weakened from within. On almost all counts, Western and Eastern Europe can be contrasted in respect of national issues – not least because in the one the self-conscious nation-state is becoming redundant, whereas in the other national identities are being rediscovered.

Party labels, the outcome of initial elections, and the welcome given to democracy are not sure guides to how parties develop and how voters will behave in the future. Any widespread disillusion with the fruits of the market system and Western-style democracy need not show itself in social unrest and political polarisation, at least not immediately. A first reaction to perceived failures may take the form of a passive turning-away from politics and the new political class, shown for instance by low levels of electoral participation. Party rule might remain intact, but the parties would become increasingly out of contact with popular needs and aspirations. Apparent quiescence, a deceptive stability, may then give way to more active expressions of discontent among voters. Electoral volatility encourages political instability, with parties striving to keep or attract support engaging in 'the politics of outbidding'. An unstable electorate is also inclined to experiment: new parties based on populism or protest and fired by demagogic leaders make the task of responsible parties and leaders more difficult. It remains to be seen whether this scenario of ensuing electoral and party instability will constitute the next phase of transition in Eastern Europe.

CONCLUSION: THE QUESTION OF RESPONSIBILITY

The preceding account of the problems facing Eastern Europe – the politics of post-dictatorship – has not been pitched in particularly optimistic terms. It has also taken a perspective of transition as viewed from Western Europe on the argument that it provides the model for the new democracies and that Western Europe is the most significant outside influence affecting the course of change. A successful transition to stable liberal democracy depends on the individual countries themselves, but should Western Europe also shoulder the responsibility?

It is important not to underestimate what has already been achieved without external intervention: the toppling of communist regimes, the introduction of democratic processes, a partial dismantling of the old state apparatus,[15] the initial moves towards a market system. Even though there are wide differences in the extent and pace of change, the pointers are all in the same direction, and it would be difficult to suggest radically different ways in which the transition should have proceeded. Yet the problems to be overcome are formidable. The political consequences of the switch to an 'electoral market' are uncertain as are those of the economic market. The social infrastructure has to bear the weight of fundamental political and economic change, and it is apparent that the stabilising effects of social pluralism are not available.

Estimates of how long it may take Eastern Europe to make a successful transfer to a market economy are expressed in decades rather than years, and even then living standards could trail far behind those by then attained in Western Europe. It is conceivable that the gap might become permanent and that some countries, saddled with foreign debt, could become dependent clients of western creditors. It is within this possibly extended period of economic restructuring that the political risks are greatest. Prolonged hardship and instability would lead to the questioning of the fitness of parliamentary institutions and demands for their replacement by strong, decisive leadership. Far from liberal democracy and the market system being valued, they could be actively resented.

Much discussion in terms of 'responsibility', the rhetoric of interdependence, and a European 'common house' may distort reality – there is little sense in which Western Europe is now 'dependent' on Eastern Europe. It is also reasonable to hold the view that the new democracies have to be held responsible for their own future: the only sure way for a people to learn to handle liberal democracy is in being prepared to court the perils of failure. If only one country were involved, or if Eastern Europe could be sealed off, then such a detached judgement might be tenable. But the politics of post-dictatorship affects half a continent, and history has shown us that massive failure of democracy in one part has had serious consequences for the rest. The political imperative for Europe is for it to grow together, because neither side can afford to let it grow apart.

NOTES

1. Of particular interest is Dankwart Rustow's, 'Transitions to Democracy: Towards a Dynamic Model', in *Comparative Politics*, April 1970.
2. Other characteristics – such as a common history, cultural inheritance, and linguistic affinities – link some countries but not others.
3. K. J. Newman, *European Democracy Between the Wars*, London, 1970.
4. For details of the first free elections held, see *Electoral Studies* Vol. 29, No. 108, Winter 1990.
5. On the American perspective, see Lewis T. Preston, 'Reforms in Eastern Europe – A US View' in U. Ramm (ed.), *Challenges of Global Finance*, Mainz, 1991.
6. Thus the new European Bank for Reconstruction and Development has made a specific link between furthering economic development and progress towards democracy, in limiting lending to countries 'committed to and applying principles of multi-party democracy.' *The Times*, 14 April 1991.
7. On migration pressures, see Jonas Widgren, 'International Migration and Regional Stability', in *International Affairs*, October 1990; and Judy Dempsey, 'The Long March Westwards', in *Financial Times*, 12 February 1991.
8. Klaus von Beyme, 'Transition to Democracy – or *Anschluss*? The Two Germanies and Europe', in *Government and Opposition*, Spring 1990.
9. Mattei Dogan, 'How Civil War Was Avoided in France', in *International Political Science Review* (Special Issue on 'Political Crises'), Vol. 5, No. 3, 1984.
10. Geoffrey Pridham, 'Political Actors, Linkages and Interactions: Democratic Consolidation in Southern Europe' in *West European Politics*, October 1990.
11. For a comparison between the Soviet Union and Spain, see Dominic Lieven, *The Soviet Crisis*, Research Institute for the Study of Conflict and Terrorism, May 1991.
12. Even the extent of electoral volatility destructuring in Western Europe can be questioned to the extent that electoral volatility is continued *within* broad groups of related parties. Stefano Bartolini and Peter Mair, *Identity, Competition and Electoral Availability*, Cambridge, 1990.
13. Gordon Smith, 'Core Persistence, System Change and the "People's Party"', in *West European Politics*, October 1989.
14. Arend Lijphart, *Democracies: Patterns of Majoritarian and Consensus Government in Twenty-one Countries*, Yale, 1984, p. 129.
15. However, the record is uneven. See Joachim Jens Hesse, *Administrative Modernisation in Central and Eastern European Countries*, Centre for European Studies, Nuffield College, Oxford, February 1991.

2 Bulgaria

Richard Crampton

When the bulk of this chapter was written, April 1991, Bulgaria had not yet enacted a new constitution – though one was under discussion and a number of drafts had been produced – and consequently its 'institutional architecture' was only under construction. For this reason, the main focus of the piece is on how political power and authority had shifted since 1989, and on the role in the new political process, and the establishment of a new political consensus, of parliament, the presidency, the Communist and other parties, and the extra-parliamentary forces. In a postscript at the end of the chapter, account is taken of constitutional and other changes which have taken place since 1991, and which are beginning to give Bulgarian politics a more stable institutional character.

HISTORICAL OUTLINE[1]

On 9 September 1944 the war-time underground coalition, the Father-land Front, 'seized' power in Sofia. The Bulgarian Communist Party (BCP) became part of the new administration and within three years had eliminated any real opposition force. The only remaining non-communist political group was the Bulgarian Agrarian National Union (BANU). In return for its compliance BANU became part of the coalition which remained in office until 1990.

The dominant personality during the BCP's rule was Todor Zhivkov who was made first secretary of the Central Committee in 1954. At times he showed originality in domestic affairs but in external policy his rule was characterised by a slavish subservience to Moscow. For this he received the backing of the Kremlin in any domestic contest he encountered. All this changed in March 1985 with the advent of Gorbachev, for whom Zhivkov was irredeemably associated with the Brezhnev era.

By 1985 Zhivkov was experiencing mounting political difficulties. Abroad Bulgaria's alleged implication in unsavoury scandals such as the assassination of Georgi Markov in London in 1978 had tarnished the country's image whilst at home a deepening crisis was made much worse by Zhivkov's tendency to respond to its problems by tinkering with the administration rather than the structure of the economy.[2] In the mid-1980s Zhivkov also launched his 'regenerative process', a euphemism for the attempted bulgarisation of the country's million or so ethnic Turks. Internal opposition was already stirring in Bulgaria and by the late 1980s it was able to exploit the anti-Turkish campaign as well as questions such as environmental degradation.[3] By 1989 mounting frustration and the changes elsewhere in Eastern Europe had frightened many members of the BCP hierarchy who therefore deposed Zhivkov on 10 November. His successor was Petr Mladenov, who had been his foreign secretary for seventeen years.

During the final years of the old régime some oppositional associations, including an independent trade union, *Podkrepa* (Support), human rights organisations, environmental groups, and quasi-political parties, had appeared, but now their number mushroomed. On 14 November 1989 fifteen of them came together to form the Union of Democratic Forces (UDF). Since then the composition of the UDF has varied somewhat but it has always been the main group opposed to the BCP and to its successor, the Bulgarian Socialist Party (BSP).

Mladenov's new administration declared its intent to reform Bulgaria and on 29 December bravely announced the abolition of recent anti-Turkish legislation. Mladenov also moved, though not without some pushing from the public and from the opposition parties, towards the dismantling of the BCP's leading rôle over the state and society, as a part of which he resigned as party leader. To reinforce this point, Andrei Lukanov, his close associate and former minister of foreign economic relations, was made prime minister rather than head of the party; the latter post went to Aleksandr Lilov. Lukanov took a full part in the round table discussions which were then in progress and which in April 1990 produced the framework for the holding of general elections in June for a Grand National – or Constituent – Assembly. By that time, however, Mladenov's position had become compromised and he resigned on 6 July. He was replaced by Zheliu Zhelev, an academic philosopher who had been persecuted under the old régime and who in November 1989 had become the first leader of the UDF.

After the elections, from which the BSP appeared as the largest party in the assembly,[4] Lukanov attempted to form a coalition but the opposition refused, forcing the incumbent prime minister to reconstruct his one-party administration on 20 September. Two months later he resigned following student sit-ins, demonstrations and strikes. He was succeeded by a 'Government to Guarantee the Peaceful Transition to a Democratic Society'. Its leader was the non-party figure, Dimitr Popov. After securing an agreement from all major parties on 20 December to guarantee this peaceful transition Popov's government promised to prepare a new constitution and to enact the economic reforms necessary to reconstruct the economy on market lines. In January 1991 a social agreement between government, the trade unions, and the managers/employers was also concluded, the basic function of which was to guarantee all-round cooperation to control and contain the tensions which would inevitably result from economic restructuring.

PARLIAMENT

After the fall of Zhivkov a BCP plenum of 11 December promised that there would be a revival of parliament and its authority. Mladenov told the Central Committee: 'The first and most important step along this road is the establishment of a true socialist parliament, which should become an embodiment of the people's self-management in the spirit of the best national and democratic traditions, by entirely restoring the supremacy of the National Assembly.'[5]

There were two immediate difficulties. In the first place language such as that used by Mladenov was too redolent of the old vocabulary of politics and could not pacify those who wanted real change, including the scrapping of Article 1 of the constitution which guaranteed the BCP a leading rôle in society and government. The second problem was that of how a new parliament was to be chosen. Only parliament could change the electoral system, yet the present parliament was unrepresentative, being entirely the product of the old order. A means of making parliament legitimate extra-parliamentary mechanisms, reflecting popular opinion, had to be found. The answer, as in Poland, was the round table for which the opposition had been calling since shortly after the fall of Zhivkov.

Serious round table discussions were under way by the middle of January 1991. At the beginning of the discussions the BCP was willing to concede that the new system could incorporate the experience of the constitutional parties and the social democracies of the west as well as that of the workers' parties in the socialist camp. By the end of March the ruling party had gone much further; on 29 March Lilov told the round table that, 'Our state needs a new, profoundly democratic constitution.'[6] For this reason, continued Lilov, his party was anxious that the nation should elect a Grand National Assembly in a free, multi-party election.

The procedures for that election were worked out in the round table. The GNA to be elected in 1990 was to consist of four hundred deputies. There had been considerable discussion over the method by which they were to be elected. The UDF favoured proportional representation which they regarded as the most democratic procedure; it was also a more sure means of countering the influence exercised by communist-appointed local officials who would oversee the voting. The BSP, meanwhile, argued that this would prevent the return of a sufficient number of 'qualified and capable people', its euphemism for pro-BSP members of the *nomenklatura*. The BSP also calculated that if the opposition forces were divided then in a significant number of constituencies socialist candidates would receive the largest number but not the majority of votes; under the first-past-the-post system they would be returned wi thout any oppositionists accompanying them. The eventual compromise was that half the deputies would be elected by PR and the other half by a majority system. The conduct of the election was to be managed by electoral commissions, with a central electoral commission overseeing the whole operation. There was also to be extensive foreign monitoring of the polls.[7]

For a country which had had few genuinely open electoral contests, the last being in 1931, those of 1990 were a considerable achievement. There were some irregularities but the general consensus was that these were isolated and did not have any material bearing upon the final result. There was much more dispute, however, about the campaign. Here, it was widely alleged, the BSP had consistently threatened rural voters that the opposition, if victorious, would sell land to rapacious foreign capitalists and would refuse to pay peasants their pensions. In effect the elections had been free but not fair.

The ceremonial opening of the GNA took place on 10 July in the old capital, Trnovo, in an atmosphere of considerable tension. Students were already protesting at the electoral commission's refusal to publish full details of alleged irregularities. Also, when the assembly convened, there were loud complaints at the presence of the twenty-three deputies from the Movement for Rights and Freedom (MRF), an organisation whose aim was to protect human rights in general but which was particularly concerned with the interests of the Turkish minority; this, said the nationalist pro-testers, contravened the electoral law which proscribed parties based on religious affiliation or ethnic identity.

There was little improvement after the assembly moved to Sofia and as the months dragged on the GNA, and even more so the social-ist government, squandered its own authority and the respect which it might otherwise have expected from the populace. The deputies showed an initial reluctance to begin serious discussions and wasted time in seemingly unimportant procedural wrangles. A further inhibitor of the GNA's reforming potential was the inability of Lukanov to persuade the opposition to join him in government or, later, to give open support to his package of reform proposals. Lukanov hoped that popular discontent would be contained if all major political groupings showed support for the tough economic medicine which would have to be administered. Even when it did enact important laws on local government, and on the depoliticisation of the army, the police, the judiciary, and the foreign service, the government was often felt to be responding more to external pressures than to its own internal dynamics. Furthermore, in the autumn there was a significant shift in public opinion. This was primarily the result of the deepening economic crisis which in turn was caused by the lack of hard-currency credits, the loss of oil from Iraq, the collapse of Comecon trading structures, and the general uncertainty as to future economic policies.

The change in public opinion left the assembly open to accusations that it had ceased to be properly representative. At the end of November the prestige of the GNA reached its lowest point when it was pressure from student sit-ins and strikers rather than a vote of no confidence from the assembly which drove Lukanov from office. The actions of the Popov government early in 1991 did something to restore public confidence in the GNA but by April there were once again signs of serious disenchantment, particularly amongst *Podkrepa* and some of the constituent parties of the UDF; they could not shake off their conviction that the BSP-dominated assembly would never enact wide-ranging constitutional and economic reform.

If the GNA has failed to fulfil all expectations it had nevertheless become the one of the main *foci* of political life. It was in the debating chamber rather than the office of the party secretary that laws were made or not made; and, the emergency of November 1990 notwithstanding, it was still the assembly which ultimately sanctioned ministerial appointments.

The assembly had also seen the emergence of a number of important and at times powerful parliamentary committees whose composition generally reflected the composition of the GNA but whose chairmen or chairwomen did not always come from the BSP. A few instances may be cited. In 1990 it became known that the labour camps in Bulgaria had been more numerous, more brutal and more long-lasting than had previously been thought; a special parliamentary commission was established to enquire into them and its report was of considerable political significance for the electoral prospects of the BCP/BSP. After the confrontations of December 1989 to January 1990 over the Turkish issue a public council was established which ended its labours by recommending the establishment of a parliamentary commission on human rights and the nationality issue. Under the political agreement of December 1990 an important rôle was given to other committees, not least that enquiring into the extremely sensitive question of connections between MPs and the security forces under the old régime. There are also commissions dealing with other delicate political problems such as the property holdings of the parties, primarily the BSP, and on the abuse of power by the BCP during the years of communist rule. It is hardly surprising that when a parliamentary delegation visited Italy in March 1991 they were said to have shown particular interest in 'the statutes and the powers granted to the parliamentary commissions'.[8]

The future evolution of parliamentary life in Bulgaria will depend greatly on how far the GNA can proceed with its major function of constitutional definition, but the vitality of its subsidiary institutions does indicate a potential for the natural development of parliamentary institutions.

THE PRESIDENCY

Soon after 10 November 1989 it was obvious that the State Council, which along with the Politburo exercised executive power, was to be an early casualty of the coup. Speaking to the opening session of the BCP Central Committee of 11 December 1989, Mladenov questioned 'whether it was necessary to have a State Council under the conditions of a permanently working national assembly and whether it would not be feasible to introduce the institution of head of state'.[9]

The round table did not dispute that Bulgaria should have a president but there was disagreement on how he/she should be chosen. The BCP favoured a direct election simultaneous with the voting for the GNA. The UDF was more cautious and argued that the president should be elected by the national assembly. The final compromise was that the existing *sobranie*, or assembly, should nominate the president until the GNA met; the latter would then make its choice of head of state. After this agreement had been reached the State Council was dissolved and Mladenov elected president on 3 April.

He was never confirmed in office by the GNA. On 14 June a video tape was discovered showing Mladenov suggesting the use of tanks against demonstrators on 14 December 1989. After initial attempts to deny its authenticity he resigned on 6 July. Not until 1 August, and after six votes in the GNA, was Zhelev chosen as his successor.

A quiet, even lugubrious man, Zhelev will never be accused of charisma, but he has bought genuineness, dignity, and power to the office of president. As a philosopher who had suffered under the *Zhivkovshtina*[10] and as a former leader of the UDF, he had the support of most of the opposition, and many others welcomed the fact that he ostentatiously made the USA not the USSR the object of his first foreign visit. Zhelev also rapidly created around him a team of young and able advisors.

In view of the relative ineffectiveness of the GNA, at least until January 1991, the presidency was bound to become important, but its power and influence grew all the more through Zhelev's sensible handling of recurrent political crises, a process in which he was much helped by his own creation, the Political Consultative Council (PCC) attached to the Presidency. First suggested in his presidential address of 5 August 1990, this was basically a continuation of the round table. It brought together members of all parliamentary groups as well as appropriate figures not represented in the GNA. It was a purely consultative body in which a variety of opinion was solicited and expressed; it took no formal decisions but was there to provide the president with information. Although it had no constitutional status and was at times criticised by all the main political groups it was of vital importance in steering the country away from complete political breakdown. It was through the PCC that Zhelev engineered the compromises which dissipated the tensions of the summer of 1990 when students and other members of the intelligentsia in many towns had established tent encampments, 'cities of truth'. On 26–27 August these tensions literally burst into flames when demonstrators looted and then burned part of the BSP party headquarters in Sofia. It was through the PCC that the ensuing perils were contained. A month later it was in the PCC that Lukanov was persuaded to form another one-party government. And, most important of all, in November it was the PCC which charted the way out of the extreme dangers which surrounded the fall of Lukanov.

In October 1990 the PCC had stressed that it was not setting itself up as an alternative to parliament but that its work was essentially consultative and 'aimed at overcoming contradictions with a view to helping the parliamentary groups and the GNA work more rapidly on the basis of previously prepared materials'.[11] But to others its very success meant that they inevitably looked to the PCC for salvation.[12] The PCC also began to take the initiative, setting conditions for convening the GNA and proposing its agenda.[13] At the end of January 1991, in the expectation of the massive price rises which would come with deregulation on 1 February, the PCC created a special group to draft the text of an agreement between the political parties in parliament, 'on the basis of which they should commit themselves to promoting a favourable social atmosphere'.[14] It is possible, therefore, that in set-ting up the PCC Zhelev has created a constitutional institution of great importance.

THE PARTY

As the centre of political attention moved to the GNA and as the presidency accumulated more authority, the BCP/BSP declined in power, prestige, unity, discipline, wealth, membership and confidence.

For some diehards the removal of Zhivkov and the promise of democratisation in the party was enough; with these moves and with BANU as a separate political entity Bulgaria would have a democratic, pluralist system. The radicals in the BCP would not tolerate such casuistry. They joined with non-party elements to demand the replacement of the party's leading rôle and of the 'administrative-command' system by a truly democratic society and a market economy. At the December Central Committee plenum the radicals carried the day and the BCP set out along the reforming path, beginning with a promise that it would abolish Article 1 of the constitution in which was enshrined the party's leading rôle.

It was then that the BCP began to exhibit a pattern which alarmed many reformists, within as well as outside the former ruling party, of making concessions in principle but then watering them down in detail, or even forgetting them. In its detailed proposal over Article 1 the BCP proposed to remove only paragraphs two and three, leaving the first paragraph which stated that Bulgaria was 'a socialist state of the working people of the towns and the countryside led by the working class'. This was not to the taste of many oppositionists who had no desire to be citizens of a socialist state or to be led by the working class. After a number of demonstrations and furious media and assembly debates the BCP gave way.

Before the recurrent pattern could be seen again the BCP undertook to put its own house in order. Its 14th Extraordinary Congress met from 30 January to 2 February 1990. Mladenov presented to the congress a document, 'On Restructuring the Party and Building a Democratic Socialist Society', which promised a multi-party democracy and the complete separation of state and party. The promised economic reforms included privatisation, decentralisation, demonopolisation, a reorientation of external trade and convertibility for the Bulgarian *leva*. Much of this had by now become little more than the common currency of political debate and it caused little excitement outside the ranks of the party.

The 14th congress, however, also engineered the formation of new government, not an encouraging sign for those who were supposedly set on separating state from party. Ironically, the new administration was the first in Bulgaria's communist history which contained members of no other party than the BCP. This was because BANU dared not rejoin the coalition. In November a new agrarian party had been established, the

Bulgarian Agrarian National Union – Nikola Petkov. A party named after the agrarian martyr to communism would lose no time in excoriating any agrarian group which went into government with the BCP.

Another decision of the 14th congress had been to call a referendum in May on the question of whether the party should change its name. In conformity with its established interpretation of democracy the BCP decided the result before the vote had been taken and on 3 April the BCP renamed itself the Bulgarian Socialist Party (BSP). Part of the motivation for this change was to escape the image of the old BCP, not least in preparation for the forthcoming electoral battle. The revelations concerning the labour camps had been damaging, and there was mounting frustration at the failure of the BCP/BSP to admit responsibility for the failed policies of the past, or to punish any of those who had applied them. Yet despite these disadvantages the BSP emerged as the largest party in the GNA taking 48 per cent of the vote and two hundred and eleven of the four hundred seats. It had been helped by its use of intimidation in the rural areas, and by the services of a British advertising agency.[15] However, the distribution of both votes and seats indicated that the BSP had failed to win the confidence of the workers in the towns; in September Lilov told the BSP's 39th congress[16] that theirs was 'no longer a working-class party' and that in future they should look to the intelligentsia and the nation's youth for their natural supporters.[17]

The difficulty was that it was precisely in these groups that suspicions of BSP intentions were strongest. It had taken considerable popular pressure to shift the BCP leadership over Article 1 of the constitution, and demonstrations were again needed in March 1990 to force the BCP government to dilute its near monopoly over the press. In the summer there was growing anxiety that the BSP was continuing to dominate national institutions despite the legal abolition of the leading rôle its predecessor had enjoyed.

The pattern of non-fulfilment of promises and the political suspicions which flowed from it were typified in the affair of the BCP archives. On 17 August 1990 the BSP Supreme Council decided to comply with the recently-enacted law on the state archives which required that all BCP records be deposited in public collections. By 30 October this had not been done and it had become known that one prominent BSP MP had told the party's Supreme Council that it should not be done and that 'while we are in power it is we who shall decide what to do with our archives'.[18] In the meantime he suggested local party officials should hide their records. Not only did these statements provide yet more fuel for suspicion of the BSP's intentions but there was a real fear that important records would be destroyed. Some had already disappeared, including those concerning certain police activities immediately before and after the communist takeover in 1944,[19] and there was concern that identification of those communists responsible for the present disastrous state of affairs in Bulgaria would become impossible. In January 1991 it was revealed that the records of the old sixth department of the Ministry of the Interior, which had responsibility for political superveillance, had disappeared.

These were not the only causes for continuing suspicion of the BSP. In 1991, despite its avowed commitment to privatisation and economic reform, the party delayed the passage of the vital bill for the decollectivisation of the land. It had also wasted time in precipitating parliamentary crises by its insistence that the discredited Lukanov be made chairman of the parliamentary committee on foreign affairs, and by questioning the validity of the election of a leading UDF deputy. And in March 1991 there was yet another example of the BSP failing to fulfil the expectations raised by its own promises. It was announced that the party would at last accept full responsibility for the policies pursued by the BCP and that officials guilty of incompetence and the misuse of power would be named. Yet when the BSP finally published its much-awaited document it went little further than previous statements and most of the officials named were either dead, decrepit, or already in the dock. At the same time there were disturbing rumours from Sofia that despite all its agreements on dismantling the old system the BSP members of Popov's cabinet had insisted on the reinstatement of a number of functionaries from the Ministry of the Interior.

The question of whether the BSP had managed to change the BCP's spots was a real one which generated much passion in Bulgaria. It was also an important one is assessing the institutional changes which occurred in the country since 10 November 1989. Compared with the situation in Romania or the Soviet Union at the same time, however, there can be no dispute but that the communist power structure in Bulgaria was much reduced by April 1991. Its supervision of the state had been considerably trimmed. Even in December 1989 some BCP primary organisations dissolved themselves, and on 24 January 1990 the Politburo issued an order banning party cells in the armed forces and in the workplace. The depolitisation bill of September meant that the BSP members in the army, the police, the judiciary and the foreign service had to chose between their party membership and their career; it seems that all but a handful opted for the latter.

The great social institutions which were once communist transmission levers were also separated from the party. Most important of all in this respect were the trade unions. Soon after the fall of Zhivkov the leader of the official Bulgarian trade unions declared them independent of the BCP. The separation was completed by the formation of the new-look organisation, the Confederation of Independent Trade Unions in Bulgaria (CITUB), on 17–18 February 1990, since when CITUB has played an important, and at times a decisive rôle in Bulgarian affairs. Another organisation which divested itself of party control was the Dimitrov League of Communist Youth, the *Komsomol*, which was reformed, again in February 1990, this time into the Bulgarian Democratic Youth Social Organisation. The former leading rôle of the party has also been diminished by the reappearance of other, older social organisations such as the boy scouts and societies attached to the churches.

Despite these changes the BSP retained considerable popular support and its membership of five hundred thousand in March 1991, even if it is only half the figure for November 1989, left it as the largest party in the country. As such it clearly had the right in a democratic system to play a major part in the nation's affairs. On the other hand, the BSP no longer enjoyed the level of public support which enabled it to secure its majority in the GNA.

The BSP was undoubtedly weakened by the appearance of factions and divisions within its ranks. As early as the December 1989 Plenum the party had committed itself to open internal debate; the abandonment of democratic centralism at the 14th congress merely accepted a *fait accompli* because by then there were a number of distinct factions within the party, including the Road to Europe, the Alternative Socialist Organisation, and the Club for Radical Change.

THE PARTIES

By the elections of June 1990 there were at least eighty registered political parties and movements in Bulgaria, and by Easter 1991 their number had topped the hundred mark. Many parties are extremely small and some are little more than lobby groups on particular issues. There is also a high degree of volatility with some parties changing their leaders and their alliances with at times bewildering rapidity.

The law on political parties, worked out by the round table and put into operation in April 1990, places few restrictions on such organisations, the major one being that no party should be based solely on religious affiliation or ethnic identity. The assertion that the MRF contravenes this regulation forms one of the main planks of Bulgarian nationalist organisations such as the Fatherland Party of Labour (FPL). The MRF

Table 2.1   Representation of Bulgarian Parties in 1990 Parliament

Bulgarian Socialist Party	211
Union of Democratic Forces	144
Movement for Rights and Freedoms	23
Bulgarian Agrarian National Union	16
Fatherland Union	2
Independents	2
Fatherland Party of Labour	1
Unaffiliated Social Democratic Party	1

responds by saying that it is a movement and not a party and that its membership includes Bulgarians and other racial groups as well as Turks, and the MRF is no doubt too powerful and well organised for it to be suppressed or restricted. In fact the regulations on religious and ethnic identity have been breached by other parties, not least those – and there are at least two – which represent the interests of the gypsies.

An equally interesting and contentious case was that of the group calling itself Ilinden. Named after a rising against the Ottoman authorities in Macedonia in 1903 this group represented the interests of what they claimed was the Macedonian minority in Bulgaria. Bulgaria refuses to recognise the existence of a Macedonian nation and could certainly not tolerate a party which advocated the alienation of Bulgarian territory. Ilinden was refused recognition by a Sofia court and when it attempted to hold its constituent congress at Oshtava in Bulgarian Macedonia on 31 July 1990 that too was forbidden.

Ilinden had not been able and many of the smaller parties had chosen not to take part in the elections to the GNA; see Table 2.1 for the results. The main groups returned to the GNA, the BSP, the UDF, the MRF and BANU, remain the most important parties. Of these the MRF maintains a steady support amongst the Turkish population and is much aided by the skill of its leader, Ahmed Dogan. Dogan has fiercely resisted any sign of excessive Turkish nationalism, and in particular any indication of autonomist or secessionist inclinations, which would inflame yet further chauvinist Bulgarian fears.

That BANU secured fewer seats in the GNA than the MRF surprised a number of observers. BANU should have been the natural party of the rural population but its position was and remains ambiguous. It has attempted to shake off its collaborationist past and has adopted many of the policies of BANU-NP, saving only that it refuses to enter the UDF; yet if it does not do so it stands little chance of exercising influence. This means that radically inclined peasants will tend to vote for BANU-NP which is still within the UDF, and which, in terms of membership, is the second largest party after the BSP. For the conservative minded peasant BANU is now too radical and he/she is therefore just as likely to vote for the BSP.

The major political grouping opposing the BSP is the UDF which brings together some seventeen separate bodies, both parties and interest groups. It is an unwieldy and a not entirely logical combination, whose policy making and executive body is the Coordinating Council. The first chairman of the Coordinating Council was Zhelev who led the UDF until his election to the presidency. Zhelev's successor was Petr Beron, a well-liked and competent member of the environmental group Ecoglasnost, but on 6 December 1990 he was forced to resign following revelations that he had acted as a minor police informer. The Beron affair showed how destructive the legacy of the old régime could be, and it seriously weakened the UDF. Beron's successor, Filip Dimitrov, is not a member of the GNA.

The UDF is inevitably weakened by its varied composition, and in many ways it is a minor political miracle that it has held together for so long. The largest constituent group, the Social Democratic Party (SDP), is unhappy that the UDF agreed to join a government with the BSP, even if Popov's government is studiously not referred to as a coalition; when Ivan Pushkarov agreed to take the industry, trade and services portfolio in the Popov government he was expelled from the SDP by its leader, Petr Dertliev. The SDP also finds it difficult to coexist with the Alternative Socialist Party, a breakaway from the BSP and a recent addition to the ranks of the UDF; the SDP suffered fierce persecution during the communist purges and finds any association with former members of the BCP extremely distasteful. At the same time, constituent organisations of the UDF differ in their policies on such vital issues as the land, with BANU-NP calling for socialisation (ownership by those who work it) rather than the all-out privatisation favoured by other groups. There are also differences about the degree of social welfare which should be provided for those who will suffer as a result of the economic reforms, and serious potential rifts over when the GNA should dissolve itself and call for new elections.

By April 1991, the contest for political power remained essentially that between the BSP and the UDF though both were enfeebled by internal division, and splits within both groups were a possibility. Should that occur a centrist combination of splinters from both major institutions could emerge.

THE EXTRA-PARLIAMENTARY FORCES

At a number of major turning points in Bulgaria's evolution since 10 November 1989 it has been popular action on the streets or organised trade union activity which have proved decisive. This was most notably the case with the deposition of Mladenov and the removal of Lukanov, but it also brought about the eventual sacking of the chief of Bulgarian television Pavel Pisarev. It was demonstrations in early January 1990 over the Turkish issue which forced the BCP and the UDF to recognise the common ground uniting them against the threat of uncontained chauvinism and which then enabled them to make progress, albeit faltering, in the round table discussions. On 23 February two hundred thousand UDF supporters marched in complaint at what they saw as BCP delaying tactics in the round table discussions, and a month later another large UDF demonstration forced the BCP government to make concessions over the press. On 5 March a protest by Bulgarian Turks and Pomaks, Bulgarian-speaking Muslims, secured more concessions on the restoration of Muslim names.

In the face of these disorders and of the mounting tension in the summer the government promulgated the decree on the maintenance of public order which was used to close down the 'cities of truth'. It could not, however, contain the massive pressure which built up against Lukanov in the autumn and it was the exercise of street and trade union power at that time which did much to concentrate Bulgarian political minds and to make possible the moves towards consensus in December 1990 and January 1991. The BSP were clearly frightened of the streets, and particularly those of Sofia, the more so in that opinion in the cities held Lukanov and his party responsible for an economic situation which, everyone knew, would become much worse in the near future. The UDF also sensed the danger of social conflict and it, as a democratic organisation, could not condone continuing disorders even if it had been to some degree the beneficiary of recent ones. These agreements did prevent further disorders on the streets though the danger of disruptive activity remained from one of the two large trade union organisations, *Podkrepa*, which was instructing its membership to prepare for strike action to force a dissolution of the GNA and fresh elections.

Podkrepa has played an important and at times a destructive rôle in events. It was the *Podkrepa* chief, Konstantin Trenchev, who denounced Petr Beron, and the organisation has not made life easier for the UDF since attaining observer status within it in the autumn of 1990. On the other hand, *Podkrepa*'s membership remains buoyant, and public approval of it remains only slightly lower than that for its rival, the more moderate CITUB.[20]

POLITICAL CONSENSUS AND THE PROSPECTS FOR THE FUTURE

It was one of the achievements of Zhelev and Popov that they were able to bring the extra-parliamentary forces into the consensus worked out at the end of 1990. CITUB, though not a political party or represented in the GNA, signed the agreement guaranteeing the peaceful transition; *Podkrepa* refused to do so because it was not a political organisation but nevertheless welcomed the agreement.

In October Lukanov had stressed that his government was anxious 'to maintain a constructive dialogue with the parliamentary forces and with the forces outside parliament. It attaches particular importance to its cooperation with trade union and employer organisations, including those in private business.'[21] The BSP leader did not have the public confidence to bring about that dialogue but Popov did, though he had first to secure unity within parliament.

This was achieved on 20 December with the 'Agreement among the Political Forces Represented in the Grand National Assembly on Guaranteeing the Peaceful Transition to Democratic Society'. In it the parties confirmed their commitment to parliamentary democracy and individual liberties, and they outlined a schedule, ambitious as it turned out, for the enactment of political and economic reforms. The agreement also attempted to bury a number of political hatchets. The BSP, as successor to the BCP, agreed to assume 'the political responsibility for the government of this country over the past several decades', and it also agreed that its records should be handed over to the official archives. All parties promised to provide full information on their property, and there were agreements on other outstanding issues such as the statutes of the state radio and television services.[22] On 8 January the government, both main trade union organisations, and representatives from employers' and managers' groups signed a tripartite social agreement. Under this the trade unions promised not to organise strikes for a period of two hundred days and the government undertook to provide an appropriate safety net for those affected by the economic reforms; the industrial managers declared they would show maximum sensitivity for the workers when applying the economic reforms.[23]

These moves towards consensus, particularly in the economic sphere, were encouraged to no small degree by the need to comply with conditions which the IMF had laid down for granting Bulgaria a much-needed loan, but the moves were widely welcomed and gave the country an essential release from the tensions which had been plaguing it. 'What matters most', Lilov told a news conference on 9 January, 'is to work together'.[24] But how secure is the consensus? The shock of the economic reforms, and above all of price deregulation on 1 February 1991, put an immediate strain upon the social agreement. Within days CITUB had expressed its concern that the price rises were thirty per cent above the predicted levels, whilst *Podkrepa* demanded that because the price rises had been so steep the government should redefine the poverty level and should consider reimposing some price controls.[25] The government gave way to this pressure and said the tripartite commission on coordinating interests, a permanent body established as part of the social agreement, would meet to consider some reimposition of price regulation.[26]

There were also political tensions within the consensus. When the nationalist FPL announced it would join the political agreement it urged the authorities, 'not to make biased decisions on the national and ethnic issues which will only result in social destabilisation and tension . . . . '[27] CITUB, on 13 February, was reported to have suspended its participation in the tripartite commission because of alleged violations of the agreement and because the government, it said, had allowed the television to be used to give an unbalanced view of the trade unions, a reference to a programme which had carried a statement from a prominent *Podkrepa* official.[28] For its part *Podkrepa* complained that the government had pushed through some of its economic reforms by decree rather than as legislation in the GNA. On 12 February the official news agency reported that the UDF was becoming anxious at the lack of movement on issues such as the drafting of a declaration on the BSP's responsibility for the national catastrophe, and the problem of the property of political parties, both questions which, it had been hoped, had been laid to rest in the 14 December political agreement. The UDF also said that BSP delaying tactics over the land bill threatened the political agreement.[29]

The delays over essential legislation such as the land bill and over the production of a draft constitution, together with continuing suspicion of the BSP, are serious threats to the democratic institutions of post-Zhivkov Bulgaria. Yet one should not discount the progress already made. No blood has yet been shed in Bulgaria, despite the resentment at the former abuses of power, and despite economic deprivation probably worse than anywhere in Eastern Europe. And this in a state and society which had no Hungarian 1956, no Czechoslovak 1968, no Polish 1980–81. Though by April 1991, the 'gentle revolution' had still failed to produce a new constitution, institutional change had nonetheless taken place: state had

been divorced form party, political power had been separated from social
control, political pluralism had flourished, democratic bodies and modes of
behaviour discovered, and individual liberties have been respected for the
first time in over forty years.

POSTSCRIPT: THE SPRING OF 1991 TO MARCH 1992[30]

The year which has elapsed since April 1991 has seen considerable institutional change in Bulgaria, the most of which was the introduction of a
new constitution, though this was not achieved without further difficulties
and tensions.

Some embarrassment was occasioned when the GNA, on 5 June, revoked
a decision to call a national referendum on the future state system, in
effect a plebiscite on the monarchy. A more serious dispute arose over
whether any constitution approved by a BSP-dominated GNA would be
truly democratic. Thirty-nine UDF deputies walked out of the assembly
in support of their demand that it be dissolved and new elections held so
that the constitution might be devised by representatives properly reflective
of current public opinion. Their action was solidly backed by two national
conferences of the UDF. Yet another confrontation arose from the demand
that the MPs take an oath of loyalty to the new constitution before its
contents had been agreed; a number of deputies staged a ten-day hunger
strike rather than conform to this requirement.

The new constitution was finally approved by the GNA on 12 July. It
declared Bulgaria to be a republic and also a 'democratic, constitutional,
and welfare' state. The doctrine of the separation of powers was clearly
stated and a constitutional court were established to arbitrate in any future
contests. The head of state was to be the president who was to be chosen
by direct election and all candidates for the office had to have been resident
in the country for a minimum of five years, a condition aimed at preventing
King Simeon II standing as a presidential candidate.

Having defined the political structures for the country the GNA dissolved
itself, calling elections for a regular *sobranie* for late September, though in
the event squabbles over the precise form of PR to be used meant that the
vote had to be postponed until 13 October. On that day thirty-eight parties
contested the vote, in which a four percent threshold was necessary to
secure representation in the 240-strong *sobranie*. On the basis of an 83.87
per cent turnout the results were as set out in Table 2.2.

That the BSP did so well, despite the damagingly ambiguous attitude
many of its leaders had shown to the Moscow coup in August, was in

Table 2.2   Representation of Bulgarian Parties in 1991 Parliament

UDF	34.36%	of votes cast	110 seats
BSP	33.14%		106 seats
MRF	7.55%		24 seats

part because its support was still solid in the rural areas where youth was less prominent in the electorate. Furthermore, the BSP was assiduously courting nationalist sentiment, forming an electoral alliance with a number of minor chauvinist parties including the FPL. The BSP also benefited from the fissures which ran through the ranks of all its opponents. The Agrarians were hopelessly divided; of their increasingly numerous factions only BANU-United, a combination of the old 'official Agrarians' and some of the BANU-NP group, came anywhere near representation in the assembly with 3.55 per cent of the vote. The UDF also split. The UDF-Liberals coalesced around a number of intelligentsia-based factions such as the Club for the Support of Democracy, whilst the UDF-Centre resulted from the fears of a number of groups, especially the Social Democrats, at what they believed to be the rest of the alliance's flirtation with monarchism.

The new government which followed from the election was headed by Filip Dimitrov of the Green Party, who became the first Green Party leader to become head of a European government. His cabinet was dominated by the UDF. Its minister of defence was the first civilian to hold that portfolio since 1944. The government did not include any MRF representatives but it was the support of this group which gave the administration its majority in the assembly. The new government also appointed three deputy prime ministers, one from each of the parliamentary groupings.

Political reconstruction and constitutional redefinition was completed in January 1992 when presidential elections were held. As in the parliamentary elections in October the electorate surprised the experts. President Zhelev was widely expected to achieve an absolute majority over the twenty-one other candidates in the first round of voting on 12 January. He did not. He polled 45 per cent of the votes cast, with BSP-backed Volko Volkanov taking 30 per cent, and the maverick candidate Georgi Ganchev, a returned exile, businessman, showbusiness personality, former fencing champion and fencing master at Eton, attracting 17 per cent. In the run-off elections against Volkanov seven days later Zhelev's 53 per cent support, though sufficient to secure the presidency, again disappointed his followers.

The preoccupation with political processes did not mean that the non-parliamentary forces which had emerged after November 1989 disappeared. Although rising unemployment had deprived the strike threat of much of its potency, as was seen in the lukewarm response to a general strike called for 8 January 1992 by CITUB, the trade unions continued to play an active rôle in national affairs, and the social peace agreements concluded in December 1990 and January 1991 survived until early in 1992. The agreements had been weakened by tensions between CITUB and *Podkrepa*, but also by the fact that the government was showing itself more willing to re-intervene in the economy to regulate prices of essential commodities and so protect the most vulnerable members of society from the enormous economic pressures being exerted upon them. Most importantly, however, the decline of the agreeements was the result of the successful transition to parliamentary democracy; political power now resided in the parliament and the major social forces seemed ready to recognise the fact.

That political power had been effectively transferred from the streets to the parliament was a considerable achievement made greater by the background against which it took place. 1991 saw price rises seldom below four hundred percent even for essential commodities; in the late autumn there were renewed interruptions of power supplies; unemployment rocketed from 27,000 to 420,000; and for most people real wages fell drastically. In addition to this there were continuing difficulties between the Bulgarians and the Turks. Nationalist passions could also have been aroused over the consequences of the alarming destabilisation of the Balkans following the collapse of Yugoslavia, for Macedonia can be an emotive issue in Bulgaria. Yet despite these internal tensions, and despite international and Balkan instability, Bulgaria has not seen the emergence of a demagogic, authoritarian movement; there is, as yet, no Bulgarian Le Pen.

Bulgaria's difficulties are certainly not all overcome. The BSP is showing signs that it can fish in very murky waters for electoral and political advantage; social tensions have not all dissipated; there is a danger that attempts to prevent a recrudescence of communist authoritarianism could turn into a witch hunt and/or vengeance, as, for example, in the attempt to deprive CITUB of its property on the grounds that the organisation was created by the old régime; there are signs that the BSP's connivance with chauvinist elements might produce an over-reaction by the MRF where even the previously circumspect Dogan has called for the banning of the BSP, an absurd notion when the party polled a third of the votes in a free election; and there is scope for further constitutional dispute as was shown by a recent (February–March 1992) confrontation between president and parliament over control of the intelligence services.

Yet despite these dangers Bulgaria can claim a unique achievement in post-communist Eastern Europe. It has seen two general elections, the second of which removed the communists or socialists from office. Although problems remain it seems that Bulgaria has absorbed the most important lesson of parliamentary democracy: that what matters most is not the solution but how it is achieved, that the means are more important than the ends.

NOTES

1. For English-language treatments of Bulgaria since 1945, see R. J. Crampton, *A Short History of Modern Bulgaria*, Cambridge, 1987, pp. 145–209; John D. Bell, *The Bulgarian Communist Party from Blagoev to Zhivkov*, Stanford, California, 1986, pp. 77–147; John R. Lampe, *The Bulgarian Economy in the Twentieth Century*, London, 1986, pp. 121–222; Robert J. McIntyre, *Bulgaria: Politics, Economics and Society*, London, 1988, which takes an indulgent attitude to the Zhivkov régime; and for a more detailed but earlier treatment of the years up to 1970, J. F. Brown, *Bulgaria under Communist Rule*, London, 1970.

2. See Richard J. Crampton, '"Stumbling and Dusting Off," or an Attempt to Pick a Path Through the Thicket of Bulgaria's New Economic Mechanism', *Eastern European Politics and Societies*, Vol. 2, No. 2 (Spring 1988), pp. 333–95.

3. See R. J. Crampton, 'The Intelligentsia, the ecology and the opposition in Bulgaria', *The World Today*, Vol. 46, No. 2 (February 1990), pp. 23–26.

4. For further details of the results, see below.

5. British Broadcasting Corporation, *Summary of World Broadcasts, Eastern Europe*, 13 Dec. 1989. This source hereafter cited as *SWB EE*, with appropriate piece number and date. These reports have formed the basis for the information contained in this essay, but to save repetition and paper precise references have in the main been given only for direct quotations.

6. *Ibid.*, 29 March 1991.

7. See R. J. Crampton, 'The Bulgarian elections of 1990', *Representation*, Vol. 29, no. 108, (Winter 1990), pp. 33–35.

8. *SWB EE*, 29 March 1991.

9. *Ibid.*, 13 December 1989.

10. In Bulgarian the suffix *shtina* is the equivalent of the Russian *shchina* and means the times, the polices, the atmosphere associated with the person to whose name the suffix is added.

11.   *SWB EE*, 26 October 1990.
12.   As with, for example, the tensions between nationalists and ethnic Turks. See *SWB EE*, 18 January 1991.
13.   *Ibid.*, 3 December 1990.
14.   *Ibid.*, 29 January 1991.
15.   See Misha Glenny, *The Rebirth of History; Eastern Europe in the Age of Democracy*, London, 1990, p. 176.
16.   The numbering of congresses had reverted to that used for the socialist party founded in 1891.
17.   *SWB EE*, 25 September 1990.
18.   *Ibid.*, 30 October 1990.
19.   Kostadin Chakrov, *Vrtoriya Etazh*, Sofia, 1990, pp. 21–50 *passim*.
20.   In March 53.6 per cent approved of CITUB and 48.8 per cent of *Podkrepa*. Their respective disapproval ratings were 19.1 per cent and 26.2 per cent. *Debati*, 12 March 1991.
21.   *SWB EE*, 12 October 1990.
22.   For a full English text of the agreement see, *The Insider: Bulgarian Digest Monthly*, February 1991, pp. 13–15.
23.   *SWB EE*, 10 January 1991.
24.   *Ibid.*, 11 January 1991.
25.   *Ibid.*, 4 February 1991, and 7 February 1991.
26.   *Ibid.*, 7 February 1991.
27.   *Ibid.*, 11 January 1991.
28.   *Ibid.*, 19 February 1991.
29.   *Ibid.*
30.   This concluding section is based upon the relevant papers from SWB/EE, the Bulgarian Telegraph Agency's daily reports and various Bulgarian newspapers.

3 Czechoslovakia

Judy Batt

Czechoslovakia is unique among the post-communist states of Central and Eastern Europe in its parliamentary-democratic heritage. The First Republic of the inter-war years remains source of national pride and self-confidence. As Edward Taborsky, who was personal secretary to President Edward Benes, wrote in 1945 when the country was just re-emerging from the trauma of the Second World War:

> If it is true that the supreme test of successful government lies in its practical achievements, then Czechoslovak parliamentary democracy has passed the test with flying colours. It is indeed considered to be one of the best developed in the world by those foreign students of government who have given it a close and objective study.[1]

The importance of the inter-war experience in the national memory was demonstrated in 1968, during the brief period of eight months when Czechs and Slovaks attempted to revive their democratic heritage. Public opinion polls at the time showed how vivid was the memory of the First Republic in people's minds as one of the most glorious periods in their history.[2] And today too, this heritage is frequently cited as a reason for optimism about the outcome of the political transition. Parliamentary democracy is argued to be more deeply rooted in Czechoslovakia's political culture than is the case in any of its Central and East European neighbours.

One of the many interesting questions to be asked when we compare the course of transition to democracy currently under way in post-communist states is whether this assumption will prove correct: to what extent will past experience really prove a decisive factor in securing a smoother political transition in Czechoslovakia than elsewhere? It is of course too early to make a conclusive judgement, but I am rather sceptical about this. The First Republic, for all its undoubted merits, also had unresolved ambiguities and flaws which are often glossed over in the rosy accounts of its more enthusiastic proponents. Today's drafters of the new Czechoslovak constitution will need to address these problems. Moreover, it has to be recognised that while the new generation of politicians in Czechoslovakia may derive understanding and self-confidence from reflection on their national past, they enjoy no greater experience of the practical business of politics and are not obviously better prepared for the responsibilities of power than their colleagues in neighbouring countries.

There is not space here to dwell at length on the inter-war constitution, but we should note some of its problems. The excessive number of political parties represented in parliament as a result of the proportional electoral system made coalition government inevitable. Moreover, the role of the parties was extraordinarily powerful; the use of party lists in elections in multi-member constituencies made parliamentary deputies very dependent on their party, and even after their election, drastic party discipline could be enforced because the parties were legally able to recall individual deputies and replace them with alternatives from the list. While coalition fostered pragmatic compromise in government, it required much behind-the-scenes negotiation between party bosses on policy issues, weakening the role of open debate in parliament. A certain unease about the role of parties and their compatibility with the democratic ideal lingers on in Czechoslovakia today.

Another feature of inter-war politics was the role of the presidency. The constitution-drafters of the First Republic had intended the post to be a weak one, weaker than that prescribed in the constitution of the French Fourth Republic, which in most other respects had been taken as a model. This was due to the deep anti-monarchist bias of the time in reaction against the heritage of Austrian rule. But the personality of the first President, Thomas Garrigue Masaryk, revered as the father of independent Czechoslovakia, in practice lent enormous authority to the post. As Taborsky recalls: 'Though the fact was not realised by the common man, the trend was away from parliamentary democracy in the direction of presidential democracy.'[3] Today too, the question of the role and powers of the presidency has to be addressed anew.

But undoubtedly the biggest problem in the past, present and future constitutions of Czechoslovakia is the determination of the proper balance between the centre and the regions, which is part of the still unresolved controversies over national identity and Czech-Slovak relations. The unsatisfied demand for Slovak autonomy must be counted, after the Sudeten German question (which is no longer an issue today), the key internal weakness of inter-war politics. Subsequent post-war constitutions proved no more satisfactory in this respect. Indeed, the 1960 constitution seriously eroded what little autonomy Slovakia had enjoyed and thus contributed to the particular grievances which activated Slovaks in the political crisis of the 1960s. The post-invasion regime led by the Slovak Gustav Husak introduced constitutional amendments which promised full federation in order to buy Slovak support for the restoration of communist rule after 1968, but these rights remained on paper only as long as real power was wholly monopolised by the strictly centralised Communist Party. This constitution remained in force after the collapse of communist rule, and determined the framework for decision-making by the new democratic politicians. Not only were the constitution's federal provisions unsatisfactory to the Slovaks from the point of view of the degree of autonomy secured, but they also resulted in a fragmented and unwieldy structure for decision-making in the Federal Assembly itself, which could only work in the past because it was purely a facade and had no real life of its own.

One of the most significant – and un-revolutionary – features of the 'velvet revolution' of November 1989 was the intense commitment to legality and constitutional procedure displayed by the leading figures who took on political responsibility for the transition. Thus despite the dubious origins and problematic content of the existing legal and constitutional framework, it has been adhered to as far as possible. But both its unsatisfactory features and the fact that it is generally agreed that it must be completely rewritten and replaced with a new one mean that adherence to constitutional procedure and strict legality are not enough to ensure the legitimacy of the existing decision-making structures or to build and sustain consensus. The transition period is thus characterised by a large amount of uncertainty, *ad hoc* improvisation, and intractable conflict which have already begun to erode the massive popular goodwill and optimism with which the new regime started out.

PARTIES AND THE ELECTIONS

A new electoral law was one of the first pieces of legislation put before the reconstituted Federal Assembly in early 1990. Debate on the specific provisions of the law was curtailed by the pressure of time, and although many people had reservations about it, it was generally recognised that some system had to be found as quickly as possible in order to get the electoral process under way. So the most obvious solution was to turn to the previous pre-communist system for inspiration, with the understanding that this would only be used for the first election, and that a full reconsideration of the electoral system would be made after the election by the democratically elected assembly as part of its task of drafting a new constitution. The system adopted was a proportional one, which divided the country into twelve large multiple-member constituencies based on the existing regional administrative units (*kraje*) and the cities of Prague and Bratislava. Candidates would be put forward by registered parties which were to draw up regional lists, circulated to the voters three days in advance of polling day. Voters would select one of the party lists, and also would have the option of indicating particular preference for up to four candidates if they wished to alter the order in which the parties placed candidates on the list. Voting was to take place simultaneously, on the basis of the same constituencies, for deputies to each of the two Houses of the Federal Assembly and to the Czech and Slovak National Councils (the legislatures of the Czech and Slovak Republics). In order to qualify for the allocation of seats after the ballot, a party had to win at least five per cent of the total votes cast in either the Czech or the Slovak Republic. For election to the Czech National Council, the same five per cent hurdle applied, but for the Slovak National Council, the hurdle was lowered to three per cent. After eliminating those parties which failed to clear the hurdle (whose votes would then be lost), seats were allocated in each constituency proportionately to each party, and candidates from the list were chosen to fill the seats according to the order in which they appeared on the list, taking into account the expressed preferences of voters.

Twenty-two parties finally qualified to register and thus present lists at the election, although many more parties were in existence. In order to register, a party had to prove it had 10,000 members, or, more realistically given the situation, were allowed simply to present a petition of supporters' signatures to bring up their total numbers to 10,000. The major party in the Czech Republic was the Civic Forum (CV), which had first emerged in the crisis in the autumn of 1989. Its leading core of activists comprised long-time oppositionists of Charter 77 and other human rights groups, but it won massive numbers of enthusiastic supporters from among the previously inactive, intimidated Czech population. In Slovakia, a similar movement had sprung into life simultaneously in November 1989, called Public Against Violence (PAV). Both CF and PAV were broad coalitional 'umbrella movements', uniting a very diverse range of individuals and groups (including not a few recent converts to democracy from among those who had been communists until 1989). In fact both strove to avoid describing themselves as 'parties', and even as 'political' organisations, as if the notions of party and politics were irretrievably morally tainted. At first, some even denied that CF would play any conventional political role, such as participating in elections, but would act in some ill-defined way as a forum for spiritual regeneration and social re-education. Moreover, the adherents of CF and PAV were for a long time deeply resistant to organisation, hierarchy, and even to formal membership. Thus internal structures remained informal and *ad hoc*, giving the movements a refreshing vitality, but at the cost of a lack of discipline, coherence, and satisfactory channels of communication and accountability between leaders and the rank-and-file, problems which were not fully appreciated until after the election. In many respects, CF and PAV at this time were comparable to Solidarity in Poland, especially in its heyday in 1980–81, as spontaneous mass movements uniting society against communist rule. These were all clearly democratic movements, but in an important sense were *pre-pluralist*, claiming to represent the whole of society, and tending to imply that sectional interests were somehow of inferior moral worth. As a noted CF election slogan put it, 'Parties are for party hacks, Civic Forum is for everyone.' While this was not inappropriate, and proved very successful for the first election which was in essence a plebiscite against communist rule, as a longer term proposition it was an illusion which later would have to be painfully abandoned.

The main alternatives to the CF/PAV bandwagon were the Communist Party (CP) and the Christian Democrats (CD). The Communist Party rather surprisingly did not collapse completely after November 1989, as occurred in Poland, nor did it undergo the traumatic self-redefinition that struck the Hungarian Socialist Workers' Party. It did not even rename itself, but it did 'federalise' itself by establishing a Communist Party of Bohemia and Moravia to complement the Communist Party of Slovakia which had always existed. But links between the two rapidly weakened as the Slovak communists proceeded to rename themselves the Party of the Democratic Left, following the example of the East German communists. The non-communist social-democratic left was to prove as ineffective in Czechoslovakia as in neighbouring Hungary – divided by personal conflicts and rivalries, and by the strategic question of whether to fight the election under the CF umbrella or independently. It was, moreover, difficult to find a space on the left of the political spectrum not already occupied by the much better organised and equipped Communist Party.

Christian Democrats emerged in both the Czech Republic and Slovakia, and attempts were made to forge links across the national divide, but by and large these links did not flourish. The People's Party, which had existed in the Czech provinces all through the period of communist rule as a manipulated partner of the CP, revived and purged itself of its most clearly compromised leaders, and was accepted as a partner in the electoral campaign by the Christian Democrats. But just before polling day, its new leader was exposed as having been for years a paid informer of the communist security forces, which badly damaged the CD's chances

Table 3.1   Distribution of Seats in the Federal Assembly[9]

HOUSE OF THE NATIONS (150 seats)
Czech Section (75 seats)

Civic Forum	50
Communist Party	12
MSD/SMS*	7
Christian and Democratic Union	6

Slovak Section (75 seats)

Public Against Violence	33
Christian Democratic Movement	14
Communist Party	12
Slovak National Party	9
Coexistence	7

HOUSE OF THE PEOPLE (150 seats)
(101 from Czech Republic)

Civic Forum	68
Communist Party	15
Christian and Democratic Union	9
MSD/SMS*	9

(49 from Slovak Republic)

Public Against Violence	19
Communist Party	8
Christian and Democratic Movement	11
Slovak National Party	6
Coexistence	5

---

*MSD/SMS – Movement for Self-Governing Democracy/Society for Moravia and Silesia

in the Czech Republic. The Christian Democratic Movement in Slovakia, however, was to prove a powerful challenger to PAV, drawing on the strong cultural traditionalism and devout Catholicism of Slovak society, and enjoying able and prestigious leadership under the Carnogursky brothers, scions of a well-known Bratislava conservative political dynasty. Lastly, nationalist and regionalist parties were gathering steam in the spring and early summer: the noisy, intolerant, separatist, and chauvinistic Slovak National Party, and a surprising new force challenging CF's dominance in Moravia, the Movement for Self-Governing Democracy/Society for Moravia and Silesia, demanding greater regional devolution.

The election itself was pronounced by the teams of international observers sent by various organisations to check up on the poll to have been the best run and most happily conducted of any witnessed in Eastern Europe.[4] The turnout of 96 per cent of registered voters was indeed worthy of the

Table 3.2   Distribution of Seats in the Czech and Slovak National Councils

Distribution of Seats in the Czech National Council *(Total 200 seats)*	
Civic Forum	127
Communist Party	32
MSD/SMS	22
Christian and Democratic Union	19
Distribution of Seats in the Slovak National Council *(Total 150 seats)*	
Public Against Violence	48
Christian Democratic Movement	31
Slovak National Party	22
Communist Party	22
Coexistence	14
Democratic Party	7
Green Party	6

'velvet revolution' of the previous year. Civic Forum won over 53 per cent of the votes in the Czech Republic, and its nearest rival proved to be the Communist Party, with 13.5 per cent. The Christian Democrats in the Czech lands won under 9 per cent. PAV carried off the most votes in Slovakia, with 32.5 per cent, doing rather better than had been expected against the Christian Democratic Movement, which won just under 19 per cent, and the Communist Party, which won nearly 14 per cent. The MSD/SMS performed very strongly with nearly 8 per cent support in the Czech Republic, and the SNP in Slovakia won just under 11 per cent, but in Bratislava, their support went up to almost 17 per cent, higher than either the CP or the Christian Democratic Movement and second only to PAV. A further party emerged in Slovakia, Coexistence, a party representing ethnic minorities (mainly Hungarians) which won 8.6 per cent of the vote.

In the two years between the June 1990 and June 1992 general elections, the parties and party-system of Czechoslovakia underwent rapid change. As elsewhere in post-communist Europe, this change took the form of fragmentation through splits in the existing parties, with little convincing evidence of realignments to rebuild effective unions or coalitions of political forces. Moreover, the Czechoslovakia has exhibited increasing divergence in the bases of party competition between the Czech Republic and Slovakia, and the failure to form any truly federal party with a strong presence in both republics and an organisational structure transcending the divide between them.

Both Civic Forum and Public Against Violence split, and had effectively ceased to exist by early 1992. This was only to be expected given their heterogeneity, but it occurred much sooner than most people had anticipated. Three key overlapping issues polarised opinion within CF, leading to the formation of organised factional groups which were the embryos of new parties. The first issue concerned the CF's identity: should it remain a rather broad, informal, spontaneous mass movement, or develop into a structured, disciplined party to support the new government? The second issue related to the strategy and pace of economic transition: although there was broad agreement on the need for a radical approach to the economy, the rhetoric of 'shock therapy' tended to provoke anxiety about the neglect of welfare considerations and ruthless commercialisation among a significant number of CF supporters. And lastly, these issue-based divisions began to crystalise around specific personalities. One of the most forceful and distinctive new politicians is the Minister of Finance, Vaclav Klaus, an enthusiastic neo-liberal economist. Despite rumours in June, at the timing of forming the second Calfa government, that Klaus did not enjoy the full confidence of President Havel, he was nevertheless elected Chairman of CF in October 1990. This accelerated the split in CF, and Klaus became leader of a CF faction which constituted itself as the Civic Democratic Party at a founding congress on 23 February 1991. The party stands for determined radicalism in the approach to economic transformation, strongly supporting the policy of the Federal Government, in which Klaus is Minister of Finance. It follows naturally that this faction wants to develop into a traditional, hierarchically-organised political party in order to mobilise support for the government's economic policy. A closely allied grouping in policy and ideological terms, but preserving a certain distance from Klaus personally, is the Civic Democratic Alliance (CDA) which has existed since before the June election within CF as a conservative-liberal ginger-group. Leading figures in it are parliamentary deputies Daniel Kroupa and Pavel Bratinka, later joined by Federal Minister of the Economy, Vladimir Dlouhy and the Deputy Chairman of the Czech assembly, Jan Kalvoda. By early 1992, both these right-of-centre parties had also come to represent a rather outspoken position in defence of Czech national interests in opposition to what they identified as the excessive willingness on the part of some federal and Czech politicians to conciliate Slovak nationalism at the expense of the federation and the Federal government's economic policies.

The other major party to emerge from the break-up of the CF was the 'centrist' Civic Movement (CM), which sought to represent a 'gentler' social-liberal tendency which, while supporting the broad thrust of government economic policy, would prefer to temper its harsher aspects and defend welfare interests where practically possible. The Civic Movement was founded on the basis of the looser, more spontaneous and informal concept of organisation characteristic of CF at its origins. In some respects it can be regarded as the continuation of the traditions of Charter 77, and it contains many former 'dissident' activists. Its leading figures include Foreign Minister Jiri Dienstbier and Czech Republic Prime Minister Petr Pithart, and its approach to most political issues is very much in line with President Havel's sympathies, although there is no formal connection. By early 1992, the CM was also beginning to take a distinctively different line from the Christian Democratic Party (CDP) and the CDA on the federal issue. Petr Pithart, closely involved in negotiating with Slovak partners on constitutional reform, has become associated with an unusually (for a Czech) sympathetic approach to Slovak demands for autonomy, and appears far more ready to concede the necessity of a looser, confederal constitutional framework than is acceptable to the CDP and CDA.

The split in PAV occurred suddenly and very bitterly in the spring of 1991 as a result of conflict within its leadership precipitated by the personality of the then Slovak Prime Minister, Vladimir Meciar, a PAV member. The underlying issue was inevitably the position of Slovakia in the federation, and, closely connected to it, the question of support for the Federal government's radical economic policies. During autumn 1990, Meciar discovered the political advantages of nationalist rhetoric, and began to employ them to great effect as the various Slovak parties found themselves competing for support in an environment increasingly charged with nationalist emotion. But this provoked deepening division within the movement, a large proportion of whose original core activists were liberal intellectuals who, while by no means unresponsive to demands for greater Slovak autonomy, nevertheless were committed to the federal framework. They found Meciar's increasingly populist political style and his provocative behaviour towards his Federal and Czech government counterparts objectionable.

At the same time, deep divisions emerged over the issue of economic reform. Meciar favoured 'special treatment' for Slovakia on the grounds of its peculiarly weak economic starting point; his arguments seemed more and more to marry potent nationalist rhetoric with the anti-market appeals of the communists, still a politically significant force in Slovakia. This line was fiercely resisted by other PAV leaders, for example, the Minister of the Economy in Slovakia, Kucerak, a strong supporter of the radical economic policy line of the Federal Government.

Conflict within the PAV over these two key issues, federalism and economic transformation, produced paralysis in the Slovak government, which was eventually resolved by the dismissal of Meciar from his post as Slovak Prime Minister by the Presidium of the Slovak National Council, which has the function of a kind of collective presidency in Slovak politics. Jan Carnogursky, leader of the Slovak Christian Democratic Movement, was appointed in his place. Meciar himself proceeded to mobilise his considerable personal following in mass protest demonstrations on the streets of Bratislava. He then broke away from PAV to form his own Movement for a Democratic Slovakia (MFDS), propagating a mixture of populist, nationalist, and anti-capitalist rhetoric with obvious wide appeal. The rump of PAV, which renamed itself the Civic Democratic Union (CDU), joined as junior partners in the new governing coalition in Slovakia under Carnogursky, and continued to defend the case for constitutional reform within the federal framework, and to support the economic policies of the Federal government. This does not appear to be a recipe for electoral success in Slovakia, and the prospects for this party are bleak.

Thus pluralisation within the Civic Forum and PAV has produced a set of successor parties which are much less able to form effective coalitions across the republican divide. The strongest parties in the respective republics, CDP and MFDS, are diametrically opposed on the key issues of the economy and the future of the federation. The CM, for all its softer, more flexible and conciliatory approach towards the economy and towards Slovak aspirations, cannot work with the MFDS's opportunistic and ill-defined policies, still less with its leader Meciar. Although the CDP has much in common with the PAV-CDU, a coalition between the two is unlikely to be fruitful given the weakness of Slovak support for the PAV-CDU.

Three other major political groupings which might have been expected to have great potential for developing cross-republican links are the Social Democrats and the Christian Democrats. But neither of these has succeeded in building up a strong presence in both republics: the Social Democrats, although rather weakly represented in legislative bodies elected in June 1990, could turn out to be the second strongest electoral force in the Czech Republic, but they are still very weak in Slovakia (despite Alexander Dubcek's recent decision to join them). The Christian Democrats are relatively strong in Slovakia, where they have been the main party in the government coalition since March 1991, but are weaker in the Czech Republic, where they are divided into two, the Christian Democratic Party led by the veteran Charter 77 activist Vaclav Benda, and the Christian Democratic Union, an alliance incorporating the Czechoslovak People's Party. Moreover, it is characteristic of both Social Democrats and Christian Democrats that contacts between the Czech and Slovak counterparts are at best sporadic and barely organized. While the leader of the Czech Social Democrats, the economist Valtr Komarek, is one of the most popular Czech politicians among Slovaks in general, Slovak Social Democrats mistrust their Czech counterparts and will not form an electoral alliance with them, largely because the Czechs insisted on calling themselves *Czechoslovak*. Christian Democrats in the two republics are fundamentally at odds over the constitutional issue: the Christian Democratic Movement in Slovakia is strongly autonomist, and aims ultimately to achieve separate Slovak statehood by gradualist and peaceful means; while the Czech Christian Democratic deputies are allied in legislative bodies with the 'Conservative Bloc' of parties, which includes the CDP and which has taken a strongly pro-federal line on constitutional issues. The Slovak Christian Democrats themselves split in March 1992 into a more radical, nationalist group led by Jan Klepac, and a more pragmatic group led by Carnogursky, committed to furthering the cause of Slovak independence through gradualism and negotiation with the Czechs.

THE FEDERAL ASSEMBLY

The Federal Assembly is a bicameral legislature, comprising a House of the People and a House of the Nations, each with 150 seats. Seats in the House of the People are distributed across the whole territory of Czechoslovakia according to size of population: at present, 101 deputies represent the voters in the Czech Republic, and 49 represent Slovak voters. The House of the Nations is designed to give equal representation to the two Republics, and is divided into two sections, Czech and Slovak, each comprising 75 deputies. This division of the House of Nations in some respects makes the Assembly tri-cameral, for the Czech and Slovak sections vote separately on major items of legislation (including economic plans, the budget, taxation, price regulations and foreign economic relations), on constitutional issues, and on the presidency. Moreover, there are exceptionally demanding rules on voting for the passage of major pieces of legislation. Support of three-fifths of the total deputies *elected* (not just of those present in a quorate session) in each of the House of the People and the two sections of the House of the Nations is required for the election of the President, for the enactment of the constitution and constitutional amendments, and declaration of war. Other major legislation requires the vote of a majority of all elected deputies in each of the House of the People and the two sections of the House of the Nations. These rules have had a great impact in the current extraordinary period of transformation of the economic and political systems, when most legislation is precisely of the kind which is subject to these very stringent voting requirements. The rules in fact give the power to block or veto legislation to small numbers of deputies in the sections of the House of the Nations. On the other hand, a vote of no-confidence in the government or any of its ministers individually can be passed with the support of the majority of deputies present in a quorate session of *any one of* the House of the People, the Czech section or the Slovak section of the House of the Nations, again giving great potential power over the government to rather small numbers of deputies.

Thus despite the fact that CF/PAV together enjoyed a clear majority in both Houses, PAV only had 33 of the 75 deputies in the Slovak section of the House of Nations (see Table 3.1). It was therefore essential, after the June 1990 elections, to draw in other parties into a coalition government. The need for coalition was further heightened by the internal structure (or lack of it) of the CF and PAV, both of which embraced a very wide range of political views and neither of which could rely on the disciplined support of their deputies for their government.

THE FEDERAL AND REPUBLICAN GOVERNMENTS

Forming the government is the task of the President, and a very challenging business it was for President Havel after the June 1990 elections, although in fact it was completed relatively efficiently. Marian Calfa, who had been installed following the collapse of the communist regime, remained as Prime Minister. The choice of Calfa was conditioned by several factors. Against him might have been the fact that he was a former communist, and had actually been Minister without portfolio in the last communist government. Although a popular campaign had built up significant anti-communist momentum, President Havel had come to respect him as a competent legal and administrative expert, and valued his personal contribution to the transition from communist rule. The choice of Calfa also symbolised President Havel's personal commitment to social reconciliation and his rejection of past communist practice of blocking the careers of able individuals on account of their (or their parents') political pasts. In any case, because Communist Party membership had been a *sine qua non* of a professional career under the old regime, there were indeed very few qualified, competent and experienced people available who were not so tainted. In the meanwhile, Calfa had disowned his communist past and had joined PAV. No doubt it was also of more than passing significance that Calfa was Slovak, who thus balanced the Czech Havel in the presidency.

But Calfa as Prime Minister was always overshadowed by Havel and dependent on his support, and was unable to build up much independent personal authority except as a recognised administrative expert.

The same task of balancing party affiliation, ethnic identity, personal competence and professional expertise was involved in finalising the government team as a whole. CF/PAV were allocated 8 of the 16 posts, including that of the Prime Minister and two Deputy Prime Ministers. CF/PAV secured the participation of the three members of the Slovak Christian Democratic Movement in the government, one as a Deputy Prime Minister and two as Ministers. A further six ministerial posts were given to non-party experts. The government contains six Slovaks, including the Prime Minister and one of the four Deputy Prime Ministers, the rest being Czechs.

In the Czech Republic, despite the convincing majority of CF in the Czech National Council (with 127 of the 200 seats), it was decided also to seek a coalition in order to secure the broadest possible support for the Czech government. Thus CF took 21 of the posts, including that of the Prime Minister, which went to Petr Pithart, a long-time Charter 77 activist. Two posts went to People's Party candidates, one to the MSD/SMS, and seven independent experts were brought in. In the Slovak National Council, PAV's position was rather less secure than that of CF in its Czech counterpart. As PAV had only 48 of the 150 seats, coalition was not a luxury but a necessity. Coalition partners were found in the Christian Democratic Movement and the Democratic Party (one of the former puppet parties which had survived as partners of the Communist Party under the old regime). PAV took 13 of the 23 posts in the Slovak government, including that of Prime Minister, while the CDM took seven posts and the DP three. After the crisis in the Slovak government in April 1991, the dominant party became the Christian Democrats, with Jan Carnogursky as Prime Minister.

THE PRESIDENCY

The presidency has become once again, as in the inter-war years, the lynchpin of Czechoslovak politics, and, as before, this is due far more to the personality in the post than to the formal definition of the powers attached to the post in the constitution. Vaclav Havel's proven moral integrity and strength of character forged in decades of consistent and conscientious opposition to the communist regime are happily combined with modesty and charm, generosity of spirit and a warm sense of humour. He is uniquely

well suited to the task of, in his own phrase, the 'rehabilitation of politics'
– the restoration of public confidence and respect in the highest political
office in Czechoslovakia. The exercise of power and political leadership
is not something which he was seeking; he accepted the office out of an
overriding sense of duty, and initially declared he would only remain in
it until free elections had taken place. But he was prevailed upon to stand
for reappointment after the June general election, and won overwhelming
support in the Federal Assembly – characteristically, he particularly valued
the 50 votes cast against him as evidence of the revival of 'normal'
politics. It is characteristic of him that he freely – and with unnerving
openness – admits to an awareness of his unpreparedness and anxiety
about his suitability for these tasks, which would tax even the most
politically-sophisticated and experienced statesman.

Nonetheless, the circumstances of the time are serving to augment the
authority and influence of the presidency. In a time of acute national crisis,
regime change, and mounting centrifugal pressures, when all existing
institutions and mechanisms for resolving conflict are open to question
if not shattered, the burden of responsibility tends naturally to gravitate
towards a single centre and a single person. Havel may have envisaged
his role as President as that of figurehead, but increasingly he has been
drawn into direct participation in shaping the government's approach to key
issues of the economic and political transition. The role of the Presidential
Office on the Castle (*Hrad*) in Prague has grown as Havel has appointed
teams of advisers to help him, and this has led to accusations that he is
setting up a parallel cabinet. Indeed, evidence of conflict between Havel's
economic adviser and leading members of the government over the strategy
of economic transition did appear at one point shortly after the June 1990
election but, by and large, Havel has used his authority to support the
government rather than compete with it (in contrast to Walesa in Poland).

President Havel is not helped in managing the personal and political
challenges he faces by the constitutional definition of his powers, which
is vague to the point of unworkability. The constitutional position of
the President is in fact very weak. He elected by and responsible to
the Federal Assembly; it is not clear in the constitution but it seems
likely that that the Assembly could recall the President. The President
has no right to dissolve the Assembly except in the case where the
two Houses are unable to reach agreement on the budget. The President
nominates the Prime Minister and other government ministers, including
assigning specific posts, but his nominations are all subject to a vote
of confidence in the Federal Assembly. The Assembly may express no
confidence in specific members of the government, and in this case the

President is obliged to recall them. Crucially, he cannot challenge the Assembly by calling a general election. Moreover, he has no right to veto legislation.

THE FEDERAL CRISIS

The first indication that Czech-Slovak relations would once again erupt to become the major political issue came in March and April 1990 with the unexpected (at least to the Czechs) controversy in the Federal Assembly over the renaming of the country. President Havel started with the seemingly innocuous proposal that the Czechoslovak Socialist Republic be renamed the Czechoslovak Republic, but this immediately opened the way to a debate not on the word 'Socialist' but on the word 'Czechoslovak'. This was found to be unacceptable to many Slovak deputies since it smacked too much of Masaryk's 'Czechoslovakism' of the inter-war period, and as such was resented by nationalist Slovaks as an affront to their distinctive, separate identity. An acrimonious debate ensued over whether or not the word should be hyphenated as 'Czecho-slovak' and further, whether there should be a capital 'S' in 'Czecho-Slovak'. After prolonged debate in the spring of 1990, agreement was reached on the new name of 'Czech and Slovak Federal Republic', but the debate served to fuel Slovak nationalism which contributed to the electoral performance of the Slovak National Party (SNP) in June.

After the elections, the Slovak Prime Minister Vladimir Meciar lost no time in making the issue of the distribution of powers between the Federal Government and the Republics central to the political agenda. He insisted that the issue could not wait until the new federal and republican constitutions had been drawn up, which was expected to occupy a large part of the two-year term the new legislatures had allotted themselves. A constitutional amendment should be drafted to resolve the question of the division of powers, he argued, and should be passed by the end of the year, for many of the key decisions which the Federal Government had to take straight away – especially on economic policy and privatisation – would inescapably touch upon the rights of the Republics. Thus came about a protracted, and more than occasionally rancorous and mistrustful series of meetings between the three governments, starting at Trencianske Teplice on 8–9 August 1990. A draft amendment was produced on 13 November, but tension and uncertainty about the draft persisted right to the very eve of the Federal Assembly's 12 December session, at which the constitutional amendment was finally passed.[5] It had been a bruising battle, and the content of the amendment was recognized as unsatisfactory on many counts.

Meciar had proved a very hard bargainer for his Federal and Czech Government counterparts, and his abrasive style did not help matters – although it won him a considerable personal following in Slovakia. Many Czechs felt unhappy with the terms of the amendment because they felt it was the product of an unstable compromise and represented an incoherent mix of federal and confederal elements. The Federal Government would retain control over defence, foreign affairs, and foreign trade; but, to Czech irritation, the Slovak government nevertheless set up its own Ministry of International Affairs. It was finally agreed that the Republics would in fact enjoy the right to make treaties with foreign powers, but 'subject to Federal Government permission'. It is far from clear whether and how the Federal Government could effectively prevent a Republic concluding a treaty to which it objected.

Much energetic debate surrounded economic matters. The Slovaks originally had raised demands for complete control over economic policy, floating the ideas of separate banking systems and even a separate currency. However, they were finally induced to accept a single central bank and currency, and federal control over taxation, customs, and price reforms. It was agreed that the Federal Government should have the right to raise its own income from direct taxation, rather than depending on transfers from the Republics as the Slovaks had proposed. Open conflict broke out over the question of general control over economic policy: the Federal Minister of Finance, Vaclav Klaus, and the Federal Minister of the Economy, Vladimir Dlouhy, both ardent free-market economic reformers, accused the Slovak side of attempting to slow down and divert the course of economic transformation by demanding that Republican control over economic matters be so extensive as to deprive the Federal Government of the instruments to enforce its economic policy in practice. Slovaks in turn retorted hotly that Klaus and Dlouhy were displaying classic symptoms of overbearing Prague centralism, and ignoring the very real differences in the economic conditions in the two Republics. Federal economic policy would, they felt, continue to be based on assumptions which suited the Czechs, and Slovaks would pay a disproportion price.

Everything else not specified as belonging to the Federal Government was to fall within the Republics' powers. They would raise their own revenues directly, and no redistribution of resources would be allowed between the Republics by the Federal Government. It was the Slovaks who insisted on this, despite the fact that as the weaker economy, Slovakia was almost certainly the net recipient of resource transfers. No consensus was reached on some key questions, which were simply postponed: for example, the mechanism for declaring a state of emergency, control over TV and radio and transport policy, and the ownership of natural resources. The entire constitutional amendment itself was an interim measure, all of whose provisions are open to further debate in the course of the drafting of the new constitution.

By the time the amendment was to be put to the Federal Assembly at the end of 1990, President Havel had become aware of a looming danger; if the Federal Assembly were unable to approve the constitutional amendment, the existing constitution provided no means for resolving the deadlock. In an attempt to avert this possibility, Havel addressed the Federal Assembly before it dealt with the amendment, and pleaded for it to consider the immediate introduction of three possible mechanisms for resolving deadlock in the Assembly: the resurrection of a constitutional Court with appropriate powers to adjudicate; the introduction of national referenda to decide key questions; the extension of the powers of the presidency, which, as noted above, are particularly deficient in this respect. In the event, the deputies heard Havel out politely, but rejected his proposals, or rather, decided to postpone debate on them. Fortunately however, his dramatic address had at least served to bring home to them the highly precarious nature of the situation and their grave responsibility. As a result, the debate in the Assembly on the constitutional amendment proceeded in a remarkably efficient and dignified manner, considering the intensity of the emotions its drafting had aroused, and it was passed by a substantial margin.

After this, from the beginning of 1991, work began on drafting the new constitutions for the federation and the two republics, with the intention of completing the drafts in time for them to be put to the voters in the June 1992 elections. As was prefigured in the 1990 negotiations over the constitutional amendment, conflict was as bitter over questions of procedure as over the content of the drafts, and eventually these negotiations ended in failure in March 1992. At the heart of the conflict is an apparently irresolvable difference of views about the origins and nature of legitimate authority. The Czechs wish to preserve the legal continuity of the Czechoslovak state, and thus view the process of constitutional reform as one which has to proceed from the assumption of the preservation of the federation, even while radically redefining its constitutional contours. The Slovaks, on the other hand, have deeply ambivalent views about the legitimacy of the Czechoslovak state in any of its previous constitutional forms, including the current federal framework. Their view is that legitimate authority ultimately resides in the national unit – that is, the Czech and Slovak

Republics. The authority of the federation, in the Slovak view, can only be derived from the national units, since they do not accept the existence of a 'Czechoslovak' national identity. Correspondingly, the Slovaks began from the starting point that the federation must be re-negotiated 'from below', implying that the existing federal state should first be dissolved into two independent states which would then be in a position of equality to negotiate afresh the terms of their association. This was and remains unacceptable to the Czechs.

However, as a form of compromise, it was agreed that the representatives of the national republics could play a direct and primary role in drawing up a 'state treaty'. This was strongly supported by Jan Carnogursky, and eventually conceded by the Czechs, but divergent interpretations of the status of this treaty were never reconciled, even though a draft text of the treaty was eventually produced.[6] The Slovaks wanted this treaty to have the force of international law, as an agreement between independent states, but the Czechs strenuously resisted this interpretation. As a compromise, it was agreed that the treaty would not be concluded between the republics, but between the two peoples, and would express the willingness of the Czechs and Slovaks to live in a common state. It would set out agreed basic principles of the division of powers between the federal authorities and the national republics.[7] These principles would then be incorporated by the Federal Assembly into its draft of the federal constitution. The Federal Assembly's draft in turn would be referred back to the republican National Councils for approval, before being put to the public for general approval.

The text of the draft treaty was finally produced in February 1992, but the whole constitutional reform process was brought to a halt when the Presidium of the Slovak National Council rejected the draft. This occurred because four members of Carnogursky's own party, the Christian Democrats, voted with the representatives of the more radical nationalist parties on the Presidium, thus precipitating a long simmering but submerged conflict within the Christian Democrats between more radical nationalists, developing informal links with Meciar and possibly contemplating a coalition with his Movement for a Democratic Slovakia, and Carnogursky's more moderate and pragmatic faction.

As it became clear that the negotiations between the republican representatives on the State Treaty were going to end in failure, attempts were made in the Federal Assembly to pass constitutional amendments adjusting the relative powers of the Federal Assembly, the Federal Government, and the presidency in order to overcome some of the critical weaknesses of the existing constitution. But these efforts were thwarted by the power

Table 3.3   Public Opinion on the Best Form of State for Czechoslovakia[10]

	CSFR	CR	Boh	Mor	SR
Unitary State	31	38	41	35	16
Federation of CR and SR	32	31	31	32	34
Multi-member territorial federation*	14	18	13	26	6
Confederation	11	4	4	4	25
Independent states	9	6	8	2	15

Table 3.4   Opinion in Slovakia on the Best Form of State[11]

	April '91	Sept. '91
Federation based on two sovereign equal republics	59	50
Federation as it is today	8	8
Multi-member territorial federation*	4	3
Confederation	6	8
Unitary state	8	11
Independent Slovak Republic	13	18

*In Czech 'spolkova republika', equivalent to the German 'Bundesrepublik'.

of veto effectively exercised by deputies of the Party of the Democratic Left (ex-communists), the Movement For a Democratic Slovakia, and the Slovak National Party in the Slovak section of the House of the Nations. A state of impasse had been reached.

BY WAY OF A CONCLUSION

Czechoslovakia faces its second election of the post-communist era in a state of extreme uncertainty. It is difficult to draw a conclusion at this point, but all the signs are that the composition of the federal and republican legislative bodies which will emerge from this election will be even less favourable from the point of view of resolving the conflicts between Czechs and Slovaks within the framework of a federation. Although public opinion polls appear to show a quite encouraging degree of popular support, even in Slovakia, for a continuation of the common state in some form (see Tables 3.3 and 3.4), paradoxically, popular support for the various parties in Slovakia does not follow this trend (see Table 3.5).

Table 3.5 Voting Intentions for the June 1992 Elections[12]

Czech Republic	
Civic Democratic Party	21
Czechoslovak Social Democracy	10
Communist Party of Bohemia and Moravia	7
Liberal-Social Union (Agrarian Party, Green Party, Czechoslovak Socialist Party)	7
Christian Democratic Party-Czechoslovak People's Party	5
Civic Movement	4
Movement for Self-Governing Democracy	3
Republican Party	3
Civic Democratic Alliance	3
Christian Democratic Party	2
Slovak Republic	
Movement for a Democratic Slovakia	27
Christian Democratic Movement	15
Party of the Democratic Left	10
Slovak National Party	10
Public Against Violence-Civic Democratic Union	4
Coexistence	4
Democratic Party	3
Green Party	3

The two most clearly pro-federal parties in Slovakia, the Civic Democratic Union and the Democratic Party, appear likely in the next election to fall below the minimum level of 5 per cent of total votes cast set by the electoral law in order to qualify for the allocation of seats in either the Federal Assembly or the Slovak National Council.[8] The most popular party seems to be Meciar's Movement For a Democratic Slovakia. In the Czech Republic, the strongest party in Klaus's Civic Democratic Party. These two parties and their leaders are very far apart in philosophies, policies and style. It is difficult to see how they could work together to hammer out an agreement for the future of the federation where such exhaustive negotiations by rather more compatible political forces have failed. A result of this would be an early declaration of Slovak sovereignty by the Slovak National Council, a move which was been attempted several times in 1991 and 1992 but was averted by Carnogursky's refusal to support it, and by the presence of a sizeable cohort of PAV/CDU and DP deputies in the Slovak

National Council. With these obstacles removed, the balance of forces seems to be tipped decisively in favour of the dissolution of Czechoslovakia into two independent states.

NOTES

1. E. Taborsky *Czechoslovak Democracy at Work*, London, 1945, p. 154.
2. See J. Piekalkiewicz, *Public Opinion Polling in Czechoslovakia 1968–9*, New York, 1972.
3. Taborsky, *op. cit.*, p. 157.
4. On the election, see J. Batt 'After Czechoslovakia's velvet Poll', *The World Today*, August/September 1990; and G. Wightman, 'Czechoslovakia' in *Electoral Studies*, special issue on Elections in Eastern Europe, edited by S. White, December 1990.
5. On the course of the negotiations, see P. Martin 'Relations between the Czechs and Slovaks' in *Report Liberty Report on Eastern Europe*, 7 September 1990; J. Obrman and J. Pehe, 'Difficult Power-Sharing Talks' in *ibid.*, 7 December 1990. The text of the constitutional amendment as passed by the Federal Assembly was published in *Svobodne Slovo*, 20 December 1990.
6. See 'Navrh smlouvy o zasadach statopravniho usporadani spolecneho statu' *Hospodarske noviny*, 11 February 1992, p. 4.
7. See J. Pehe, 'The State Treaty between the Czechs and Slovaks', *Radio Liberty Report on Eastern Europe*, 6 June 1991.
8. The only amendment to the electoral law has been the raising of this minimum for the Slovak National Council from 3 to 5 per cent.
9. Sources for Tables 3.1 and 3.2, *Svobodne slovo*, 12 June 1990; *Lidové noviny*, 14 June 1990.
10. *Lidové noviny*, 1 November 1991, p. 2.
11. *Lidové noviny*, 18 September 1991, p. 1.
12. *Lidové noviny*, 29 January 1992, p. 2.

4 The East German Legacy

Karen Henderson

The German Democratic Republic (GDR) ceased to exist at midnight on 2 October 1990, when its territory acceded to the Federal Republic of Germany. East Germany nevertheless remains a particularly fascinating case study in the history of communist states. In the past, because Germany had been divided, it was unique in Europe in providing an opportunity to analyse what happened to the same nation under the conditions of Soviet-type socialism and under the conditions of western liberal democracy. It thus acted as a 'control case' in the effects of communism, and most comparative work on the GDR contrasted it not with its neighbours in Eastern Europe but with West Germany.

In the 1990s, East Germany still acts as a control case, but of a different kind: it demonstrates how a society which has been distorted by forty years of communism fares when confronted, almost overnight, with a complete set of Western European institutions. This is important in the East European context because its fate is likely to be viewed in the rest of the ex-Soviet bloc either as a model or a warning. East Germany has all the advantages the other states lack: it can share the material resources and democratic experience of the strongest economy in the European Community. So if liberal democracy and a social market economy cannot be transplanted successfully there, its neighbours may argue, what hope do they offer to Eastern Europe?

Since the German Democratic Republic has now dissolved itself and become part of the Federal Republic of Germany, it is impossible to investigate institutional change there within an analytic framework applicable to the other formerly 'socialist' countries. Its new institutional architecture has been adopted in ready-made form, complete with a highly complex set of bureaucratic procedures which are rendered doubly confusing to the populace by the simultaneous presence of transitional arrangements laid down in the Unification Treaty. The discontinuity of its development since 1989 is therefore even more marked than elsewhere in the East of Europe. The replacement of the old élites has been more far-reaching, and the dislocation of employment and social structures affecting the average citizen has been far more intense.

It is not the aim of the current contribution either to present an account

of the the revolution in the GDR and German unification, or to describe
the political system of the Federal Republic of Germany. However, it is
necessary to touch on each in order to understand the contradictions which
currently affect the functioning of the new institutions in East Germany,
for on the territory of the GDR, two separate processes of institutional
change have been taking place since the fall of the communist regime.
The first encompasses the decisions leading to German unification, that
is, the acceptance in principle of West German structures by the East
German population. The second derives from the East German legacy: it
is an on-going process in which the established West German system of
government is having to adapt in order to permit the creation of a new and
truly unified German state and society.

THE ABANDONMENT OF THE OLD INSTITUTIONS

Four distinct periods can be identified from the beginning of the revolutionary changes to the end of the GDR in October 1990. A common
basic pattern emerges, whereby society was running ahead of the old
institutional structure. By the time unification was achieved, however,
institutional change had overtaken the transformation in society's political
demands, and it was society that was left to catch up.

The Revolutionary Period

This period started with the emigration wave in the summer of 1989, and
ended in early December 1989, with the beginning of the round table
discussions between the old political parties of the communist regime and
representatives of the new opposition groups and parties, which represented
the first structure formed to reconcile the old and new political forces in the
GDR.[1]

The time up to early December 1989 had been marked by radical shifts
in power within GDR society. As late as 7 October 1989, the communist
Socialist Unity Party (SED) had been celebrating the fortieth anniversary
of the foundation of the GDR while at the same time steadfastly refusing
to address the political causes that had led to an emigration wave in which
over 50,000 citizens had left the country in the previous two months alone.[2]
Popular demonstrations followed the lead of opposition groups such as
New Forum, for whom dialogue was a major demand; they did not have
a ready-made programme for reform, but appealed to all citizens to enter
into a democratic discussion about the contradictions in their society, so
that they could try and formulate what the tasks of reform should be.[3]

The slogan on a banner in one of the early demonstrations summarised the politics of this period: 'The people lead, the Party limps along behind'.[4] The GDR was characterised by what could be called 'institutional lag': the political momentum was neither controlled nor articulated through any institutional framework. The creation of the Round Table on 7 December 1989 was a belated attempt to formalise the consultation processes which had been forced on the state by society; but by the time it was created, the legitimacy of the state as an entity was being called into question.

The Pre-Election Period

It had been in the first, revolutionary, period up to December that the old institutions began to lose their power. The second period was characterised increasingly by their dissolution, and it ended with the first free elections to the *Volkskammer* (GDR parliament) on 18 March 1990. Whereas, in December, the legitimacy of the GDR state was being challenged, by the time of the elections in March, reform of the existing system had been replaced by reunification as the dominant political issue. As the inevitability of reunification became accepted by all political groupings, discussion centred on the constitutional mechanics whereby it could be achieved (see below).

Within East Germany, the process of party formation was accelerated when the election date was brought forward to 18 March from 6 May. This was in part a domestic problem for the East Germans, as hastily founded groups had to negotiate electoral alliances, but it was also a West German problem, as the established parties in the Federal Republic sought 'sister' parties in the East. On a broader front too the political initiative was passing to Bonn, as it became clear that the emigration wave had not been halted so that the introduction of the D-Mark into the GDR was increasingly viewed as an imperative to prevent the influx of East Germans from disrupting West German society.

Hence as in the revolutionary period, the real political decisions on fundamental questions were not being made within the existing institutional framework. The old *Volkskammer* was ceding decision-making to the Round Table, but both suffered from the problem that their decisions lacked authority. In other words, no East German institution – neither the revitalised *Volkskammer* nor a transitional creation like the Round Table – was strong enough to withstand the pull of West Germany. This could be most simply explained by two factors. Firstly, as the full extent of the GDR's economic problems became known, there was little faith that anyone but the West Germans could put them right. Secondly, in spite of the blossoming of independent groups at this time, the all-embracing nature of a communist regime had nevertheless left an enormous vacuum on its demise.[5] This has been true in the whole of Eastern Europe, but for the GDR there was a set of German political and economic structures already in existence which could fill the gap.

The De Maiziere Government

The third period ran from the elections on 18 March to the Currency, Economic and Social Union on 1 July 1990, when the D-Mark was introduced into East Germany. It was in this time that the only democratically elected government in East German history – led by Minister President Lothar de Maiziere – wielded most of its power, although it actually remained in office until 3 October.

The election results were, above all, a clear endorsement of the Christian Democrats in the West German government – via their East German namesake – and therefore also a vote for the D-Mark and reunification as soon as possible. De Maiziere, the East German Christian Democrat leader, went on to form a broad coalition government which, inter alia, included Social Democrats,[6] and it had to tackle many contentious domestic issues such as the legacy of the notorious *Stasi* secret police. Yet its essential mandate was to negotiate the country's incorporation into the Federal Republic, and economic weakness severely limited its room for manœuvre.

What needs some explanation at this point, though, is the failure of New Forum and its partners in the elections. It is certainly true that groups such as the Czech Civic Forum and the Romanian National Salvation Front were rewarded for their role in ending communist rule by success in the first free elections. New Forum never underwent this success because, for East Germans, the image of West Germany presented a competing focus. What people sought was a moderately prosperous life on the West German model. After forty years of communist attempts to create a new sort of German society, they did not want more experiments or attempts to create a 'third way' between socialism and capitalism. The proven success of West Germany's stable democracy and flourishing economy enjoyed an authority with which neither the communists nor the newly formed political groupings could compete.

The Pre-Unification Period

The fourth period runs from the Currency Union on 1 July to German Unification on 3 October 1990, and can be called the pre-unification period. The major international obstacle to reunification, which had been Soviet opposition, had been removed by Gorbachev during his meeting with Chancellor Kohl in July, a couple of weeks after the currency union, and from here on attempts to find transitory, domestic solutions to East German problems seemed increasingly futile. The major political issues were the terms of the unification treaty, as well as the date of the first all-German elections and formal constitutional unification.

The pre-unification period was characterised, like previous periods, by the fact that East German institutions were not setting the political agenda. Many East German ministers found their areas of competence severely limited by the effects of the Currency Union, and the West Germans could barely conceal their impatience with some of their inexperienced East German counterparts, particularly on economic issues. Even the breakdown of the governing coalition scarcely seemed to matter, since real decision-making power was already gravitating to West German institutions.

Unification had taken place much more quickly than had been expected for a number of reasons. The speedy resolution of the international questions involved is certainly one, and Kohl's desire to be elected the first all-German chancellor in the December election was also a factor. A further reason is that the establishment of new political structures is a lengthy process, which involves not just constitutions, with elections, parties, central and regional government and local council administration, but also judicial and education systems, taxation law and the whole panoply of economic structures. In the GDR, all these were in desperate need of overhaul, and to have established what were known to be transitional structures in all these areas would simply have been too much wasted effort.

THE CONSTITUTIONAL FRAMEWORK OF THE NEW GERMANY

In the early part of 1990, there were many debates about merging substantial or symbolic aspects of West and East Germany into the new German state, yet they all withered away almost to nothing. In constitutional terms, the East German legacy in the new Federal Republic is minimal.

Mechanics of Reunification

'The entire German people are called upon to achieve in free self-determination the unity and freedom of Germany.'[7] This final sentence in the preamble to the 1949 Basic Law (Constitution) of the Federal Republic of Germany committed the state to the idea of unification, although the word itself was not at that point used: to have done so would have anchored the notion that Germany was divided in a document that was initially conceived to be temporary in nature.[8]

The issue of reunification had decreased in prominence for West Germans over the decades,[9] to re-emerge with startling speed at the end of 1989. By the early months of 1990, the political debate in Germany began to centre on the mechanics of reunifying the two German states. The framework for achieving unity had to be the West German Basic Law: the Constitution of the GDR had contained no reference to reunification since it was amended in 1974, and it was not in any case generally regarded as a legitimate document. Consequently, like so many political debates in West Germany, reunification was discussed in terms of paragraph numbers from the Basic Law.

Two alternatives presented themselves: one was Article 146 of the Basic Law, which stated that 'This Basic Law shall cease to be in force on the day on which a constitution adopted by a free decision of the German people comes into force.' This route to unification would have proved quite problematic, however, for it would have entailed the writing of a new constitution, to be approved by a simple majority in a popular referendum, and some West Germans were of the view that their present constitution was perfect.[10] Many others thought that its role in creating democracy and stability had been too valuable to justify the risk of tampering with it.

The second alternative for reunification was Article 23 of the Basic Law, which talked of the Basic Law coming into force in other parts of Germany on their accession. This was a quicker and simpler variant, since the GDR merely had to reconstitute itself into five states (*Lander*) like the eleven existing in West Germany which could then exercise their right to join the Federal Republic.[11]

The constitutional aspects of reunification were largely settled in principle by the election result in the GDR in March 1990. Although accession under Article 23 was labelled 'annexation' by its opponents, it was the option favoured by the victorious 'Alliance for Germany', which consisted of the parties supported by the Christian Democrats who led the government in Bonn. The alterations to the Basic Law necessitated by the Unification Treaty were not substantial,[12] and although the treaty recommended that other alterations or additions should be made within two years, obtaining the necessary two-thirds parliamentary majority in order to do this will require complex political manoeuvering.

Symbols of Statehood

The absorption of East Germany into the Federal Republic also put an end
to discussions about incorporating other symbolic elements of the GDR
state into the new Germany. Debates about a new national anthem led to
nothing. There had for a time been an expectation that the new Germany
would have a new name – maybe the Republic of Germany[13] – yet it
remained the Federal Republic of Germany. In this sense the new Federal
Republic represents continuity in identity for West Germans, but not for
East Germans.

The one debate which remained heated even after unification concerned
the capital of Germany. The relatively insignificant town of Bonn had been
chosen as the capital of the Federal Republic after the war in order to
emphasise that it was merely a temporary replacement for the real capital
of Berlin, which would revert to its rightful status when German unity was
attained. However, as unity became a reality, voices were raised against
moving the apparatus of government from Bonn. Although the Unification
Treaty states that the capital of Germany is Berlin, the question of where
the seat of parliament and government were to be was left to be resolved
after unification.

The arguments in favour of keeping the government in Bonn were presented as rational: the sheer cost of moving civil servants and their families,
and preparing suitable accommodation, at a time when there are so many
other pressing economic problems; the desirability, in a federal country,
of splitting the representative and governmental functions of the capital
between two different areas of the country; and the negative memories
of Berlin as capital of the German *Reich*.[14] Yet the underlying question
also concerned the willingness of West Germans to abandon the familiar
structures of their statehood to which they became accustomed over forty
years.

The final decision to move the German government to Berlin was made
in a free vote of the German parliament (*Bundestag*) on 20 June 1991. The
closeness of the result – 338 to 320 – reflects the conflict in identity of the
newly enlarged country, but also the gradual acceptance by West Germans
of their own need to adapt.

Political Culture and Identity

The reasons why the structures and symbols of the GDR state have largely
been obliterated are twofold. Firstly, there was the contempt with which the
West Germans viewed the political system of the GDR. This was matched

on the East German side by a craving for the perceived antithesis of their previous system, coupled with the political weakness of the forces who wished to preserve the 'better' part of the East German legacy.

Another equally crucial factor, however, has been the strength of the West German political culture which has been developing since 1949. The most eloquent proof of this is the meteoric rise in the public prestige of the Basic Law in the course of forty years. Over the decades since 1949, initial indifference to a constitution which had not been put to the vote in a popular referendum was superseded by informed and positive approval on the part of the Federal Republic's citizens,[15] and its crucial role in the reunification process have granted it ultimate legitimacy. It can now no longer be considered the temporary document of a state lacking full sovereignty.

THE ELECTORAL SYSTEM AND POLITICAL PARTIES

At first sight, the electoral and party system in the new Germany appear to have been directly inherited from the old Federal Republic. The East German legacy leaves its mark not in the institutional framework within which party politics is conducted, but in the effects of the unification issue and the in the impact of new voters on electoral politics nationally.

The Electoral System

Four elections took place in East Germany (except in East Berlin, where there were only two) during the course of 1990. The *Volkskammer* elections on 18 March and the local elections on 6 May were carried out using new GDR election laws based on proportional representation, with seats allocated to party lists according to their strength both in the country as a whole and within individual constituencies. However, although twelve parties gained seats in the *Volkskammer* in March, a party constellation similar to that in the Federal Republic had already developed at this early stage.

De Maiziere's coalition government contained representatives from all the alliances and parties with West German partners: the 'Alliance for Germany' supported by the Christian Democratic Union/Christian Social Union (CDU/CSU), the League of Free Democrats supported by the Free Democratic Party (FDP) and the Social Democratic Party of Germany (SPD). Together, these comprised over three-quarters of the deputies in the *Volkskammer*. The main forces not to be represented in the government at any stage were the Party of Democratic Socialism (PDS), which succeeded the communist SED, and the Alliance '90 comprising New Forum and two other citizens' groups.

It is therefore hard to maintain that the introduction of the West German electoral system for the last two elections – the state (*Land*) elections on 14 October and the all-German federal elections to the *Bundestag* parliament in Bonn on 2 December – has been a major factor in the formation of the party system within East Germany. The electorate's preference for West German parties had been established in the months immediately following the fall of the communist regime.

The most contentious issue connected with the electoral system concerned the implementation for the federal election in December 1990 of the 'five per cent' clause, which excludes parties with less than five per cent of the vote from any seat allocation under proportional representation. This was an argument closely linked to the timing of formal unification, since if Germany were to be unified at midnight after the election, the five per cent clause would operate separately in East and West Germany, so that parties which had not merged with West German counterparts would only need five per cent of the East German vote in order to send deputies to Bonn. If it were united beforehand, however, East German parties like the communist PDS would have to gain twenty-three per cent of the vote in the ex-GDR in order to have the required five per cent of the vote in Germany as a whole.

The Electoral Law upon which the major West German parties finally agreed was so finely tuned to produce the party constellation they desired in the *Bundestag* that it was rejected by the Federal Constitutional Court in September 1990. Article 38 of the Basic Law stipulates that elections to the *Bundestag* must be 'general, direct, free, equal, and secret', and it was felt by the judges that the five per cent clause would present the parties and political groupings which had only been founded after the 'peaceful revolution in the German Democratic Republic' with exceptional difficulties, so that they would not have 'equal' chances in the elections. These parties had not had time to organise in West Germany, so the Court's decision laid down that the five per cent clause should operate separately in both parts of Germany for one election only in order to ensure a fair chance for these newly-established parties.[16] The immediate effect of this has been that communists (PDS) are now sitting in the *Bundestag* for the first time since 1953. However, since the Federal Republic will be treated as a single electoral territory in all future federal elections, the five per cent clause makes it highly unlikely that any party representing specifically East German interests will gain seats in a later *Bundestag*. The early voting decisions of the East German electorate have effectively locked it into the West German party system.

Electoral Impact of Reunification

The events in East Germany have influenced the distribution of power between the established political parties in Germany on two different levels: through the impact of unification as an issue, and through the addition of a new electorate amounting to about a fifth of the whole.

A comparison of the federal election results in 1987 and 1990 does not show remarkable divergences between the two (see Table 4.1), despite the momentous changes that had taken place and the new, enlarged electorate. However, although the victory of Chancellor Kohl's CDU had seemed predictable in late 1990, it had been far from secure in 1989. His tenure in office was ensured largely by the dominance of the unification issue, which both raised Kohl's stature in the eyes of the West German voters and further marginalised the minor parties. German unity did therefore influence the outcome of the federal elections, yet at the same time, if one excludes the *Bundestag* presence of the East German communists, it did not produce a result which disrupted the general pattern of post-war parliaments.

An examination of voting behaviour of the new electorate in East Germany indicates that it has so far displayed a left-right voting balance which is superficially similar to that in West Germany. Although the Social Democrat vote was about one third lower in the East, this must be viewed in the light of the not insubstantial remaining support for the communists. The Christian Democrat vote there was actually slightly lower than in West Germany, when it is added to that of their Bavarian partner, the CSU. The East German legacy is therefore a potential rather than a current force for change in the party constellation.

Future Prospects

A crucial fact in the long term is that the Christian Democrats enjoyed a large level of working-class support in East Germany,[17] which was based to a considerable extent on a belief that the party is best able to handle the region's economic problems and encourage much-needed investment.[18] On all West German indicators, however, these voters should be predominantly Social Democrat, as many of them are low earners or unemployed.[19] This has to act as a constraint on government policy, since their support will be contingent on its ability to satisfy their aspirations.[20] There have been suggestions that there will be an East German legacy of hostility to the Social

Table 4.1   German Election Results

| | East Germany | | West Germany | | Germany |
	02.12.90	18.03.90	02.12.90	25.01.87	02.12.90
CDU/CSU	43.4	40.8	44.1	44.3	43.8
SPD	23.6	21.9	35.9	37.0	33.5
FDP	13.4	15.3	10.6	9.1	11.0
PDS	9.9	16.4	0.3	–	2.4
Alliance 90	5.9	2.9	–	–	1.2
Greens East	–	2.0	–	–	–
Greens West	–	–	4.7	8.3	3.9
DSU	1.0	6.3	–	–	0.2
DA	–	0.9	–	–	–

CDU	Christian Democratic Union
CSU	Christian Social Union
SPD	Social Democratic Party of Germany
FDP	Free Democratic Party
BFD	League of Free Democrats[1]
PDS	Party of Democratic Socialism
DSU	German Social Union
DA	Democratic Awakening

Jointly with the Independent Women's Association

Sources: *Neues Deutschland*, 24–25 March 1990; *Die Zeit*, 7 December 1990; *Deutschland Archiv* 2/1991.

Democrats because of the negative connotations of 'socialism' deriving from forty years of the GDR, but the popularity of the SPD in opinion polls taken in early 1990 indicated that this was limited in extent.[21]

In a proportional representation system like that in Germany, a change in party support of a few percentage points can have major repercussions on the delicate process of coalition formation. This means that the volatility of the East German vote introduces a large element of uncertainty into future developments although it only constitutes a fifth of the electorate. The results of the four elections held in East Germany in 1990 show a fair degree of consistency (see Table 4.2), but issue voting and the role of personalities appears to dominate over established party loyalty.

An example of this is the increase in support for the Free Democrats in East Germany between March and December, which can be largely attributed to the popularity of the party's leader, Foreign Minister Genscher. He was not only able to take credit for achieving reunification on an international level; he was also an East German by birth, and both his home state of Saxony-Anhalt and his home town of Halle produced notably good results for the Free Democrats. This increased strength of the FDP was a factor in the complexity of the coalition negotiations following the December 1990 elections.[22]

The final question must concern whether or not the West German party system will actually prove adequate for furthering the specific interests of the people in the ex-GDR. For it did not develop as a response to the political situation in East Germany, but was embraced by the citizens there as an element of the country which embodied their favoured vision of the future. If their vision does not materialise, they may seek an alternative way of articulating their political demands. There are already signs, particularly on the level of *Land* governments and the *Bundesrat* (to be discussed below), that on many issues politicians align not only on a party basis but also according to whether they represent the old or the new *Lander*. The old traditions of party confrontation may thus be adapted in the new Federal Republic.

THE FEDERAL SYSTEM OF GOVERNMENT

A further source of political power for former GDR citizens derives from the German system of federalism. In East Germany, the fifteen former regions (*Bezirke*) created by the communists in 1952 have been re-formed into five *Lander* on the West German model, each with its own government and constitution. Under Article 30 of the Basic Law, the exercise of governmental powers and the discharge of governmental functions is incumbent on the *Lander* in so far as the Basic Law does not otherwise prescribe or permit. The *Lander* also have a major role in the government of Germany, since the federal system is based on a horizontal division of functions, whereby the federal parliament in Bonn holds most legislative power, while the *Lander* are largely responsible for the implementation and administration of laws and the provision of services to the public. A majority of public officials are therefore employees of a *Land*, and most of the remainder work for local authorities rather than the central government.[23] A consequence of this is that the bulk of the problems deriving from the need to carry out totally unaccustomed administrative procedures in the ex-GDR are having to be confronted by the East German politicians at *Land* level.

The *Bundesrat*

The second chamber of the Bonn parliament, the *Bundesrat*, comprises delegations from the governments of the *Lander*. The *Bundesrat* sometimes

Table 4.2   East German Election Results (by Land, excluding Berlin)

	Mecklenburg-West Pomerania	Brandenburg	Saxony-Anhalt	Saxony	Thuringia
CDU					
18.03.90	36.3	33.6	44.5	43.4	52.6
06.05.90	25.9	24.9	30.2	35.5	33.9
14.10.90	38.3	29.4	39.0	53.8	45.4
02.12.90	41.2	36.3	38.6	49.5	45.2
SPD					
18.03.90	23.4	29.9	23.7	15.1	17.5
06.05.90	20.0	40.2	38.4	15.3	18.9
14.10.90	27.0	38.3	26.0	19.1	22.8
02.12.90	26.6	32.9	24.7	18.2	21.9
FDP					
18.03.90	3.6	4.7	7.7	5.7	4.6
06.05.90	5.5	5.5	8.9	6.4	7.0
14.10.90	5.5	6.6	13.5	5.3	9.3
02.12.90	9.1	9.7	19.7	12.4	14.6
PDS					
18.03.90	22.8	18.3	14.0	13.6	11.4
06.05.90	19.4	13.7	12.6	10.8	9.3
14.10.90	15.7	13.4	12.0	10.2	9.7
02.12.90	14.2	11.0	9.4	9.0	8.3
DSU					
18.03.90	2.4	3.3	2.4	13.1	5.8
06.05.90	1.1	2.0	1.0	7.0	3.8
14.10.90	0.8	1.0	1.7	3.6	3.3
02.12.90	0.3	0.4	0.4	1.7	1.3

CDU	Christian Democratic Union
SPD	Social Democratic Party of Germany
FDP	Free Democratic Party
PDS	Party of Democratic Socialism
DSU	German Social Union
18.03.90	Volkskammer elections
06.05.90	Local government elections
14.10.90	Land (state) elections
02.12.90	German federal elections

The citizens' movements/Greens have been omitted from the table, as they stood in different alliances in different Länder in different elections.

Sources: Deutschland Archiv, 2/1991; *Neues Deutschland*, 16 November 1990; *Das Parlament*, 50/1990.

has a different party majority party from the *Bundestag*, or lower chamber, and it has considerable obstructive powers over whole areas of legislation which fall within the competence of the *Lander*. This divergence in the party composition of Bonn's two legislative bodies arises in part because the *Land* elections which determine the composition of the *Bundesrat* do not take place simultaneously with the federal elections for the *Bundestag*, and in part because the delegation from each *Land* votes en bloc, so that the winning party or coalition of parties in each *Land* election gains all that Land's seats in the *Bundesrat*. In addition, as is common in federal systems, voters from the smaller territorial units are over-represented in the *Bundesrat*: although the number of seats varies with *Land* size, each has at least three but no more than six seats. One of the West German *Lander*, North Rhine-Westphalia, had a similar population to the entire GDR, yet now has only six *Bundesrat* votes compared to the fifteen for the new *Lander*.[24]

The East German voters have had a considerable impact on the composition of the *Bundesrat*, as four of the five new *Lander* returned governments in October who were either purely Christian Democrat (Saxony) or CDU/FDP coalitions on the Bonn model. This was in marked contrast to the results of many recent elections in West German *Lander*, which would have given the SPD a secure majority in the *Bundesrat*.

Political Autonomy in the *Lander*

The *Land* governments provide a forum where East German politicians of all parties can pursue the interests of former GDR citizens without the direct control of their party leaderships in Bonn. Although the new German government appointed by Chancellor Kohl in January 1991 contains three ministers from the ex-GDR, they have all-German responsibilities and their tenure in office is dependent on the support of their West German colleagues in Bonn. The same does not apply to the members of East Germany's *Land* governments, and even for those ministers who are West German by origin, the prime concern is promoting the welfare of their electorate in the ex-GDR.

In the months since unification, the two most vociferous East German politicians have been the Minister Presidents leading the *Land* governments in Brandenburg and Saxony, the Social Democrat Manfred Stolpe and the Christian Democrat Kurt Biedenkopf. Meetings between federal government and *Land* representatives necessitated by the catastrophic financial situation in the ex-GDR in early 1991 clearly demonstrated that politicians from East Germany had vital interests in common which transcended the traditional party divides but conflicted with the financial priorities of their colleagues from the West German *Lander*.

Furthermore, it should be noted that many of today's most prominent West German politicians have reached the highest national offices through their work at *Land* level, frequently as the Minister President of a *Land* government. It appears likely that this pattern will repeat itself in the ex-GDR, and that the *Lander* will prove the most effective stepping stone for the first generation of democratically-elected East German politicians. The significance of this is that the individuals concerned will be forging their careers through competence in handling specifically East German problems, and their performance will be judged in this context; the ability to adapt to the informal rules of West German political life in Bonn may not necessarily become the key criterion for success.

Financial Equalisation

Apportionment of tax revenue between central government and the regions had long been a major source of dispute in West Germany,[25] and in 1990 this was exacerbated by arguments over the extent to which the West German *Lander* should share the financial burden of German unity. The issue had constitutional ramifications, as Article 107 of the Basic Law stipulated that federal legislation should ensure 'a reasonable equalization between financially strong and financially weak *Lander*', and that the regional share of revenue from Value Added Tax should be divided on a per capita basis. If these provisions had been implemented without regard to the lower revenue deriving from the new *Lander*, it would inevitably have entailed a substantial reduction in income for the old *Lander*. The Unification Treaty therefore laid down that a number of articles in the Basic Law should be suspended for a transitional period until the end of 1994.

By early 1991, however, it had already become clear that the provisions made for financing the new regions in the Unification Treaty were inadequate. It was the *Lander*, therefore, where a total breakdown of services seemed imminent, which became the forum in which two major political issues finally had to be confronted: one was the sheer scale of the task of equalising living standards in both parts of Germany within just a few years; and the other was the absurdity of Chancellor Kohl's 1990 election promise that this could be achieved without tax increases in the old Federal Republic.

It was also the East German *Lander*, with their wide range of administrative responsibilities, which highlighted the true problems of imposing an entire institutional structure on a territory lacking the pre-conditions for its effective functioning. The ex-GDR has neither the trained personnel nor the money to carry out the tasks assigned to it by its new government and constitution. The old system of financial allocation between central and *Lander* government was carefully geared to produce a reasonable balance of income and expenditure under the prevailing economic circumstances, but these were radically different from those in East Germany. Unification has therefore disrupted this equilibrium. The new *Lander* require far greater resources than the old ones in order to build up the region's infrastructure and cope with the pressing social needs of many of their citizens, yet the sources of revenue upon which German *Lander* normally depend yield them a lower income. Apart from the problem with VAT apportionment, locally raised taxes are severely limited in the East by high levels of unemployment and the closing down of local companies. Consequently, federal principles of autonomy may be jeopardised as the new *Lander* become dependent on special aid from central government.

WEST GERMAN INSTITUTIONS IN EAST GERMAN SOCIETY

The difficulty of adopting West German structures in the ex-GDR has emerged in a number of areas of public life that are not directly political. The most obvious problem has been the privatisation of state-owned industry, and the growth of unemployment rates as East German enterprises prove unable either to compete with their western counterparts or to attract urgently needed investment. However, the disconsonance of West German arrangements with existing conditions in the ex-GDR affects the functioning of a number of other institutions, either for technical or for cultural reasons. Technical reasons can be taken to encompass problems related to lack of infrastructure, and might therefore be overcome by material provision at an institutional level, whereas cultural reasons relate to the different aspirations and expectations of Germans in the East. These require a gradual adaptation process at a human level, though the effects of unification more closely resemble 'shock therapy', thereby increasing the risk of widespread alienation.

Administration of Justice

The Basic Law of the Federal Republic enshrines the principles of the *Rechtsstaat* (government based on the rule of law), and lays down that recourse to the court shall be open to any person whose right is violated by public authority (Article 19), and that 'in the courts, everyone shall be entitled to a hearing in accordance with the law' (Article 103). It can be assumed that after four decades of political interference in the judicial process under communist rule, the extension of these provisions to the territory of the ex-GDR is welcomed by the vast majority of citizens, and that the main difficulties enveloping the legal system there derive from technical deficiencies in the existing infrastructure. The new *Lander* lack the structures necessary to guarantee citizens their constitutional right of access to the courts.

The administration of justice represents an acute example of East Germany's problems in implementing West German institutional procedures, as the judicial system in the GDR was inferior to that of the Federal Republic in both quality and quantity. Many East German élites are suspect in the new Federal Republic both because of their communist backgrounds and because their professional skills do not reach western standards, but the situation is extreme in the case of judges and public prosecutors. Political criteria were crucial to selection procedures at all stages in their careers, and most were involved at some stage in trials that were political in nature; additionally, even the few who can be absolved from blame by vetting committees lack the basic familiarity with the Federal Republic's law possessed by any recent law graduate in West Germany. The shortage of judges is compounded by a far greater dearth of solicitors; it has been estimated that the plethora of litigation which comes before regular and specialised courts (administrative, social, labour and fiscal) in West Germany generates employment for at least ten times as many lawyers per head of the population as are available in the new *Lander*.[26]

In the legal system as in many other areas of East German life, the inability to make provision for the population which accords to West German standards is complicated by problems specific to the ex-GDR. Even where trained personnel are available, they have to perform their duties without the benefit of modern office technology, and the repercussions of unification itself will place a particular strain on an already overburdened judiciary. If only a proportion of the million claims for the return of property illegally removed from its owners during the lifetime of the GDR were to end up in court, it is hard to envisage how the legal system could cope.

Even partial emergency provision can only be made by 'importing' lawyers and judges, particularly those who have recently retired, from the old *Lander*, but this confronts the East German population, many of whom are unemployed, with a West German élite earning far higher salaries than their local colleagues. It is fair to say that the desire of East Germans to remove the vestiges of the old SED regime and to enjoy rights and services comparable to those in West Germany may not in the short term be compatible with preserving their sense of identity and self-esteem.

Social Provision

It was the 'social achievements' of the GDR which many East Germans who were opposed to speedy reunification were so anxious to preserve. However, these achievements were praiseworthy only in relative and not in absolute terms. They related to the distribution of material resources and social rights in a society where both wealth and citizens' rights were in short supply, and these achievements were thus almost irrelevant in the West German context. What was impressive about a health service which, while comprehensive, was clearly technically inferior to that in the Federal Republic?; or an enormous multitude of creches and kindergartens staffed at ratios which would be unacceptable in much of Western Europe? Other social benefits, such as cheap rents and generous leave allowances for the parents of sick children, were simply incompatible in their previous form with a market economy where the state no longer had the majority of material resources at its disposal.

It is still unclear what the social profile of the new Germany will ultimately be, but a few preliminary comments can be made. Firstly, the total dislocation of social life in the new *Lander* is tending to marginalise issues on which attention was originally focused. As unemployment rises to levels unprecedented in German history, retaining one's job becomes the prime concern of family life. Initial statistics suggest that the birth and marriage rates fell dramatically in 1990,[27] and while this appears to be a manifestation of chronic insecurity about the future, it also radically changes the social context in which questions such as childcare are considered. Legal provisions for leave to care for sick children are at best hollow if competition for employment renders workers unwilling to avail themselves of their rights, while the reduction in the labour force presents new alternatives to state-run childcare facilities. Secondly, the financial crisis of *Lander* and local governments jeopardises the ability of the state to ensure even those services considered essential in West Germany, so that the retention of more generous social provisions appears increasingly a utopian dream.

Ironically, it would appear that it is in West Germany that part of the East German legacy may be preserved in the social field. The Bonn government has not proved completely insensitive to the social traditions of the East German state, and the new coalition formed in Bonn in

January 1991 has agreed, for example, on future extensions on the time parents can remain at home to look after small children.[28] Concessions will almost certainly have to be made on the abortion issue, although it is questionable whether the key factor here is the resistance of East German women to having doctors decide whether or not they have to have a child: the real argument stems rather from the fact that abortion is a highly contentious issue, both socially, morally, legally and constitutionally, among West Germans. West German concerns underlie the political agenda, but unification has added an important impulse for change.

The Church

Brief mention should also be made of the role of the Church in the new Germany, as it was an important factor in the opposition movement in the GDR before and during the changes of 1989, and it raises some particularly interesting issues about the legacy of forty years of communism. While the Federal Republic has no established church, religion is nonetheless institutionalised and furthered by the state to a degree which is surprising to many East Germans. The state is involved through such issues as church tax (which is raised together with income tax), religious education in schools and the presence in barracks of army chaplains.

East German attitudes to the role of the church in the Federal Republic are notable on two levels. Firstly, the pattern of religious affiliation differs markedly in the old and the new *Lander*. Whereas there is an approximate balance between the numbers of protestants and catholics in West Germany, East Germany has proportionately many times more protestants, and this in itself has some effect on the way people vote.[29] More significant, however, is the balance between Christians and atheists, since Communist systems not only discouraged active religious participation, but they also made it far more likely that agnostics would incline towards atheism rather than retaining nominal church membership. Agnostics are now confronted by a system where the GDR's assumption of atheism has been replaced by an assumption of belief: even the amended preamble to the Basic Law contains a reference to God in the first sentence, although approximately half East Germans are prepared openly to admit that they do not believe in one.[30]

The second consideration is the attitude of active East German Christians to the reunification of the church in Germany, since this minority is much more immediately affected by the religious structures in the Federal

Republic. Whatever compromises were involved in the notion of the 'church in socialism' in the GDR, the relationship between church and state was radically different to that in the Federal Republic since it was based on conflicting rather than compatible ideologies. This served to underline the independence of the church as an institution. It remains to be seen whether West German arrangements will encourage religious practice in the new *Lander*, as they take little account of the East German legacy. The considerable pacifist movement among East German protestants is disorientated by the co-operation between the church and army in the Federal Republic. And, in an environment where lack of religious affiliation is widespread and money is short, it is more likely that citizens will leave the church in order to avoid the deduction of church tax from their salary.

THE NEW CITIZENS IN THE FEDERAL REPUBLIC

A last question must be whether East Germans hold any political power outside the institutional structures. One answer is that the most powerful weapons they hold are exactly the same as those they wielded so successfully both against the SED leadership in 1989 and against the East and West German governments in early 1990: they can take to the streets and they can vote with their feet by going to West Germany. These actions reinforce the reasoned political demands made by East German politicians through the established institutional structure.

Both the currency union and German unity were hailed in 1990 as measures which would establish East German confidence in both their democratic and their economic future. Yet the private investment needed to revitalise the decaying infrastructure of the ex-GDR, and mentioned by Chancellor Kohl as early as his 10-point plan in November 1989, has been slow to emerge, and rapidly rising unemployment has increased the financial rationality of leaving for the west, which can now be treated as a temporary option less final and intimidating than the unauthorised emigration of 1989. Two widely publicised statistics in 1991 highlighted migration as an unsolved problem: first, there was the statement of the Saxon Economic Minister that ten thousand people were leaving his *Land* every month;[31] then, the prediction of the Federal Office of Labour that 180,000 East German would move westwards in the following year, in addition to over a quarter of a million commuters who will live in East Germany but work in the west.[32] Continued migration is also being accompanied by a resurgence of street protest, for as the social fabric disintegrates in the new *Lander*, this takes the form not only of mass demonstrations but also of criminal disorder.

In a democratic social state like the Federal Republic, only the illegal disturbances can be countered by force, and there is no way that the East Germans can be prevented from exercising their equal citizenship rights by moving within German territory. The frequent complaints by East Germans that they feel like second-class citizens[33] are in themselves an affirmation that their right to equal citizenship is beyond question. The Federal Republic's constitution also contains a stronger commitment than many democracies to ensuring 'uniformity of living standards in the federal territory' (Article 106).

At time of writing, debates in Germany are essentially about the manner in which unification took place: was it carried out with too much haste, are there flaws in the Unification Treaty which was negotiated, should politicians have prepared the West Germans psychologically for greater financial sacrifices, should the state intervene to save the ailing East German economy rather than spending the revenue from tax increases on unemployment benefit? Consensus exists, however, on the ultimate aim of creating an equal standard of living throughout the new Germany, and arguments are restricted to the means and the realistic time-span for achieving this.

Both the East German population and West German politicians can be accused of myopia in their assessment of the problems which would result from the unification of two societies with vastly different life styles and material resources, and it can be argued that the structures of the Federal Republic should have been, or should be, amended to take account of the East German legacy. However, the issue decided by the East German electorate in March 1990, when they voted for speedy reunification and the adoption of the West German institutional architecture through accession under Article 23 of the Basic Law, can also be viewed as a request for the same citizenship rights as enjoyed by West Germans, and this has been granted irrevocably.

The formal unification of the two German states in October 1990 was the beginning rather than the end of the process of unifying the two German societies, but what structural unification established was that the starting point for this process should be one of equal rights. It is possible therefore that the power East Germans can exercise within the framework of their citizenship of the Federal Republic will be stronger than any pressure their politicians could have exercised while negotiating unity.

NOTES

1. For an account of the work of the Round Table, see Uwe Thaysen, 'Der Runde Tisch. Oder: Wer was das Volk?', *Zeitschrift fur Parlamentsfragen*, 1–2, 1990.
2. For emigration statistics, see Volker Ronge, 'Loyalty, Voice or Exit? Die Fluchtbewegung als Ansto und Problem der Erneuerung in der DDR', in Gottrik Wewer (ed.), *DDR Von der friedlichen Revolution zur deutschen Vereinigung*, Leverkusen, 1990, p. 40.
3. 'Die neuen politischen Gruppierungen auf dem Wege vom politischen Protest zur parlamentarischen Interessenvertretung. Soziale Bewegungen im Umbruch der DDR-Gesellschaft', *Zeitschrift fur Parlamentsfragen*, 1, 1990.
4. See Ewald Lang (ed.), *Wendehals und Stasi-Laus. Demo-Spruche aus der DDR*, Munich, 1990, p. 33.
5. For a discussion of this issue, see Kurt Sontheimer, *Deutschlands politische Kultur*, Munich, 1990, pp. 79–88.
6. For the members of De Maiziere's government, see *DDR-Almanach '90. Daten Informationen Zahlen*, Stuttgart/Landsberg, 1990, p. 398; *Deutschland Archiv*, 6, 1990, pp. 983–986.
7. All quotations from the Basic Law from *Basic Law of the Federal Republic of Germany*, trs. Press and Information Office of the Federal Government, Bonn 1986.
8. For discussion of the vocabulary of reunification, see Helmut Berschin, 'Quo vadis, Wiedervereinigung?', *Deutschland Archiv*, 8, 1990.
9. Silke Jansen, 'Zwei deutsche Staaten – zwei deutsche Nationen?', *Deutschland Archiv*, 10, 1989.
10. See, for example, *Spiegel*, 9, 1990, p. 99.
11. See Josef Isensee, 'Verfassungsrechtliche Wege zur deutschen Einheit', *Zeitschrift fur Parlamentsfragen*, 2, 1990.
12. They are contained in one-and-a-half pages of the Unification Treaty. See *Vertrag zwischen der Bundesrepublik Deutschland und der Deutschen Demokratischen Republik uber die Herstellung der Einheit Deutschlands (Einigungsvertrag)*, Presse-und Informationsamt der Bundesregierung, Nr. 104, S.877, Bonn 6 September 1990.
13. See *Die Zeit*, 25–26, 1990.
14. See *Die Zeit*, 12–14, 1991.
15. David P. Conradt, 'Political Culture, Legitimacy and Participation', *West European Politics*, No. 2, 1981, pp. 18–34.
16. See *Das Parlament*, 42, 1990, p. 5; 'Verfassungsgerichtsentscheidung zum Wahlverfahren fur den 12. Bundestag', *Deutschland Archiv*, 12, 1990.
17. Forschungsgruppe Wahlen, *Wahl in der DDR. Eine Dokumentation der Volkskammerwahl vom 18 Marz 1990* Mannheim, 1990; *Die Zeit*, 43, 1990, p. 4, and 50, 1990, p. 9.
18. See, for example, *Spiegel*, 47, 1990, p. 48.

19. Dieter Roth, 'Die Wahlen zur Volkskammer in der DDR', *Politische Vierteljahreszeitschrift*, 3, 1990, p. 380.
20. Support for Kohl and the CDU/CSU began declining steadily from the beginning of 1990: see public opinion surveys in *Spiegel*, 6, 11, 12, 20, 1991.
21. Peter Forster, Gunter Roski, *DDR zwischen Wende und Wahl*, Berlin, 1990.
22. Sources: *Deutschland Archiv*, 2, 1991; *Neues Deutschland*, 16 October 1990; *Das Parlament*, 50, 1990. The citizens' movements/Greens have been omitted from the table, as they stood in different alliances in different *Lander* in different elections.
23. M. Donald Hancock, *West Germany. The Politics of Democratic Corporatism*, New Jersey, 1989, p. 63.
24. Peter J. Lapp, 'Funf neue Bundeslander – Starkung des Foderalismus?', *Deutschland Archiv*, 11, 1990.
25. See Rudiger Voigt, 'Financing the German federal system in the 1980s', *Publius*, Vol. 19, No. 4.
26. *Die Zeit*, 29, 1990; *Spiegel*, 9, 12, 1991.
27. *Junge Welt*, 27 March 1991.
28. *Das Parlament*, 6, 1991; Regierungserklarung von Bundeskanzler Dr. Helmut Kohl vor dem Deutschen Bundestag in Bonn am 30. Januar 1991 (Presse-und Informationsamt der Bundesregierung).
29. Forschungsgruppe Wahlen, *Wahl in der DDR. Eine Dokumentation der Volkskammerwahl vom 18. Marz 1990*, Mannheim, 1990.
30. *Spiegel*, 46, 1990.
31. *Junge Welt*, 5, 6 January 1991.
32. *Suddeutsche Zeitung*, 4 January 1991; *Junge Welt*, 5, 6 January 1991.
33. Surveys in early 1990 showed that upwards of 85 per cent of East Germans felt themselves to be second-class citizens: see *Spiegel*, 6, 12, 20, 1991; *Die Zeit*, 24, 1991, p. 79.

5 Hungary

Bill Lomax

INTRODUCTION

In the autumn of 1989 a spectre was seen to be haunting the state socialist regimes of East-Central and Eastern Europe, the spectre of liberal democracy and market capitalism. Hungary, as the regime that had gone furthest even under state socialism in introducing political liberalisation and economic reforms, appeared in one of the strongest positions to make a success of this transition to democracy.

Yet in 1992, although Hungary has clearly abandoned the communist party state and command economy, it would be an illusion to assume that the historical legacy of state socialism can simply be ignored, or to expect that a Western style liberal democracy and market economy can be directly grafted on to the Hungarian social system.

It may also be inappropriate to regard the events of the autumn of 1989 as revolutions, when what they represented was the collapse of an empire and the fall of its local mandarins. At the time it was easy to see in them a dramatic break with the past, but with the hindsight of history the continuities may come to stand out more. The events certainly lacked that element of innovation or creation that Hannah Arendt has identified as lying at the core of revolutionary change, and while the new political élites in Hungary are unambiguously committed to the establishment of liberal democracy, this is no guarantee that it will come about.[1] Even the success of the economic transition is far from sure, as Western capitalists appear more interested in investing in the lucrative service sector, than in modernising the country's productive capacity. So we are not necessarily witnesses to a systemic change, and it could even be that the present transition may involve less the creation of a new system than the continuing collapse of the old one. At the very least, it is safe to predict, Hungary's future will be influenced more by the legacy of her state socialist past than many commentators presently appreciate.

Starting from this perspective, it follows that any study of the current changes and of Hungary's new political system must begin with an analysis of the society from which they emerged. Although frequently described as a one-party system, it was never truly a party system at all, but a system of arbitrary power in which a political élite bound by personal ties ruled over and above not only the formal institutions of state but also the leading bodies of the Hungarian Socialist Workers' Party, that is the communist party itself. This is not only a political tradition that goes back to pre-communist times, but also one that shows many signs of surviving into the post-communist era.

THE REFORM COMMUNISTS

The first serious questionings of this structure of power in Hungary only arose after Mikhail Gorbachev's accession to the leadership of the Soviet Communist Party in 1985, and his introduction of the policies of glasnost' and perestroika. They did not at first, however, involve any demands for the abolition of either the one-party state or the leading role of the communist party, but sought to make the political élite and its decision making processes more open and responsible to society. One of the first and foremost advocates of change was the General Secretary of the People's Patriotic Front, Imre Pozsgay, who made much of Marx's remark that 'wherever the state is free, the citizens cannot be free', and called for 'government for the people' to be replaced by 'government by and through the consent of the people'.[2]

Pozsgay's proposals were not initially aimed at the abolition of the communist party's monopoly of power, but for its subjection to public criticism and accountability in the spirit of glasnost'. This did, however, imply a separation of party and state, as well as a greater autonomy for society, and possibly the establishment of a popularly elected parliament to check, if not to control, the powers of the executive. This was a model for pluralism, and for even a measured devolution of power, within the overall structure of the one-party state, but it was one in which the exercise of executive power would remain the party's prerogative.

Following Janos Kadar's ousting from power as party leader in May 1988, Pozsgay was elected to the Politburo and appointed to the Government as a Minister of State charged with the preparation of a programme for political reform. Central to his ideas remained the institutionalisation of a separation between society and power, with society gaining the right to independent representation of its interests, but with executive power remaining under the party's control. Initial proposals for constitutional reform favoured a division of powers between a popularly elected house of representatives and an executive senate and presidency, with the latter two bodies to be appointed by the HSWP. These proposals were quite similar to Gorbachev's changes in the Soviet Union, allowing for a multi-party system restricted to the legislature, but with the executive remaining under the undisputed control of the communist party.[3]

Yet instead of providing the basis for a compromise, Pozsgay's proposals served only to further polarise conflicts within the party. The introduction of a multi-party system was first debated, behind closed doors, by the Central Committee in November 1988, but the result was a stalemate and a hardening of positions on either side. The new party leader Karoly Grosz publicly resisted the pressures for change, declaring that 'communists could imagine the future only under a one-party system', and whereas Pozsgay was coming increasingly to question the entire history of socialism in Hungary, Grosz favoured 'not a change of the system, but a renewal of socialism'.[4]

Both Grosz's resistance to change, and Pozsgay's reform proposals were, however, speedily overtaken by events as a multi-party system, independent of the party-state, began to emerge regardless of the will or wishes of the authorities. The first independent political association, the Hungarian Democratic Forum, grouping together populist intellectuals, poets and historians, scientists and economists, had been formed, with the quiet support of Pozsgay himself, as early as September 1987. Aware of the HSWP's low popular legitimacy, Pozsgay was encouraging the emergence of a moderate non-communist opposition with which the communists could safely hope to share power without having to fear losing it entirely.

Soon, however, more radical forces began to appear, first amongst them an independent student organisation, the Association of Young Democrats or *Fidesz*, in March 1988. The same month also saw many of the dissidents and *samizdat* activists of the former Democratic Opposition coming above ground to form a Network of Free Initiatives that would later reconstitute itself as the Association of Free Democrats. These new political forces would soon show themselves less than willing to play the role of political legitimators envisaged for them in Pozsgay's reform scenario, while by the end of 1988 and early 1989, the historic parties of the pre-communist period had also made their reappearance on the political stage – with the re-establishment of the Independent Smallholders' Party, the Social Democrats, the Hungarian People's Party and the Christian Democrats.

In this situation the HSWP, increasingly in danger of being outflanked by the newly-emerging party system, clearly decided that if it couldn't beat them it would have to join them. The decision to concede the principle of a multi-party system, perhaps the most crucial concession of the entire period, may have been taken as early as the Central Committee session of 15 December 1988. Certainly, the parliamentary sessions of late

December 1988 and early January 1989 saw the approval of constitutional amendments establishing the basic rights of association that allowed in principle for the formation of independent political parties. It has also been suggested that further pressure to adopt a multi-party system was applied by the IMF early in 1989.[5] Finally, at the Central Committee session of 10 Fe bruary 1989, and then partly in a vain attempt to draw attention away from Pozsgay's reassessment of 1956 as a popular uprising, the HSWP declared its belated commitment to the introduction of a multi-party system.

The communists, however, were still not preparing to countenance the loss of their leading role. The line now changed from the acceptance of a limited pluralism within the framework of a one-party state to the advocacy of a limited multi-party system within which the HSWP would still hold all the aces. In Pozsgay's explicit view, the HSWP remained the only party with the capacity to govern, and free elections could not be allowed to challenge its power. Elections would be held with the participation of competing parties, but a compromise would have to be reached beforehand to assure that 'the key positions in the government would remain in the hands of the HSWP'.[6] Pozsgay was clearly thinking along the same lines as those on which the Polish elections were to be fought in June 1989. At this point the most likely political configuration appeared to be a parliament in which the HSWP and the Democratic Forum would be the two largest parties, with an implicit understanding that the communists in the person of Pozsgay would hold the presidency while a government could be formed under the leadership of a prime minister from the Democratic Forum.

NEGOTIATIONS

Barely had the HSWP agreed to the introduction of a multi-party system than it was obliged by the course of events to negotiate with the newly emergent non-communist parties about the structure of the new system and the preparation for free elections. By March 1989 an opposition Round Table had emerged from negotiations between the different independent groups and parties to promote the cause of a fully democratic transition. As one Hungarian observer remarked, the starting point of the Round Table was 'to build a parliamentary democracy and not a presidential system' as the necessary guarantee against arbitrary or personal rule.[7] From June to September 1989 the opposition parties met with the HSWP and other social organisations in a series of trilateral talks to prepare the ground for constitutional reform and the holding of free elections.

Initially, the historic parties and the Democratic Forum favoured the holding of elections on a pure list system of proportional representation, since their parties' names were well known but their candidates less so. The HSWP, on the other hand, favoured a system based on individual member constituencies, since while their party was highly unpopular, many of their politicians were well known and respected. The Free Democrats also favoured individual constituencies, but with a proportion of representatives to be elected by PR. The compromise finally agreed on was for 50 per cent of the seats to be elected by individual constituencies, and 50 per cent by PR with separate lists at county and national level. The elections were to be held in two rounds, with a second ballot wherever less than 50 per cent of the electorate voted, or if no candidate won more than 50 per cent of the votes in the first ballot.

The trilateral talks, however, reached no satisfactory agreement over the future of the HSWP's militia, the workers' guard, its workplace or factory cells, and its by no means insubstantial assets. The Free Democrats and Young Democrats also took exception to the agreement reached for the direct election of the president by popular vote in advance of the parliamentary elections. Consequently, while refraining from the exercise of their right of veto, these two parties refused to sign the final agreement of the talks.

By this stage, Pozsgay and the HSWP's reform wing had travelled a long way from their initial aim of reforms designed to save rather than to transform the communist system. Yet although they had abandoned both the principle of the one-party system, and then that of the HSWP's privileged and leading role within a multi-party system, they had not yet abandoned all hope of remaining in power. In a number of by-elections over the summer of 1989 the HSWP had consistently won around a third of the vote, and Pozsgay had continued to express the belief that although the party was unlikely to win an absolute majority in parliament, it could still emerge as the strongest party and play the leading role in the formation of a coalition government, most probably in partnership with the Democratic Forum.[8] Moreover, Pozsgay was the HSWP's official candidate for the presidency, and enjoying a massive lead in the opinion polls. Were he to win the presidency in the autumn of 1989, the HSWP's chances would be greatly improved for the parliamentary elections planned for the spring of 1990.

In the autumn of 1989, however, things started to go seriously wrong for Imre Pozsgay. First, the more radical reformists found themselves in a minority at the HSWP's party congress and were unable to force a complete break with the past, even though the party was dissolved and reorganised as a new Hungarian Socialist Party. Moreover, less than 2 per cent of former HSWP members applied to join the new party. Then, scarcely before the ink was dry on the agreement of the trilateral talks, the Free Democrats launched a campaign for a national referendum over the timing of the presidential elections and the disposal of the HSWP's assets, factory cells and workers' militia. The campaign was supported by the Young Democrats, the Social Democrats and the Smallholders' Party, and the referendum was held two weeks after the opening of the Berlin wall and at the height of Czechoslovakia's 'velvet revolution'. The result was overwhelming support for the dissolution of the workers' guard, the abolition of factory cells and the disposal of the HSWP's assets, and the narrowest of majorities (50.1 per cent to 49.9 per cent) for the postponement of the presidential elections until after the parliamentary ones.

The referendum radically transformed the political situation, and decisively influenced the future course of events. The result severely undermined Pozsgay's presidential ambitions, while the Democratic Forum's credentials as the leading opposition party were called into question, after it had called upon its supporters to abstain. The Free Democrats, up till then a small group of intellectuals rarely rating above five per cent in the opinion polls, were from this point on able to present themselves as the most radical and outspoken critics of the communist system and to do so at the very time when communist regimes were falling like ninepins throughout East-Central and Eastern Europe. Pozsgay's strategy of offering to share power in order to forestall its total loss had finally bitten the dust.

PARTIES AND ELECTIONS

The first months of 1990 saw the leading opposition parties, the Democratic Forum and the Free Democrats, competing with each other in increasingly shrill campaigns against the communists. The Free Democrats followed up their victory in the referendum by exposing the continuing surveillance of the new parties by the secret police, and succeeded in forcing the resignation of the Minister of Interior. They also attacked the government's manipulation of the press and television. While their actions confirmed their credentials as the party least prepared to compromise with the communists, their strident self-confidence and assertiveness eventually came to lose them support. At the end of the day, it would be the more moderate and restrained Hungarian Democratic Forum that would emerge the victor. The Forum had not been slow to make up for its setback in the referendum, and the election as its president of Jozsef

Antall, an astute and canny conservative, in October 1989, together with the ousting of several former HSWP members from its leadership, had distanced the party from its former period of flirtation with Pozsgay and the reform communists. Under Antall's leadership the Forum moved away from its earlier 'third road' populism towards becoming a West European style Christian Democratic party identifying itself with the social market economy symbolised by Ludwig Erhard in postwar West Germany. By the time of the parliamentary elections the Forum had established itself as a 'catch-all' party with a wider national appeal than the more ideological and programmatic Free Democrats.[9]

In the first round of the elections held on 25 March 1990 the Forum emerged as the leading party with 24.73 per cent of the votes cast for party lists, and as the only party to win any seats outright in individual constituencies. The Free Democrats came a close second with 21.39 per cent of the votes cast for party lists, and were not far behind the Forum in the number of candidates in first place in individual constituencies. The Forum's 'natural allies', the Smallholders and Christian Democrats, won 11.73 per cent and 6.46 per cent of the votes respectively, while the Young Democrats who stood politically close to the Free Democrats received a remarkable 8.95 per cent. The new-style Hungarian Socialist Party did at least as well as expected, coming fourth with 10.89 per cent of the vote, whereas both the Hungarian Social Democratic Party and the reconstituted and neo-stalinist Hungarian Socialist Workers' Party got less than the 4 per cent required for entry into the parliament. 15.85 per cent of votes were cast for parties that failed to make the 4 per cent hurdle and in most cases did not figure in the second round. In fact, in the voting in the first round for individual constituences, 22.04 per cent of votes were cast for candidates other than those belonging to the six main parties. It was the redistribution these votes in the second round that eventually determined the final outcome of the elections.

When the second round of the elections were held on 8 April 1990, the results were interpreted as a landslide for the Democratic Forum. The total votes cast for the Free Democrats and Young Democrats, who had entered into a number of electoral agreements, went up to 33.41 per cent (31.04 per cent and 2.37 per cent respectively), 6.12 per cent above their combined vote for individual constituencies in the first round. The votes cast for candidates of the Democratic Forum, however, jumped by 16.97 per cent to 41 per cent, with a further 10.95 per cent being cast for the Smallholders and 3.73 per cent for the Christian Democrats, giving the potential Forum-led coalition a clear overall majority of 55.68 per cent. The votes for the Hungarian Socialist Party remained fairly firm in those constituencies where their candidates remained in the race and the party received 6.31 per cent overall. The change in the parties' fortunes between the first and second rounds, however, was not quite the landslide that many commentators presented it as. The increased share of the votes for the Forum in the second ballot resulted primarily from a redistribution of the votes initially cast for parties that did not make it beyond the first ballot, whereas the Free Democrats were unable to benefit in the same way from the votes for the other opposition party, the Socialists.

Nevertheless, the electoral system produced a parliament the composition of which fairly reflected the votes cast for the different parties. The Democratic Forum obtained 164 seats or 42.49 per cent, with a further 44 seats or 11.40 per cent for the Smallholders and 21 or 5.44 per cent for the Christian Democrats, giving the Forum-led coalition 229 seats out of 386, a majority of 59.33 per cent. The Free Democrats won 92 seats or 23.83 per cent, the Young Democrats 22 seats or 5.70 per cent, and the Socialist Party 33 seats or 8.55 per cent. A further 10 seats or 2.59 per cent were won by independents, joint candidates or other minor parties.[10]

GOVERNMENT AND PRESIDENT

A major issue and continual debate between the elections concerned the form of coalition government to be formed once the elections were over. There were two main conceptions: that of a grand coalition between the two largest parties, the Forum and the Free Democrats, and that of a centre-right coalition led by the Forum and including the Smallholders and Christian Democrats. The United States government seems to have favoured a grand coalition, whereas the West German government looked approvingly towards a centre-right coalition. This fitted in with the outlooks of the parties: the Free Democrats with their radical liberal ideas and uncompromising commitment to capitalism being more attracted to the American spirit of freedom and enterprise, while Antall and the Forum saw Hungary's future in much closer involvement with Europe and the German economy in particular.

Antall repeatedly expressed the view that a grand coalition between parties of radically different ideologies could rarely work except in wartime, while the increasing bitterness that characterised the second round of the election campaign made it very unlikely that the leaders could have sold the idea of a grand coalition to their own parties even if they had wanted to. In the end the election result rendered the issue academic, as the Forum and its allies had a clear and workable majority for a centre-right coalition.

Its majority notwithstanding, the new government's position was not as strong as Antall might have wished for. It lacked the two-thirds majority required by the constitution for the passing of important changes in the law, and the parliament had strong powers to bring votes of confidence against individual ministers or the government itself. (These provisions had been written into the constitution by the opposition parties at a time when they wanted to limit the powers of a possible communist-led government.) In a remarkable coup, Antall pulled off an agreement with the Free Democrats which effectively gave him the advantages of a grand coalition without the drawbacks. He directly approached the highly respected writer and translator Urpad Goncz, the head of Hungary's Writers Association, who had just been elected to parliament on the Free Democratic ticket, and offered him the presidency if, in return, he could get the Free Democrats' agreement to dropping the two-thirds rule and introducing other measures to strengthen the powers of the government *vis-à-vis* parliament. The agreement was made by Antall and Goncz over the heads of their party leaderships to whom it was then presented in a way they could hardly refuse, and the pact was then entered into by the two party leaderships over the heads of their parties whose members were only informed once it was already a *fait accompli*.[11]

The major component of the pact was to reduce to a minimum those laws for which a two-thirds parliamentary majority was required to effect changes in them. The Free Democrats also agreed that they would not disrupt the proper functioning of government, and supported a change in the provisions in the constitution for parliamentary votes of censure or no confidence. In the original draft of the new constitution approved by the old parliament in October 1989, a motion of no confidence in any minister, including the prime minister, could be brought with the support of at least one fifth of the members of parliament. A vote of no confidence in the prime minister would count as a vote of no confidence in the government as a whole. This provision was now changed so as to remove the possibility of a vote of no confidence in any individual minister other than the prime minister himself, in which case this would be a vote of no confidence in the government. The support of at least one fifth of members of parliament was required as before, but in addition the motion of no confidence would have to include the name of the new prime minister to be appointed in the event of the motion's success.[12]

This change to the constitution strengthened the government's position considerably, and made it possible that even if it should lose its overall majority in parliament it would not automatically lose office. In this way the parliament came to lose some of its powers not to the presidency, as the

Free Democrats had originally feared, but to the government and the prime minister. Within less than a month of the country's first free elections in over 40 years, the new political parties had agreed to weaken the powers of parliament over the executive. Paradoxically, the new parties were already beginning to turn the clock back towards the very sort of limited and controlled democracy that had once been the aim of Pozsgay and the communist reformers.

The issue of the presidency was still not finally resolved, however, as the Socialist Party was still calling for the people to elect the president in a direct national vote. A referendum was held on the issue on 29 July but, although over 85 per cent of those who voted favoured direct elections, the result was invalid as the turnout was a mere 13.8 per cent – way below the 50 per cent minimum required. In consequence Goncz was confirmed in office by the parliament on 3 August 1990.

Although the president's powers are largely ceremonial, it is only in practice that their full potential will become clear. In the words of the constitution, the president 'expresses the unity of the nation and is the overseer of the democratic functioning of state institutions' – clearly these words could be interpreted to give the president power over and above the parliament and the political parties. The president is also the commander in chief of the armed forces, a stipulation that could be of crucial importance in the event of war or a national emergency. The possibility of conflicts between the president and the government thus cannot be ruled out, and Goncz has already made it clear on at least two occasions that he sees his office as representing the interests of the nation over and above party politics. When the foreign minister Geza Jeszenszky made a particularly vehement attack on the opposition parties, Goncz expressed his disapproval, declaring that as president he too had a certain responsibility for the conduct of foreign affairs, though he was rebuked in turn by the prime minister. Again, at the time of the taxi-drivers blockade in October 1990, Goncz came out publicly and strongly against the use of force – which as commander-in-chief of the armed forces he could have vetoed – and he may well have influenced the outcome of the events. In any case, it is clear that the possibilities for conflict between the powers of president and prime minister will continue.

THE PARTY SYSTEM

From one point of view the elections had been an outstanding success. They had resulted in a stable government with a firm parliamentary majority – an outcome few commentators had predicted. On the other hand, others feared that a parliament polarised between two major parties did not augur well for the consolidation of a new democratic system, and such observers still urged the necessity of a grand coalition. Yet, the pact between the parties appeared at first to establish a degree of consensus that removed the threat to national unity.

At the same time the parties, and the shape of the new party system, began to develop clearer profiles, with a growing similarity to the patterns familiar in Western democracies. Although his government relied on the parliamentary support of the Smallholders, Antall made few concessions of substance to them, and the Democratic Forum continued to transform itself into a West European style Christian Democratic party which some observers believe may eventually come to swallow up both the small Christian Democratic People's Party and the larger part of the Smallholders.

While introducing policies of marketisation, foreign investment and privatisation, the Antall government rejected the sort of 'shock therapy' being experimented with in Poland and favoured by the Free Democrats. This strategy strengthened the Forum's popular following with its emphasis on defending Hungarian national interests and avoiding any, at least immediate, mass unemployment. At the same time the Forum stepped up its anti-communism, calling for a purge of former communists in public office, attacking the Free Democrats for the number of ex-marxists and former HSWP members in their ranks, and at times proclaiming itself to be the only defender of the values of the Hungarian nation, Christianity and European civilisation.

One of the most remarked upon aspects of the election was the total eclipse of the Social Democratic Party. Some saw this as a result of internal leadership squabbles and party splits, followed by the disastrous election campaign of the party's new leader Anna Petrasovits who modelled herself on Margaret Thatcher and indulged in the most vacuous anti-communist demagogy imaginable. However, the failure of the Social Democrats more probably reflected the undermining of the social basis of social democracy by changes in the industrial structure and the nature of employment in Hungary during the Kadar era, not to mention the similar defeats for Social Democratic parties throughout the former East-Central and East European communist bloc.[13]

The result was a vacuum on the centre-left of the political spectrum, that led some commentators to express concern that the poor showing of the three socialist parties combined – the HSP, the old HSWP and the HSDP – effectively meant the disenfranchisement of the industrial working class – hardly a promising sign for the consolidation of a new democratic system.

Some of the lowest rates of participation in the elections were recorded in the industrial regions of the country and the working class suburbs of Budapest and other cities, suggesting that many industrial workers simply did not exercise their right to vote. At the same time, and not a little paradoxically, opinion polls continued to show strong popular support for 'social democratic values'.[14]

The new style Hungarian Socialist Party, however, soon proved incapable of turning this situation to its advantage, and it began to appear that, if polarisation towards a two-party system progressed, it would be the Free Democrats who would come to establish themselves on the centre-left of the political spectrum, and profit from the reservoir of support for social democratic values. During the election campaign, the Free Democrats had appeared to many Western observers as more right-wing, even Thatcherite, and certainly more pro-capitalist, than the Democratic Forum, and this was certainly true of their free market economic policies.[15] Yet the British Conservative Party certainly did not see them as natural allies; prime minister Margaret Thatcher having publicly snubbed them to appear with Antall in the Forum's election broadcasts. The Free Democrats are bourgeois radicals in the intellectual tradition of the Enlightenment and the French revolution, committed to the ideals of individual liberty, human rights and suspicion of authority. They are indisputably liberals, but of a radical and humanist persuasion. If anything, the term that best describes them is 'free thinkers', and their political alignment is clearly on the left of the political spectrum.[16]

One clear possibility, after the elections, was for a gradual rapprochement between the Free Democrats and the Socialist Party, as the Socialists abandoned their last remaining vestiges of marxism and the Free Democrats appeared motivated to taking on board more social democratic policies. The Socialist Party clearly could expect no future in government except in collaboration with other parties, while following their defeat in the elections the Free Democrats appeared to have few chances of raising their support alone to hope for any chance of forming a government. Closer collaboration between the two parties in unity against the Forum's otherwise likely domination of Hungarian politics, seemed a sensible strategy if either were to hope for a future election victory. Any such development would also have favoured the emergence of a two-party system along the more conventional left-right lines of Western democracies.

In practice, however, the wounds created by the hatreds and bitterness of past years have been slow to heal, and the continuing feelings of resentment and hostility on both sides have prevented any such rapprochement. Moreover, following the elections, support for the Free Democrats continued to rise, while that for the Socialists slumped yet further, weakening the case for collaboration.

At one time, another prospect for the Socialists appeared to be in collaboration or coalition with the Democratic Forum. This had been the original conception in 1988 and early 1989, when the Socialists had much to offer the Forum in terms of politicians with experience in government and international reputations. Antall's political intuition, however, held him back from any such move, while the defection from the Socialists of first Miklos Nemeth (the last communist prime minister) and then Imre Pozsgay (the reformists' former leader), to sit as independent members of parliament, has drastically reduced what the Socialists might have to offer.

The Hungarian Democratic Forum, on the other hand, stood to gain in authority on account of its election victory alone, while once in government the prominence given to its leader and prime minister Jozsef Antall could be expected to increase its standing even further. In a country with very limited experiences of democracy, but long periods of authoritarian rule in the twentieth century by benevolent conservative autocrats like Horthy and Kadar, it could well be expected that the country might accommodate itself to a system of hegemonic rule by a dominant party such as the Democratic Forum.

The prospect then arose of the emergence not of a two-party system allowing for alternation in government of two major parties, but of a system in which one dominant party, without necessarily having an overall majority in parliament, would always be substantially stronger than any of the others and would constitute the focus of any coalition government. Elections might result in changes in the composition of the government coalition, but the dominant party would always be at the helm. This would not have been a one-party system, but a coalition system in which one party would always be the dominant partner, and where opposition parties would also exist. In the summer of 1990, it looked as though such a constellation might be developing in Hungary with the Democratic Forum emerging as the permanent party of government – the focus around which the smaller parties would cluster and alternate.

The test came in the local elections at the end of September and the beginning of October 1990. The previous weeks had been characterised by increasingly acrimonious exchanges between the two largest parliamentary parties, a phenomenon that served to alienate popular support for them amongst the electorate. One consequence was an unexpected gain in support for the Young Democrats, whose parliamentary performance, parliament being shown live on TV, marked them out from the other parties because they refrained from making party political points, let alone engaging in the rancorous slanging matches favoured by the other parties, or attacking the government just for opposition's sake, but concentrated on making level-headed and professional contributions to parliamentary debate and to the law-making process. Some of their leaders like Viktor Orban and Gabor Fodor were now ranked amongst the most popular politicians in the country, and shortly before the local elections opinion polls were putting them amongst the top three parties.

For those who saw the March election results as a landslide for the Democratic Forum, the October local elections appeared as an avalanche in the opposite direction. The votes for both the Free Democrats and the Young Democrats increased throughout the country, with local alliances between the two parties sweeping them to power in Budapest and in 14 of 18 other major towns and cities. Whereas the Forum had headed the poll in Budapest in the March elections, it now held only one of the city's 22 district councils. This time it was the Free Democrats and Young Democrats who had benefitted from the workings of the electoral system. Since the turnout was in most places below the 40 per cent required in the first ballot (this itself a reduction on the 50 per cent required in March), the second ballots were generally held with all the candidates continuing to compete and with only a simple majority needed for victory. As a result the votes cast for smaller parties were wasted, not re-allocated as in March, a factor that now worked against the Forum. So although the Free Democrats and Young Democrats appeared to sweep the board in terms of seats and councils won, their combined vote nationwide still fell well below 50 per cent. Nevertheless, the most remarkable aspect of the elections was the continuing advance of the Young Democrats who won the third largest share of the votes, in many places coming in ahead of the Free Democrats. The other parties fared less well, the Socialist Party's vote falling by about a third, the Smallholders by at least a quarter, and the Social Democrats polling even worse than in March with a total vote of less than 1 per cent conveying them into final oblivion.

At the basic levels of local government, however, in communities of less than 10,000 inhabitants, the picture was somewhat different. Here almost two-thirds of the votes were cast for independent candidates, and as a result over 80 per cent of local mayors and over 70 per cent of councillors elected were independents. The parliamentary parties had clearly not established any firm implantation at this level, with votes cast nationwide of only 6 per cent for the Smallholders, 5.5 per cent for the Forum, 4.7 per cent for the Free Democrats, 3.2 per cent for the Christian Democrats, 1.4 per cent for the Socialist Party and 0.8 per cent for the Young Democrats.

Moreover, many of the candidates standing as independents were former council leaders, of whom 70 per cent who stood were re-elected.[17]

The main outcome of the local elections was to call into question some of the views about the future development of Hungary's party system discussed earlier. There was now less prospect of the Democratic Forum establishing for itself a hegemony as the dominant party of government. Together with its 'natural allies', it was now clearly in a minority in the country. On the other hand, the Free Democrats and Young Democrats had shown that the two liberal parties together were capable of mounting a serious challenge to the Forum and overtaking it and its allies in popular support, even though they had not yet managed to win 50 per cent of the vote. The decline in the fortunes of the smaller parties also appeared to favour developments that would put the possibility of a two-party system back on the agenda.

Even this scenario, however, was to prove short-lived. The Young Democrats declined offers of sharing power in local government, and their growing popular support in fact made them even less willing than before to co-operate with the Free Democrats, whom they now came to see as their main rivals for the liberal vote. At the same time, continuing price rises, increases in the cost of living, and the looming threat of unemployment, gave a new boost to support for the Socialists, who won a parliamentary by-election vacated by the newly-elected Free Democrat Mayor of Budapest, Gabor Demszky, and seemed to be finally escaping the stigma of their communist past. By the autumn of 1991, some of the most perceptive observers of the Hungarian political scene had reached the conclusion that Hungary's unique six-party system had possibly come to stay.[18]

ECONOMIC AND SOCIAL PROBLEMS

Party systems, however, do not exist in a vacuum. It is the economic and social problems that Hungary, like most other countries in post-communist East-Central and Eastern Europe, is now facing that will largely determine the future of the country's political system and, in particular, whether or not a modern and stable party system will be developed and consolidated.

Hungary does not have political parties as we know them in the West. There are no mass parties, and none have developed as institutions representing wider social and economic interests. Not only are there hardly any workers in the present Hungarian parliament, there are hardly any capitalists or businessmen either. The parliamentary parties are small élite groups of intellectuals, in most cases long-standing personal friends, many of whom were active dissidents or critics of the communist system before 1989. If any of them have had any involvement with society it has more likely been as social workers or priests rather than as involved participants in social movements, conflicts and struggles. The result has been an absence from the very beginning of any real sense of identification with the parties amongst ordinary people and a growing alienation from them as time has gone by. Both the low level of participation in the elections of 1990, and the high support for independents in the local elections, evidence the weakness of the parties and their low level of implantation in society.

This raises a serious question mark over the ability of any party system that finally emerges to maintain its authority over the country in a time of deepening economic crisis and growing social tensions. While Hungary has so far avoided anything like the 'shock therapy' that has been applied in Poland and produced such extraordinary and alarming political results there, the country's inflation rate was running at over 30 per cent in 1990–91, with particularly high rises in rents and food prices. The policies of marketisation and privatisation being introduced by the present government, and which would be no less severe were any other party in power, are likely to lead over the next two years to the closure of 30–40 per cent of Hungarian factories, and the unemployment of as much as a third of the labour force or between one and two million workers. The situation will be unbearable. Not all of those made redundant will be able to find re-employment as fast-food restauranteurs, boutique managers, satellite dish fitters or hard-porn sellers. Nor, on present form, will the political parties be able to provide channels for their discontent, let alone for its alleviation and satisfaction. In such circumstances, and particularly in the absence of effective trade unions, discontent is likely to be given direct expression outside or even in opposition to the existing political institutions and parties.

The first instances whereby such discontent has found expression and articulation have already occurred, and the most dramatic of them was undoubtedly the 'petrol war' blockade of October 1990, which broke out, to everyone's surprise, shortly after the first official anniversary celebrations of the 1956 revolution. On 26 October the Government announced a rise in the price of petrol by an average of around 66 per cent. The reaction was spontaneous. Taxi-drivers and lorry-drivers, fearing for their livelihood, launched an immediate national strike, blockading the Budapest bridges over the Danube as well as national and international thoroughfares, and carrying out similar actions in other cities in the countryside, in protest against the price rises. The blockade divided the nation. Not only the government, but most politicians of the opposition parties too, condemned it as an unconstitutional action by one group in society taking the law into its own hands to impose its sectional interests on the country. The citizens of Budapest, however, many of whom had to walk into work for the 2–3 days the blockade continued, appear to have sided with the strikers, and opinion polls showed over 80 per cent public support. The government at first wanted to use force against the strikers, preparing to send in the army to break down the barricades, but wiser counsels eventually prevailed and negotiations resulted in an agreement whereby the price rise was reduced to 32 per cent. This was very much a climb-down if not a capitulation to the strikers by the government.[19]

There are two particularly significant aspects to the blockade. The first is that the wider public were prepared to support, and take part in, extra-parliamentary action against the government initiated by one particular social group in support of its own sectional interests. The second is that the government behaved as if it had only two choices – either to use force or to capitulate. If such situations should repeat themselves in the future, and if every aggrieved sectional interest can rely on public support, while the government can find no other solution other than the use of force or capitulation, then it is difficult to see how political democracy can continue to function. Such a situation must either result in anarchy or give way to some form of dictatorship.

The blockade illustrated the fact that the legacy of forty years of state socialism will be hard to shake off, and could provide a continuing obstacle to the establishment of democratic politics for many years to come. As several contributors to a recent symposium on the revolutions of 1989 have pointed out, the communists deliberately abolished the various networks of civil society that existed between the state and everyday life and that are essential for the functioning of democracy, while state collectivism destroyed all sense of community and the common good. The result, as several of these commentators point out, is a situation in which 'society as a whole needs changes urgently, but individual social groups do not want them' – a situation that could well terminate in 'a right wing or a left wing authoritarian restoration'.[20]

WHAT TYPE OF TRANSITION

The transition away from communism in East-Central and Eastern Europe today is most frequently compared to the transition to democracy that took place in the Southern European countries of Spain, Portugal and Greece in the 1970s after the fall of their fascist regimes. At least equally valid, however, would be the comparison with Weimar Germany after world war one – an infant democracy that itself fell foul to fascism. As one commentator at the time, Carl Schmitt, pointed out, the collapse of Weimar was due in no small part to the contradictions between liberalism and democracy – between the attempt to limit power and the attempt to distribute it.[21]

Other commentators have already warned of the prospect of a 'Latin Americanization' of East-Central and Eastern Europe and the dangers of a new authoritarianism arising from the combination of a new form of economic colonial status *vis-à-vis* Western Europe with a re-emergence of older forms of nationalist hatred and violence.[22] But it is also possible that a more civilized and even liberal form of authoritarianism might arise in countries like Hungary. After all, it was the liberal philosopher John Stuart Mill who compared politicians to doctors, and argued that the patient's role was not to prescribe the cure but to take the medicine.[23] Hungarian political culture is not only lacking in any traditions of democratic behaviour but also in any practice of pluralist politics – throughout the twentieth century there has been almost no experience of popular political participation or the expression, articulation and mediation of interests through an active civil society. This has resulted in a predisposition amongst both the people and the élites towards the technical solutions offered by experts rather than the compromises produced by political bargaining.[24]

In this situation, and faced with growing economic problems, there could be a gradual slide into a non-ideological yet authoritarian regime of experts and professionals grounded in inter-party pacts, similar to those already adopted, to reduce parliament's powers over the executive still further, and such measures might even enjoy popular support. Paradoxically, such an outcome might be surprisingly close to the original proposals that were advanced by Hungary's reform communists in 1988 and 1989 for a limited pluralism within a one party state, and that would have envisaged a representative legislature alongside an all-powerful executive. It is indeed possible that, despite the revolutions of the autumn of 1989, Hungary's political future could continue to be influenced more by the traditions, norms and values of the past forty years of state socialism than by the attitudes and practices of Western democratic politics.

This is not an inevitable development but it is certainly a possible one. Marxist-Leninists have always professed that it is not possible to make omelettes without breaking eggs. The problem today, however, is not only that of getting the eggs back out of the omelette, but the naive belief that healthy young chicks will then hatch out of them. It is too early to say for sure just what the political future holds for Hungary and the other post-communist countries of East-Central and Eastern Europe, but one thing is certain – their new political institutions will prove to be both novel and unique, different and challenging both for those whose fate it is to live under them and for those whose profession it is to analyse and study them.

NOTES

1. Hannah Arendt, *On Revolution*, London, 1973.
2. Cited by Misha Glenny, *Guardian*, London, 14 November 1987 and 1 July 1988.
3. For an examination of some of the early proposals, see: Bela Pokol, 'Politikai Reformvaltozatok', *Heti Vilaggazdasg*, No. 49, 10 December 1988, pp. 52–54.
4. Cited in *Radio Liberty Report on Eastern Europe*, 29 November 1988, and *Nepszabadsag* 4 May 1990.
5. György Wiener, 'Az 1990–es valasztasok', *Eszmelet*, No. 9–10, May 1991, p. 79.
6. Interview with Pozsgay, *The Independent*, London, 16 February 1989.
7. Andras Bozoki, 'Ut a rendszervaltashoz: az Ellenzeki Kerekasztal', *Mozgo Vilag*, No. 8, August 1990, p. 31.
8. See the interview with Pozsgay, 'Hungary for Change', *Marxism Today*, May 1989, pp. 26–29.
9. For an early attempt to map out the contours of the emerging party system, see: Andras Bozoki, 'Politikai iranyzatok Magyarorszagon', in Sándor Kurtán, Péter Sándor, László Vass (eds), *Magyarorszag Politikai Evkonyve*, Budapest, 1990, pp. 184–92.
10. For documentation and analysis of the election results, see: Tamas Moldovan (ed.), *Szabadon valasztott: parlamenti almanach 1990*, Budapest, 1990; Gyorgy Szoboszlai (ed.), *Parlamenti Valasztasok 1990: politikai szociológiai korkep*, Budapest, 1990; and also András Korosényi, 'Partok es szavazok – Parlamenti valasztasok 1990–ben', *Mozgo Vilag*, No. 8, August 1980, pp. 39–51. In English: Andras Korosenyi, 'Hungary', *Electoral Studies*, No. 4, 1990, pp. 337–45.
11. For the text of the agreement, and the list of laws to which the two-thirds rule would still apply, see: Gyorgy Balo and Ivan Lipovecz eds., *Tenyek konyve '91*, Budapest, 1991, pp. 797–800.
12. For the initial, and revised, versions of the constitution, see: *A Magyar Koztarsasag Alkotmanya (23 October 1989)*, Budapest,1989; and *A Magyar Koztarsasag Alkotmanya (9 August 1990)*, Budapest,1990.
13. Several commentators have spoken both of 'embourgeoisement' and of 'lumpenproletarianization' to explain the decline in working class consciousness and solidarity in state socialist societies. I prefer the term 'deproletarianization'; see: Bill Lomax, 'The Rise and Fall of the

Hungarian Working Class', *The Journal of Communist Studies*, No. 2, 1990, pp. 45–60.

14. Gabor F. Havas and Ilona Lisko , 'Merre tart Kelet-Európa?', *Beszelo*, 24 February 1990.

15. This was certainly the view of Misha Glenny, *The Rebirth of History*, London, 1990, p. 82.

16. This is also the conclusion of Federigo Argentieri's forthcoming study 'Poland, Hungary and Czechoslovakia after 1989: Is Anything Left Still Left?', in Joan Barth Urban (ed.), *Gorbachev and the Global Left in the Era of Perestroika*, forthcoming.

17. For details of the local election results, see 'Onkormanyzati valasztasok: Mi mennyi?', *Heti Vilaggazdasag*, 13 October 1990.

18. See, for example: Laszlo Keri, *Osszeomlas utan*, Budapest, 1991; Jozsef Kiss and Eva Kovacs, *Tobbpartrendszer Magyarorszagon*, Budapest, 1991; Laszlo Lengyel, 'Hogyan jutunk 91–r 1 92–re?' *Tarsadalmi Szemle*, Budapest, December 1991.

19. Amongst other reports and analyses of the 'petrol war' blockade, see the special number of *Beszelo*, 'Megrengette-e a negy nap az orszagot?', 3 November 1990.

20. Gwyn Prins (ed.), *Spring in Winter: the 1989 revolutions*, Manchester, 1990, pp. 34–35, 53 and 184.

21. Carl Schmitt, *The Crisis of Parliamentary Democracy*, Cambridge, Mass., 1985.

22. The danger of re-emerging nationalist conflicts is particularly emphasised in Misha Glenny's, *The Rebirth of History*. The dangers of 'Latin Americanization' have also been raised by Hungarian sociologists such as Ivan Szelenyi and Erzsebet Szalai.

23. See the enlightening discussion of Mill in S. R. Letwin, *The Pursuit of Certainty*, London, 1965, esp. chap 21: 'The Creed of Progress', where it is argued that Mill believed in 'an aristocracy of intellect'.

24. The political culture of Eastern Europe as it bears upon problems of the present transition is most illuminatively discussed in Judy Batt, *East Central Europe from Reform to Transformation*, London, 1991.

6 Poland

George Kolankiewicz

> To attempt to propose today what the office of the president is to
> be in the future is like choosing a hat and adjusting the head to fit
> that hat.
>
> Lech Walesa

Poland shares with the other post-communist countries the need for nation-
state building, constitutional enactment and the creation of democratic
politics. It is doing this with the larger than life figure of Lech Walesa
and the near-mythical status of Solidarity and in a society which sees itself
as bearing the brunt for being the vanguard of the 'negotiated revolutions'.
The development of post-1989 Polish politics has been characterised by
the rise of President Walesa and the concomitant decline of the Solidarity
movement, to the point where three years after taking power another
putative government almost emerged in June 1992 headed by a prime
minister designate who had nothing whatsoever to do with the Solidarity
opposition. When the candidate was found not even to be in the country,
the last vestiges of Solidarity produced a relatively unknown nominee who
could become Poland's first woman premier.[1]

These convoluted politics are being conducted in the context of a painful
IMF monitored macro-economic stabilisation programme and the tentative
privatisation and restructuring necessary to install a market economy.
While Poland looks to be bottoming out from its recessionary spiral
this has not had any immediate effect on the turbulence of its politics.
However, as society becomes more impatient with the slow outcomes of
economic reform so grass roots pressure from peasant and workers alike is
conspiring to shift politicians attention away from factional squabbles to the
urgent issues of restructuring Poland's antiquated industry and fragmented
agriculture.

THE SOCIAL SOURCES OF POLITICS

The social legacy of communism in Poland is an amorphous social structure
and second economy, rooted in the homogenising and atomising policies of

the party-state which submerged class relations if not economic interests. On this basis, Poland is now seeking to reconstruct classes, and in particular the vital middle class on which to base a market society. In the process, however, the entrenched interests of the previous system are becoming ever more apparent. It is not just the oft stated absence of a civil society that hinders interest formation but also the existence of a distorted set of interests rooted around the planned economy and the *nomenklatura* system. The removal of these is proving as difficult as is the articulation of new interests. However, the manner in which the artificial interests generated by real socialism through the redistributive state are overcome and reshaped will provide the guide to how the reforms will progress.[2]

Against this uncertain background, there are several possible directions political competition may take. First, what will be the relationship between parties and society? Despite the antipathy felt towards the ex-communist parties with their proletarian ideologies will a 'labour' party emerge articulating the interests of the largely unrepresented working class? Similarly will a peasant class party emerge to defend the interests of a rural class rooted in fragmented and inefficient agriculture?

Second, and alternatively, because civil society is still very weak (and thus unable for example to connect individual interests with political parties), a void exists which can be filled by populist parties mobilising on single issue or rejectionist demands. The most recent case of this is the 'Movement for the Republic' which brings together the defeated remnants of the Olszewski government and other splinters rallying around the need to cleanse Polish politics of all communist influences.

Third, will populism and nationalism inform the political map of Poland in comparison to Western Europe? Single group and single issue parties may be destined to disappear in Western Europe but does the ground for broader-based political parties which are non-populist exist in countries like Poland?

PRIVATE AND PUBLIC, CIVIL SOCIETY AND CITIZENSHIP

It is in the realm of the private shaped by real socialism that the barriers to, as well as the sources of, a new civil society must be sought. Here, in the expectations and aspirations, both public and private, in the practices and predispositions of primary groups in the domestic division of physical and emotional labour, the confrontation between the old order and the new dispensation is rooted.

First, and foremost, the re-definition of the realm of the private involves not only the de-politicisation of the family and domestic realm but also its opening up to the intrusions of both Church and state. Whereas the family may have been a haven in the face of the totalising state, for that same reason it excluded from scrutiny certain domestic and family activities. Previously, for example, family networks and second economy activity were accepted as a necessary survival strategy, but now nepotism does not carry the same legitimacy and marketisation as well as taxation reforms raise new questions for the black economy.

Abortion was not as public an issue as it has become since it was symptomatic of the artificial disjuncture between the public realm of state pro-natalist policy and the private need to survive in a shortage economy. The threads connecting private need and public policy are now being reconnected and in the process raising the issues of private morality and public values.

In another vein, different sections of the population are being pauperised in different ways with the withdrawal of redistributive privileges inherited from real socialism. As such, the effect of the transition upon the individual family will be determined by the network of subsidies, informal ties, occupational appendages as well as other features of status ranking which existed under real socialism and are now being withdrawn.

The ability to externalise political opinion makes public what was once the realm of the private. However, whether this aggregate of newly liberated political opinion will have an effect on élite policies is a different matter. Although Poland is replete with associations and parties seeking to articulate needs, it is in the nature of the *revolution from above* that the space between individual and state is being constructed by political fiat. The struggle over rights is based less on their appropriation from below than in inter-factional élite conflicts in parliament and in the state apparatus. This process is further distorted by the fact that Poland has had an oppositionless transition to democracy which has culminated in Solidarity activists seeking to destroy the careers of their former associates. It is difficult to explain how one-time comrades in opposition could turn upon each other with such venom but in the politically anomic world of this élite, where all could become prime minister let alone minister, career expectations run unchecked and minor differences are expanded into major confrontations in order to fill the normless void.

The values attached to the freedoms of conscience, association, speech, person and property are thus being influenced by inter-factional political struggles. Individual and collective rights compete over property rights (divisible capital vs. worker share ownership), over minority rights (the rights of the German minority to their own language and culture which may impinge on the rights of indigenous Poles), and educational rights(the right to private, fee paying schooling ahead of improved state education). Freedom of speech is associated with burgeoning pornography, freedom of conscience with the growing power of the clergy, anti-abortion and religious education campaigns, freedom of association with peasant road blocks and occupations of government buildings, and property rights with corruption and illegal appropriation of property. All this weakens the moral dimension so critical to citizenship as the basis for societal solidarity.

THE LEGACY OF REAL SOCIALISM

Polish political culture was shaped not only by communism but by opposition to it, when it was easier to be against than for something, for conspiracy rather than construction, for intense bursts of effort rather than dull routine, and where the cult of criticism questioned everything and everyone save for your closest circle and left little room for trust and tolerance. This was the debit side of the oppositional Solidarity ethos which was transported into the political arena of post-1989 Polish politics.[3]

More generally real socialism fostered, as Mira Marody has observed, a propensity to nationalism, authoritarianism and populism.[4] While not fully exploited they remain as a resource to be mobilised by the various political actors in their power struggles. These propensities were rooted in:

1.   The search for sources of unity within the emerging moral vacuum caused by the collapse of official doctrines. It was all the greater given the atomised nature of society, and the absence of mezzo-level structures and institutions. Nationalism and religious revival provide a ready source of unifying values.
2.   The black and white, right or wrong personality-based arguments, backed up by morals, religious or secular, rather than merit, which fosters authoritarian reactions. Within this part of the legacy it is possible to seek out the origins of élite based internecine politics which have characterised Poland's negotiated revolution from above as well as the formation of political factions divided by values rather than material interests. The latter is particularly critical since the ability to negotiate, compromise, create coalitions of views, is easier when mediated through material interests rather than the more ineluctable commitment to values.
3.   The illegitimate and often socially opaque sources of inequality

emerging from the uneven movement towards the market which evoke the ingrained sense of egalitarianism. Cultivated by the communist slogan of 'we all have one stomach' these are the diet of populist movements and currently underpin right wing, anti-market ideologies of certain major parties such as the KPN.

Of course there are anti-currents which seek to limit the sources and influence of the above. Local and regional self-government is being re-asserted focusing on more traditionally delimited regions often with an ethnic underpinning as with the Silesian Germans, the Ukrainians and Lithuanians not to mention the constant confrontation with anti-semitism. National diversity as an ideology is buttressed by the sensitivity to the fate of ethnically Polish minorities in neighbouring newly independent republics.

Likewise the 'return to Europe' imperative is anti-xenophobic and demands tolerance of minorities, refugees and migrants as well as the acknowledgment of the 'Europe of regions' rather than the outmoded nationalism pedalled by both the post-communist and new right parties. This does not mean to imply that membership of a cultural, economic and political Europe is unproblematic and universally accepted. The prospective inflow of foreign capital tests this commitment to cosmopolitanism more than any other agenda as do the strictures of the IMF and World Bank in Poland's budget wrangles. Indeed as the sacrifices of 'conditionality' bear down on the population, the year 2000 entry point throws up political opposition and 'third way' chimeras.

It is more difficult to see what the antidote to moral authoritarianism is likely to be. The rediscovery of human subjectivity as the author of change and the source of discernment and responsibility, of human dignity and initiative are all part of the democratisation of Polish society. However, the continuing personalisation of politics, from the presidency downwards, where programmes matter for less than personalities, still appears to hold sway.

It is likely that this will be further embedded by the Polish version of 'lustration' or decommunisation where once again the individual will be held to account rather than the system subjected to scrutiny. Political purity and an unsullied past may be simply the outcome of being insignificant rather than the hall mark of moral rectitude. However, police files, connections and associations, have further emphasised right vs. wrong as personal attributes at the expense of right or wrong policies. This coming to terms with the past is a necessary process but when it finishes up in the hands of politicians then it becomes a personalised past rather than a common past upon which a future has to be built. That the misuse of this political tool led to the collapse of the Olszewski government in June 1992 exemplifies how it can backfire and destroy those that wield it irresponsibly and without due recourse to the rule of law.

Finally, the emerging diversity of inequality, where not all wealth stems from corrupt ties, *nomenklatura* connections or sharp practice but from diligent accumulation and market rationality, will weaken the inherited political culture of communism and opposition. The emergence of a strong private sector of employment has already highlighted the advantages and disadvantages of state guaranteed job-security vs. the gains of the market place.[5] In the process, however, the employees from within the budget sector, routine white collar as well as professionals who are casualties of debureaucratisation and hard budget constraints, provide a fertile ground for political parties as the former have done for the ex-communists (SLD).[6]

There were a multitude of expectations, aspirations and practices rooted within the economic system of the redistributive state which have been used as a blanket condemnation and explanation for the progressive demobilisation of reform impetus. In particular the orientation towards state paternalism, the 'over protective state' in welfare provision affected all sections of society in a network of payments in kind or subsidies which it is difficult to call perks or privileges since they were part of the wage structure. These reinforced the learned incapacity to take risk-bearing decisions and made it difficult to anticipate what the rational reaction to marketisation might be from any particular group and, hence, what political forces it might release.

This was particularly the case with the direct action of the land-owning peasantry which some had considered market-oriented. The increasing popularity of defensive organisations such as '*Samoobrona*', set up to represent peasants who found themselves burdened by debt and high interest payments, hark back to the inter-war period of militancy. The emergence of such grass roots protest groups is indicative of the reshaping of a post-Solidarity form of interest articulation in part caused by the absence of a left dimension to the political spectrum.

Similarly,the trade union Solidarity is under pressure not only from the martial law union (OPZZ) and the radical Solidarity '80 but from within its own ranks in the form of a revivified '*Siec*', a horizontalist organisation of 250 key large factories which, as with the rest of the forgotten constituency of workers, is now actively courted by president and premier alike. Their militancy has grown following a massive show of strength in April 1992 demanding that the various governments begin to heed the voice of organised labour and not assume that it will accept economic reform at any price simply because Solidarity initiated it.

The disenchanted state-employed intelligentsia is likewise drawn to nationalist-populist causes which hark back to para-military organisations of the inter-war period. An example is the increasing attractiveness to the young, right-wing urban intelligentsia of the '*Strzelec*' organisation, which is a form of self-defence group associated with the bearing of arms and quasi-military ritual.

All of these grass roots activities throw doubt on the feasibility of a neo-corporatist solution, particularly given the ineffectiveness of political parties and governments in articulating and reconciling increasingly strident and organised demands. It is probable that Solidarity, the trade union, combining as it does members of several different political persuasions, will be a major force in giving employees a voice denied them through the vagaries of the ballot box which produced no credible left-worker parties in the *Sejm*. The reconstruction of a left politics, of a social democratic flavour, after three years of 'liberal' governments has been hindered by certain traditional right wing parties adopting anti-market rhetoric.

Whatever the residual effect of the post-communist legacy on Polish politics nonetheless there can be little doubt that it is the activities of the post-Round Table governments that are most actively shaping political culture and practice in Poland. In understanding the nature of the élite manœuverings and subsequent governments in contemporary Polish politics, two factors stand out: first, the Balcerowicz Plan with its 'shock therapy' introduced in 1990 dissipated the legitimacy of the 'Round Table', the negotiated revolution, and of its political vehicle Solidarity;[7] and, second, Walesa's initiation of the 'war at the top' which has culminated in a 'war of all against all' amongst the political factions.

In the aftermath, all institutions, other than perhaps the president, are forced to search for identities, achievements, and followers of their own making rather than Solidarity's. The emergence for however briefly of the first non-Solidarity prime minister, Jan Pawlak, from the old communist alliance, is not just the outcome of the Solidarity factions having fought themselves to a stand-still but an indication of how difficult the task of creating a post-Solidarity political identity is proving.

HOW DID POLAND GET HERE?

It is impossible to provide a genetic unravelling of the events since the 4 April 1989 Round Table agreement[8] which has culminated in the war

of all against all', the dramatic collapse of the Olszewski government on
4–5 June 1992, and the return full-circle to a post-Solidarity government.
The battle lines have been drawn along every possible political continuum
and rivalries and animosities which had lain dormant since the sixties
have re-emerged and combined with the memories of fresh slights and
political insults.[9] Divisions between and within political institutions, social
movements, and society itself are now overlain with personal antipathies
created in the more recent past.

There has been a turbulent political evolution in the period from
the Round Table to the paralysis of three years later, from Solidarity
as a social movement to the myriad parties and competing coalitions
spawned from its womb which led to its negation in the nomination of a
prime minister with no opposition pedigree. Following this, a compromise
Solidarity prime minister has emerged who, being a woman, an ex-member
of a pro-communist party, a late-comer to the movement, and coming
from Poznan rather than the Warsaw-Gdansk hotbed, was able to stand
outside current squabbles. She is, therefore, as close as is possible to a
non-Solidarity nominee while still of Solidarity. All the above make her
appear to be the negation of personality politics.

From 1989 to 1992 there were five premiers: Mazowiecki, Bielecki,
Olszewski, Pawlak, and Suchocka. Since to understand the élite politics
which characterises Polish political life it is essential to grasp the animosities and predilections of the major actors, other personalities have to be
introduced, such as Moczulski, Kaczynski, Najder, as well as those around
whom political controversy has centred such as Parys and Wachowski.

Since 1989, major institutional divisions have arisen, between the parliament, its government and president, and in the putative struggle between
anarchic democracy and authoritarian directiveness. Most symptomatic of
the many conflicts generated along these axes was the failure of the
anti-presidential Olszewski government to put together a working coalition,
and its replacement with Ms Suchocka and her team which, while not in
open conflict with the president, is nonetheless not of his making nor at his
behest and thus preserves parliament's prerogative to choose a government.

These confrontations, to the extent that they are encoded in the constitution, will determine the nature of Poland's political regime. As such it will
not be the projects of parliamentary commissions or academic think tanks
but the raw struggle between the Belveder palace and the *Sejm* mediated
through many substitute issues (e.g. the Parys affair culminating in the
dismissal of the minister of defence at the behest of the president) which
will determine whether Poland has an Italian, French, Irish, Chilean, or US
political architecture.

FROM SOCIAL MOVEMENT TO POLITICAL PARALYSIS

The new Polish political élite perceived after the breakthrough of 1989 that the generalised rejection of communism and the prevalent vision of a affluent future would, along with the moral capital of Solidarity, be enough to impose and withstand the rigours of the transition and provide the normative underpinnings to the system. Subsequently, however, there emerged a counter-élite, which elaborated a legitimating ideology which might be called the 'politics of breaking with' the Round Table and the compromises and deals that the negotiated revolution required. As befits a group excluded from the first round of power positions, they opposed policies which sought only gradually to exclude the old communist political élite and sought to cut the umbilical cord associated with the first contract parliament of 1989 and put an end to the Solidarity era.

It is perhaps not so surprising that out of the unity of the Solidarity there has emerged a parliament which has 29 political parties, and 138 registered parties in the country as a whole. All the main parties have several internal divisions, names are already changing to disguise a previous association or identity. Personal predispositions appear to hinder coalition formation around coherent programmes of action and common oppositional origins have done little to moderate intense conflicts.[10]

Identities associated with right and left, believer and atheist, nationalist vs. cosmopolitan, market interventionist vs. liberal, were all originally submerged in the common task of overthrowing the communist system. It was only in the normal process of shaping the political terrain that divisions had to occur. Afterwards these parties formed coalitions in order to taste power only to sunder and for new parties and coalitions to emerge out of this exercise of responsibility.

The process of breakdown had a number of stages. At first, Solidarity entered the political arena as central and local Citizens Committee(s) which then became jointly organised. Once in power, however, the Citizens Committee(s) saw hitherto submerged factions – e.g., economic liberals, self-management, employee interest, agrarian – reappearing. These factions became parties, chiefly the UD (Democratic Union), PC (Centre Alliance) and Christian Democrats. Personalities predominated in the absence of competing programmes, given the public unanimity over the 'privatisation' and 'marketisation' programme as well as the continued illegitimacy of the post-communist left, and personality politics were strengthened by an election which returned a fragmented *Sejm* requiring government coalitions. In due course, post-coalition parties emerged after party splits formed under the pressure to join one or other government coalition. Out of the debris of these myriad parties and factions political movements have arisen which are embryonic parties and which are casting around for unifying ideologies and slogans.

PHASE 1

The OKP, formed out of the 161 seats won by Solidarity and the Citizens' Committee(s) at the June 1989 elections, was always a precarious structure. Not only was it formed in anticipation of being an opposition to the 65 per cent majority of the communists and their allies in the 'contract parliament', but in the process had already spawned a group of those excluded from the Walesa mandate (the famous 'photo with Walesa' seal of adoption) and therefore a likely competitive grouping within the new post-communist political class.

The OKP took power under the premiership of Tadeusz Mazowiecki, who had been installed by Walesa, but when Mazowiecki preferred to be his own man a set of events was put in train whose outcome was difficult to foresee.[11] From the outset the political machinations which installed Jaruzelski into the presidency as the guarantor of the Soviet communist interest soured the political atmosphere and provided a lasting suspicion of deals done between the élites to which society was not a party. As such it became, along with the question of security files, the political platform for the excluded sections of the political class who were to emerge in the Olszewski retinue.

Within a year of the Solidarity electoral victory at least five main groupings or factions had emerged within the OKP: Mazowiecki-Geremek, PC or Centre Alliance, a peasant lobby, a Christian Democratic Group, and a pro-worker left Solidarity faction under Bugaj, as well as a myriad of parties both elsewhere in the *Sejm* and outside stretching from extreme market liberals, nationalist-Christian, nationalist-democratic, agrarian populist, urban populist, radical independent, social democratic and post-communist.[12]

In particular the split between the Mazowiecki and Walesa factions and the formation of the PC supporting the latter under the leadership of Jaroslaw Kaczynski was clearly aimed at the introduction of Walesa into the presidency. Walesa's own avowed reason for forcing the rupture was to provide a counter-weight to the dominance of one group in parliament and thus to lead Poland into the normal politics of government and opposition. But, from the very outset, even Jaruzelski had been aware of the dangers of Walesa being left outside of the power structures with only his union presidency to back him.

PHASE 2

The gradual splitting of Solidarity followed the poor 42.4 per cent turnout in the May 1990 local government elections which, apart from signalling the political weariness of the population, nonetheless highlighted the continuing power of the local Citizens' Committees in returning Solidarity candidates and excluding those from outside its provenance.

It was symbolic of the change in Polish politics that these grass roots organisations, so critical in the first days of Solidarity power, gradually atrophied as élites prevailed and local government shifted to newly empowered local councils. During the early 1990 period there existed the distinct possibility that these committees could emerge either as a new party, perhaps becoming the basis for a presidential party owing allegiance to Walesa or as an autonomous horizontal grouping of local interests. The 'war at the top' of June 1990, however, which was fought in part over who was to control them, split the committees and effectively forced them to withdraw from politics. In this way a key constituent of the nascent civil society, which was intermediary between individual and state – geographically, politically and socially – was removed together with an obstacle to the autonomisation of élite politics. The departure of local citizens' committees from high profile politics, in turn, gave lie to the belief that Poland would not need party politics of the traditional kind.

Since then local politics has seen an unwarranted turnover of local politicians.[13] In part this is caused by an inability to decide where the prerogative of the centre ends and local government begins and partly by the desire of key coalition groupings with large apparatuses such as the PSL to reward local activists even if nominations to the cabinet are not available.

It is possible to conclude that the Citizens' Committees had achieved their role of clearing the local ground for democratic politics in a population inexperienced in such procedures. However, they could not fulfil their local umbrella function because the membership were forced to spell out their allegiance to one or other wing of Solidarity, specifically Mazowiecki or Walesa. As with many of the ideals of the original Solidarity intellectual leadership, the notion of the 'self-governing republic' granting greater autonomy to the periphery over the centre withered in the face of political reality and today local government activists complain of a state apparatus as centralised as its communist predecessor.

A power struggle over the central Citizen's Committee also ensued. The removal and subsequent resignation of key opposition figures such as Kuron, Michnik, and Geremek signalled the beginning of the end of a unified Solidarity.

There followed an artificially created debate focussed upon the need to stimulate or accelerate the privatisation process, to purge the last strongholds of the old communists through a 'de-communisation' policy, and to adopt a more aggressive stance towards the crumbling Soviet Union. Into this was interwoven the question of the role of the church in politics, in the constitution, and indeed in everyday private life as well, as was evident in the 'true Pole' slogan and incipient anti-Semitism.

In the face of the growing pressure from an increasingly discontented working class and a disillusioned peasantry, as well as from Walesa, Mazowiecki had to start to remove the by now ex-communists (the PUWP was dissolved in January 1990) from the sources of power. Again the question of *nomenklatura* capitalists helped to focus debate upon who was likely to gain from the privatisation process rather than on the process itself.

In sacking five key 'contract coalition' ministers including Kiszcak and Siwicki – interior and defence respectively – and some of those from the post-communist parties, the gradualist strategy which emanated from the round table unravelled. Walesa, having created two major groupings within the OKP, then went onto the offensive to remove Jaruzelski and called presidential elections prior to general elections and the drafting of a new constitution. The latter had originally been slated for adoption by parliament before the historic anniversary of May 3 1991. However, the question marks over parliament's legitimacy to enact this basic document deferred its drafting. By July 1992, the best that could be hoped for would be the so-called 'small constitution' which would clarify some issues of prerogative between the legislature and the executive.

Mazowiecki and the Solidarity figure Bujak at the head of the ROAD and Jaroslaw Kaczynski's PC were by now at loggerheads, contrary to the wishes of a population which could not understand either Walesa's rationale for instigating the split or what actually divided these one time allies. Whether it was a genuinely different level of commitment to the democratic ethos, their differing attitude to the post-communists' collective responsibility and therefore the latter's exclusion from any form of participation in the Third Republic, or whether it was simply a struggle for power by a group which saw its opportunity to unseat the 'fathers' of the round table is still unclear.

In fact the manner in which the Polish revolution was ostensibly falling behind Czechoslovakia and Hungary on all fronts was made much of, but the political splits only served to distract attention from the real issues of marketisation and restructuring and eventually contributed to the so-called 'wasted years' of 1989–91.

The presidential elections called for 27 November 1990 were seen to formally include Walesa in the institutional political process. This was seen by many as a means of preventing a Pilsudski-like figure emerging as in 1926, by giving Walesa responsibility rather than being allowed to adopt a posture of splendid isolation as had Pilsudski in Sulejowek. His inclusion may have been a success; when Walesa was faced two years later by 70,000 workers demonstrating outside the presidential residence he acknowledged that he would have been at their head if he had not in fact been president himself.

The acrimony of the presidential election campaign, the populist and nationalist rhetoric deployed by Mazowiecki's opponents – who included, apart from Walesa himself, Cimoszewicz the ex-communist, Moczulski of the KPN, Bartoszcze of the peasant constituency, and Tyminski the emigre dark horse – further discredited élite politics. It soon became clear that despite slogans to the contrary there was no real alternative to the Balcerowicz Plan save for some minor adjustments to handle the severity of the ensuing recession.[14]

However, the substitute issues more than compensated for the lack of real policy differences. Heated controversies involved the population in the debate as to the role of the church in education and abortion, anti-Semitism as well as the position of the German minority and indeed foreign influence in Poland's economy, the exit of the Soviet-Russian forces, popular privatisation and Walesa's promise to hand out 100 million zloty per head. These substitute issues were not only more comprehensible to the post-censorship media and its audiences but also provided material to those who sought to create a portfolio of differences with which to distance themselves from the incumbent regime.

Walesa's eventual triumph, despite the scare offered by the second stage run-off against Tyminski, saw the resignation into opposition of the newly formed Democratic Union under Mazowiecki and the removal from the political centre stage of what all opinion polls still considered to be the party of government – if not under Mazowiecki's publicly lacklustre leadership.

PHASE 3

The incoming government of Bielecki, formed after the unsuccessful efforts of Olszewski, appeared to be very much a caretaker affair in anticipation of fully free elections promised for May 1991. But despite criticism of the anti-inflationary policies he continued very much along the tough path of his predecessor, with Balcerowicz very much on board but less in evidence.

The Liberal Congress government was now faced with an increasingly obstructionist post-communist parliamentary rump, which was heartened by the relatively good showing of its candidate Cimoszewicz in the first round of the election. There also existed an extra-parliamentary grouping being mobilised around the KPN, the less predictable populist currents of Tyminski's party 'X', and the peasant lobby. Once again, the turn out at the presidential elections of 53 per cent appeared to indicate that the electorate either doubted their relevance or suffered continued societal *ennui*.

For his part Walesa now possessed greater legitimacy than the *Sejm* given his popular mandate. However, once again Polish politics was to seek refuge in the agenda of elections rather than tackling the mounting problems of the economic transition – not least the 110 pieces of legislation which had accumulated in the *Sejm* by 1992 and which had been the basis of demands for special powers for the executive. The constitutional arrangements inherited from the previous regime were an obstacle to presidential rule but its spectre was constantly deployed to limit the efficacy of the Bielecki government.

Nevertheless the election of Walesa served to clarify the picture within the post-Solidarity camp. While Walesa appeared to dispense with a parliamentary based party and sought to stand above the political chaos he had initiated, a clear grouping was now forming around Olszewski and Najder, the leaders of the Citizens' Committee, with some support from the PC. Mazowiecki's DU was to join up with ROAD and also take on board the FPD (Democratic Right Forum). As such the DU was still a movement-party containing a left, under Zofia Kuratowska (which was often an embarrassment to a party which sought to marry a staunchly pro-market philosophy with its Solidarity and therefore essentially workerist origins) and a liberal pro-market right. They were united nevertheless in their opposition to Walesa and by their commitment to democratic, secular politics.

All attention now switched to the date of the general election and the nature of the election regulations. When 7 March 1991 had come and gone without the announcement of the expected May 27 ballot day, it was apparent that the voting would be deferred until after the papal visit. At the same time confusing proposals for what manner of proportional representation would be adopted culminated in the defeat of Walesa's proposals by a house keen to ensure its own re-election. However, the adopted variant – the Hare method, combined multi-mandate party lists (345 MPs) with a single mandate national list (115 MPs) which was guaranteed to produce a fragmented upper chamber – played into the hands of Walesa who could manipulate the resulting assembly's divisions.

As had been the case a year previously, the election campaign scheduled for 27 October 1991 was dominated by the usual substitute issues of clericalism vs. secularism, nationalism vs. Europeanism, de-communisation vs. gradualist exclusion. All parties sought to distance themselves from Balcerowicz, the long-suffering Finance Minister and guarantor of international financial probity, as too did some members of his own government. The popularity of Solidarity also showed a radical decline as the costs of the transition were placed at its door rather than sought in the communist past.

This time around the church was more evidently in the fray than during the presidential election and the so-called Catholic Action grouping (subsequently reverting to its Christian National Union title) which was to form the basis of the incoming government was highly favoured by the clergy in their pulpit admonitions to their flock.

PHASE 4

The outcome of the 'war at the top' split was that over the intervening months both groups, the UD and the PC, had accumulated partners which clarified their political as opposed to personal identity. However, as with previous elections the pundits and polls were again found wanting, not least in the 57 per cent abstention rate and where only 37 per cent of the population cast valid votes.

Again the population saw parties coalesce not on the basis of common values or of jointly produced economic programmes (save for some slogans about combating recession) but simply to take power. Walesa's first reaction to the configuration of party strengths was to seek to put together a government under Mazowiecki or Geremek. The UD was the party which had been tipped to win, and had in fact the most seats, and as such it sought to present itself as the natural party of government. Both figures, however, failed as did the attempt to bring back a KLD government under Bielecki. The stunning success of the post-communist PSL and SLD as well as the nationalist KPN did much to undermine the status of the UD and legitimate a search for a non-communist but also non-Solidarity option.

Ultimately Jaroslaw Kaczynski emerged in the king-making role and

Table 6.1   Results of the 1991 Sejm Elections[18]

	% vote	# seats
Democratic Union (UD)	12.31	62
Democratic Left Alliance (SLD)	11.98	60
Catholic Electoral Action (ZChN)	8.73	49
PSL-Programme Alliance	8.67	48
Citizens' Centre Alliance (PC)	8.71	44
Confederation for an Independent Poland (KPN)	7.5	46
Liberal Democratic Congress (KLD)	7.48	37
Peasants' Alliance PSL 'S'	5.46	28
Trade Union Solidarity	5.05	27
Polish Beer Party	3.27	16
Christian Democracy	2.36	5
Union of Real Politics	2.25	3
Solidarity of Labour	2.05	4
German Minority	1.17	7
Party of Christian Democrats	1.11	4
Polish Western Union	0.23	4
Party 'X' (Tyminski)	0.47	3
Movement for Silesian Autonomy	0.35	2

Note: 11 other parties received 1 seat apiece.
Total 29 parties.

proposed an alliance between his PC, the ZChN, KPN, and the KLD under the leadership of Jan Olszewski much to the annoyance of Walesa who had successfully vetoed such a government in January 1991 after his presidential success. As pointed out above, this grouping, while possessing some Solidarity opposition credentials, was very much a shadow cabinet and had failed in the original élite distribution in 1989.

The KLD reneged at the last minute as did the KPN when the defence portfolio was not offered to Moczulski. At this juncture the post-communist PSL offered its services which after some hesitation was accepted, although no portfolios were offered to its highly successful young leader, Jan Pawlak, or any member of his party. Although accepted by a substantial majority, this configuration soon ran into trouble when presenting its budget and economic programme to the *Sejm* in March 1992 at which point the 'coalition of seven', as it had become, had to seek further support to survive. In the search for such support and in an effort to undermine opposition to it from the post-Solidarity groupings, it played the 'security files' card and fell.

COALITIONS OF COALITIONS

UD was the major casualty of the election because of its inauguration of the controversial Balcerowicz Plan and the poor showing of the candidate himself. A second casualty was the KLD of Bielecki, very much the party of economic liberals and young turks from Gdansk, whose popularity increased during the first months of the Bielecki premiership only to drop just as dramatically. Their major appeal was to the emerging but as yet minuscule middle class and entrepreneurs and demographically speaking they must bide their time. The KLD had made enemies of the powerful peasant grouping, particularly the PSL, for their opposition to minimum prices and continued subsidies. This animosity, which was at least indicative of emerging economic rather than purely rhetorical differences, was to undermine the attempts to form the fourth government in June 1992.

The two parties KLD and DU became linked together in the months of political paralysis after November 1991 after the KLD had left Olszewski in the lurch when a government appeared to have been formed. It was the UD insistence that the KLD be included in any 'grand coalition' combining the seven parties of premier Olszewski's government with the three from the small coalition, that allowed the ZChN of Chrzanowski and PSL to scotch the chances for a broader based government.

A further casualty was the PC of Jaroslaw Kaczynski, who soon after the elections finally broke with Walesa. It was the PC which then nearly fractured under the pressure of whether to move towards the UD. After the collapse of the grand coalition in April 1992, the PC and the Solidarity peasants, now renamed and seeking a broader centre-right constituency, proposed a consolidation government which would include all democratic forces, including the KPN but excluding the post-communist 'social democrats'.

Both the UD and the PC, as could be predicted, did in fact split after the collapse of the Olszewski government in June 1992, although the former less conclusively. The right of the UD under Alexander Hall moved into a temporary alliance with the PC. The Christian Democratic part of the PC formed a new party with the ex-premier Olszewski and other casualties which came to be known as the 'Movement for the Republic' aimed at cleansing Poland of the '*nomenklatura* and police collaborators'.

It is the emergence of the PSL, the descendant of the communist coalition ZSL peasant grouping, as well as the rising popularity of the right-nationalist KPN which was making inroads into the working-class constituency, that has been the major development of the first six months of 1992. As part of a bloc – which could potentially include the ex-communists SdRP – opposed to the stringent policies of all the three post 1989 governments, parties which would never have been considered as potential allies are responding to the rising discontent amongst the peasantry, workers, and the impoverished white collar employees.

The inclusion of the PSL and KPN into the Pawlak coalition alongside their major opponents the KLD and DU was symptomatic of the extraordinary lengths to which parties would go in their élite struggles, although, as was shown three weeks later, unity in overthrowing a government did not ensure the ability to form one.

It is generally accepted that the impasse could only be broken by a new general election, but this would in turn require a new electoral law with a 5 per cent threshold, which the parliament is loathe to grant.[15] The alternative of presidential rule is limited by the absence of a presidential party within the *Sejm*, although Walesa has always claimed that he could easily raise one. The collapse of the Olszewski government under his direct instigation using the presidential powers available to him is evidence of this.

A POLISH DE GAULLE?

There is little doubt that much of the political commotion centres around the figure of the presidency, his staff and their declared and undeclared intentions. If, as is indicated, Walesa is seeking a Gaullist solution to the nature of his presidency then it will require the formation of a presidential party or a stable presidential bloc. Co-habitation as a long-term *modus vivendi* is not considered feasible unless this exists. However, his many supporters are also drawn from those who favour parliamentary rule with limited powers for the president.

Walesa has demanded the power to call and disband a government, leaving the *Sejm* with the vote of confidence. Likewise he insists on greater executive powers particularly as regards the military. As a result of the Olszewski débâcle and the rumours of the use of the military, appointments in the Defence, Interior and Foreign Ministries have in effect passed to the president. However, in the light of the events surrounding the Olszewski government's collapse, constitutional reform is now a priority recognised by all parties.

A parliament which had the greatest difficulty in passing a budget and which could only foster determined unity in the desire to remove Olszewski who they saw as threatening state stability, may find it difficult to agree on a constitution. Not least they will be tested by the church's desire for a preamble referring to the Christian nature of Polish society to which Walesa is committed but to which the DU and KLD as well as some other key groupings may find it hard to agree. While awaiting constitutional reform, the standing of all political institutions, apart from the military and police, is declining. It is the de-legitimation of the institutions of democracy which provides the greatest cause for concern. Coalition manœuverings have not improved the popular will to support particular parties. One person in five would still not vote and a similar number do not know who to vote for – and the proportion is increasing.

CONCLUSION

To paraphrase a well-worn dictum, 'when events change quickly conclusions should crafted carefully'. The facade of Poland's new institutional architecture has emerged in a variety of styles but the interior is far from complete. The problem is that there is no agreement on the design, whether presidential, parliamentary, coalitional or majority. At the same time there are those who argue that Poland must develop its own style, rather than following the well tried formulae of the West; however, here the problem is that no plans exist and the costings are not clear.

What are the constraints facing Polish governments in the transition and what are the dangers?[16]

1. Consensus over the current pro-market economic policy and perceived adherence to IMF and other international guide-lines is an essential platform for any government.

2. Governments have rested upon the remnants of post-Solidarity political groupings which have shown themselves to be the only source of a working majority within parliament. However, there is every likelihood that if new elections are called that the populist parties (KPN, PSL and SLD) will increase their representation. Only 6–7 parties would make it into the *Sejm* on a 5 per cent threshold, and a UD-based coalition could at most expect 25 per cent of the seats.

3. For this reason the post-Solidarity coalition is under pressure to take on board parties or political forces which represent constituencies central to Poland's continued adherence to reform. This involves the trade union and peasant lobbies in particular in some neo-corporatist solution, as well as the church.

4. There is no evidence that a society based upon citizenship and the market can be achieved by any third way and here the Latin American exemplars of Mexico and Argentine are increasingly instructive for the Polish élite. Thus populist rhetoric must be treated as a symptom rather than a solution to the problem. However, anti-market, anti-capitalist, anti-European voices will become more vocal and pose the greatest problem for Poland today.

Poland's politics has thus far withstood the many travails of transition. It has successfully incorporated a powerful presidency, and produced a parliament which has given public voice to many private concerns. The security apparatus and defence establishment has been overhauled, and the judiciary appears to be holding its own against the wave of corruption and political scandals.[17]

Parliamentary legislative work, however, is obviously considerably behind in its tasks which constantly raises the question of special powers to a branch of the executive (cabinet and president), taking the more difficult decisions out of the parliamentary arena. Foreign intervention, while strengthening the argument of the pro-reform forces, also fuels the engine of xenophobia and nationalism.

Poland may not split like Czechoslovakia but it may yet have to learn the lessons of economic nationalism before it accepts that limitations on national sovereignty are concomitant with the commonwealth of economic and political integration.

NOTES

1. E. Szemplinska 'Skazana na wladze', *Wprost*, 19 July 1992, pp. 19–20.
2. See David Stark, 'Path dependence and privatisation strategies in East Central Europe', *East European Politics and Societies*, No. 1, 1992, pp. 20–21. For an instructive indication of the problems raised by the 'legacy of socialism' issues, see W. D. Connor and P. Ploszajski (eds), *Escape from Socialism: The Polish Route*, Warsaw, 1992.
3. There is a considerable literature on the 'ethos of Solidarity' debate but one of the most convincing studies of the ideologies underpinning the Solidarity movement during 1980–81 which must form the basis for any subsequent analyses is Sergiusz Kowalski, *Krytyka Solidarnosciowego Rozumu*, Warsaw, 1990.
4. Miroslawa Marody, 'The political attitudes of Polish society in the period of systemic transitions' in *Escape from Socialism*, loc. cit., p. 266.
5. There have been many attempts to integrate the fledgling business community in Poland and provide it with a lobby. Considerable attention is paid to the burgeoning wealth of Poland's financial élite and the gains to be made from the market, e.g. '100 Najbogatszych Polakow' in *Wprost*, 21 June 1992.
6. The KPN has shown a steady increase in its popularity amongst the electorate by the populist policies of anti-recessionary it espouses. Likewise the PSI and to a lesser extent the ex-communist SLD have shown continued strength in the polls. However the poll popularity of the UD which has strengthened by more than any of the above parties since the 1991 elections, is greater than that which it actually achieves at the ballot box whereas the reverse is the case for the SLD. *Demoskop. Przeglad*, Jan.–Feb. 1992. Warsaw also showed UD as the most popular party in June 1992 with 18%, KPN 12.1%, SLD 8. 1%, and PSL 7.9%. NSZZ Solidarnosc at 7.1% was also slightly more popular.
7. Jan Pakulski, 'Rewolucje Wschodnioeuropejskie', *Kultura i Spoleczenstwo*, July 1991.
8. For a study and summary of attitudes during the 1980's see *Polacy '90*, IFis and ISP, Warsaw 1991.
9. Miroslawa Grabowska, 'System Partyjnyow budowie' *Krytyka*, No. 37, 1991.
10. For a glance at the variety of parties on the market – erotic, ecological and eccentric, see Magdalena Grochowska, 'Kwestia smaku', *Przeglad Tygoniowy*, 14 June 1992.
11. Ironically, three years later in July 1992, the option on offer was exactly that foreseen earlier by Walesa, namely that he and Mazowiecki rule in tandem. However they were by now both faced by a more assertive parliament and both were of diminished authority.
12. A. Friszke, 'The Polish political scene', *East European Politics and Societies*, No. 2, 1990, pp. 305–41.

13. A belated recognition of the loss of local self-governing impetus is provided in an interview with T. Mazowiecki, 'Szansa poprawy zycia publicznego', *Wspolnota*, 31 May 1992.
14. For a recent statement of how far according to its author Poland has travelled towards the market see L. Balcerowicz, 'Czarna robota zostala juz zrobiona', *Rzeczpospolita*, 22 June 1992.
15. B. Nowotarski, 'W Strone Wyborow', *Polityka*, 20 June 1992.
16. A studies assessment of the political exigencies facing Poland is provided by J. Kofman, 'Komentarz na wiosne', *Krytykano*, 38 Spring 1992.
17. The Minister of Justice, Z. Dyka, who survived the Olszewski collapse, provides an update on the rule of law issues in *Katolik*, 21 June 1992.
18. Apart from the election to the *Sejm*, there were also those to the upper chamber or senate which had much diminished in authority since it had been elected with a 99 per cent Solidarity majority in June 1989. The 1991 senate elections produced 21 seats for the UD, 11 for the trade Union Solidarity. 9 for Catholic Action, 9 for PC 7 for PSL, 6 for KLD 4 each for the SLD and KPN and 5 for Solidarity peasant.

7 Romania

Jonathan Eyal

INTRODUCTION

Romania was the only Eastern European state to undergo a violent revolution in 1989. Yet, far from signifying a complete break with the communist past, the Romanian revolution has created a hybrid of democracy and authoritarian rule. It is ruled by a curious mixture of communists turned 'democrats' who, although still able to prevent opposition forces from assuming power, are not powerful enough to suppress dissent. The country is therefore in a legal and political limbo: it has ostensibly democratic institutions, all radically overhauled since 1989, but no democracy. And the gulf between realities and appearances in state institutions is as wide as it has always been. A country ruled by probably the harshest communist regime in Eastern Europe is still headed by a president who was a notable functionary under the old regime. As a result, the internal political fight in Romania is not merely between personalities and parties. Instead, it continues to be a confrontation about the very nature of the state, its character and even its ultimate territorial frontiers.

REVOLUTION AND THE BEGINNINGS OF A NEW REGIME

Interpretations of the Romanian revolution usually concentrate on two conflicting scenarios: whether Ceauçescu's overthrow was the result of a coup d'etat or a popular rebellion. However, the December 1989 events represented both a palace putsch and a revolution at the same time. The real problem with the Romanian revolution was that it was a prime candidate for hijacking from the beginning.

By the 22 December 1989, Ceauçescu was already doomed. Betrayed by the army, deserted by the Securitate, and lied to by his closest advisers the President was persuaded to flee the capital, only to be delivered straight into the hands of a military unit loyal to the revolution. For the next few days, Romanians were treated by a hysterical mass media (and especially the television) to a gripping account of the 'hunt' for the fleeing dictator. In practice, everything was a charade: Ceauçescu was safely in the hands

of those who commandeered the revolution from the beginning and was
executed together with his wife and with the minimum of legal niceties on
Christmas Day.

When Ion Iliescu appeared on the balcony of the Central Committee,
a newly anointed leader was facing his people. Those who supported
him were precisely the same institutions which were the mainstay of
Ceaucescu's rule and Romania started its new life with the biggest lie of
all: an ostensibly radical change which, at least in the first month, amounted
to no change at all.

ROMANIA'S FIRST POST-REVOLUTIONARY INSTITUTIONS

Romania's new leaders were all former communist notables. Those who
knew Romania's new leaders argued that the outcome could have hardly
been otherwise: Ceaucescu's rule was so complete that it was only natural
for former communists to inherit the mantle.

The National Salvation Front was supposedly formed out of 145 personalities from 'different walks of life', as a temporary ruling body, intended
to govern Romania in the lead-up to free, multi-party elections. In its first
proclamation, the Front dissolved all the country's institutions and assumed
complete control over all state affairs. The press was freed from party
control, all political movements were liberalised, the country was promised
a free and impartial judiciary, the rule of law and, most preciously, freedom
from travel restrictions, cold, hunger and fear. Yet, right from the start,
apprehensions about the Front's real intentions appeared. First, the full
list of the Front's membership was not published,[1] and the biographies
of those included were never released. Indeed, it subsequently emerged
that some – such as the dissident Doinea Cornea – were included without
their prior consent. Furthermore, the full body of the Front had no powers.
Instead, the mythical 145 members 'delegated' control to a 'council' which
also appeared to do nothing. This council, in turn, established an executive
body which was the real power in the land. Control remained concentrated
in the hands of the few: Brucan, Iliescu and Roman.

More disturbing was the fact that these leaders decreed the separation
of powers but continued to hold both executive and legislative functions.
Government ministers were made responsible to the Front, rather than
to the newly appointed Prime Minister Petre Roman, and 'decree-laws'
were issued without any reference to the cabinet. The Front talked about
the independence of the media, yet it appointed the head of radio and
television as its spokesman. It promised that all political parties would be

allowed to function freely, but at the same time suggested that Romania required 'consensus' within one Front, a notion not very different from 'democratic centralism'. Crucially, leading members of the Front vowed to remove Ceauceşcu's 25-year dictatorship but not a word was said about the 40 years of communist rule. Nobody wanted even to talk about the fate of the Communist Party. Its vast organisation, its funds and structures stretching back to the smallest village, simply 'disappeared'. The party was never, however, officially dissolved and when this was demanded the Front simply refused to respond. Within weeks after the revolution, dissidents such as Doinea Cornea left the Front, accusing Romania's government of being dominated by communists and Securitate officers.[2]

Meanwhile, other political parties were created. Interestingly, at least at the beginning, these parties, such as the National Peasants Party and the National Liberal Party, were revivals of the political movements which existed before 1945. The Peasants, led by Iuliu Maniu, a Transylvanian Romanian of great distinction and personal integrity, traditionally stood at the left of the political spectrum. The Liberals, historically representing town dwellers and small merchants, stood on the right. Nothing illustrated Romania's real condition better than the recreation of these two parties. Bereft of any organised opposition to Ceauceşcu, those who already mistrusted the Front had no other choice but to look to a new point of reference, extinguished no less than four decades earlier. And the old-new parties were re-established by men and women in their late sixties or early seventies, many of them returning to the country for this purpose. The newly established political parties immediately asked to share power with the Front. Yet the Front's members, many of whom were responsible for sentencing the leaders of the Peasants and Liberals to long-term imprisonment decades ago,[3] prevaricated for as long as possible by promising 'round-table' discussions which did not materialise.[4] The Front, originally established as a temporary institution, then announced its intention to guide the country towards free elections, and decided to take part in the parliamentary elections as a distinct party with all the advantages of representing the new state authority.[5]

The total absence of any dialogue between government and opposition led to the first post-revolutionary outbreak. On 12 January 1990, exactly 21 days after Ceauceşcu's overthrow, thousands came on to the streets, demanding the abolition of the Communist Party, an enquiry into the events surrounding the revolution, and the reinstatement of the death penalty, abolished by the Front in a move widely regarded as shielding former communists from punishment. Eager to calm the population's anger, the Front swiftly published a series of proclamations outlawing the Communist

Party and confiscating its property, instituting a special committee tasked with investigating previous communist crimes and calling for a referendum on the question of the death penalty.[6] Yet immediately thereafter they changed their minds yet again: instead of banning the communist party outright (as they had promised to the demonstrators) the Front called for a referendum on the issue.[7] In what became a litany of false promises, neither the referendum on the death penalty, nor that called in order to decide the fate of the Communist Party were ever held.

Deceived opposition parties enlarged their demands to include not only the posponment of elections but also the creation of a government of 'national unity' which could ensure their fairness. Yet the Front refused to accept any of these demands: in a meeting with the foreign press in Bucharest, Silviu Brucan, the government's *eminence grise*, accused journalists of being 'victims of 19th-century ideological prejudices' when they pointed to the inherent contradiction between the Front's promise to hold free elections and its desire to compete as a distinct political movement.[8] Having been surprised by the speed of the challenge to their newly established rule, Romania's leaders were clearly moving to the offensive. They did it with the only instruments they knew: mass mobilisation and violence. A meeting of Bucharest factory workers was called at the behest of Ion Iliescu, the Front's president. The participants duly asked Iliescu to stand in the forthcoming elections, in an atmosphere which reminded many Romanians of Ceaucescu's rallies. Ostensibly at the opposition's behest, the Front postponed the parliamentary elections to 20 May 1990, a small respite for parties recreated after four decades of dictatorship. But at the same time, electoral rallies were restricted to weekends only, in specific public parks.[9] And on sharing power with the opposition there was no compromise: the Front, claiming to be the revolution's creation, also intended to remain its only keeper.[10]

This string of decisions led to another bout of rioting, culminating in a vast rally on 28 January, when crowds besieged the Front's headquarters in Bucharest. Not for the last time, it appeared that the Front's rule was doomed.[11] Yet the government implemented a strategy which was subsequently destined to become Romania's original contribution to Eastern Europe's post-communist history: the miners. Transported by the state-owned railways,[12] miners descended on demonstrators with chains and sticks. From representing the opposition to the communist regime, the Front became the newly contested state power. Octavian Paler, one of Romania's foremost commentators, aptly called it democracy 'which lasted only a month'.[13] The mistrust between those governing and those governed, the personal confrontation between political partners, the heavy mist of suspicion which permeates Romanian society all have their causes in the events of December 1989 and January 1990.

THE PROVISIONAL BECOMES SEMI-PERMANENT

The confrontation between government and opposition ultimately resulted in the compromise of a Provisional Council for National Unity to provide Romania with a temporary parliamentary assembly able to draft, with the participation of all opposition parties, an electoral law. The agreement, however, called for the equal participation of all newly created political parties, but the Front coupled this with another decree which required only 250 signatures from potential supporters in order to register a new political party. With remarkable speed, over 100 parties were registered for the May 1990 elections. In the period after the elections, the number of parties continued to grow, reaching more than 1000 by 1991. Indeed, the entire exercise in democracy became a farce: some registered their own family as a political movement, mainly in order to gain financial advantages.[14] In the Council, the Front reserved for itself half of the seats. With the aid of other parties – many actually established with the government's support or connivance – the Front continued to retain an absolute majority. The Council therefore became an instrument for Front rule under a different guise. Yet there was a difference: decisions could now be taken with the semblance of a democratic debate. In practice, the Council confined itself to voting on the electoral law; the country continued to be governed by the Front's leaders who very seldom reported their decisions to Romania's rudimentary parliament.

The sessions of the Council had a serious impact. Romanians concluded that, apart from the Front's leaders who enjoyed constant exposure on television and appeared knowledgeable, no one else was fit to govern. The electoral law which the Council adopted contained all the usual safeguards of any democracy. In practice, the law was irrelevant, for Romania's future rulers were already chosen after the first televised Council session.[15]

Yet the Front itself was undergoing some transformations. Having realised after the events of January that any attempt to retain the overt signs of communism would be forcefully resisted and could create a severe reaction in the West,[16] its strategy changed. The aim, observable only with the benefit of hindsight, was actually very simple: the prevention of any recrimination against former communist notables through the smooth transformation and adaptation of old institutions in the new political context. Few Romanians were aware that when the communist regime was toppled, the Front decided to change the country's name from the Socialist Republic of Romania to, simply, Romania. The change avoided the thornier issue of whether Romania should revert to its monarchist traditions. Alone in Eastern Europe, Romania still had King Michael, a monarch whose rule was extremely popular and whose removal in December 1947 signified the beginning of the communist rule. The Front was not worried about King Michael's challenge; it knew that after decades of communist indoctrination the former sovereign could initially count on precious little support in his country. Instead, it feared that any discussion on the King's return could trigger off a wider process of reckoning with former communist officials and galvanise the opposition.

Instead of confronting the issue of the monarchy directly, the Front tackled it piecemeal. The avoidance of mentioning the republic in Romania's name neatly bypassed the issue, and the distribution of posts immediately after the revolution maintained this careful silence. Thus, Ion Iliescu was merely the president of the Front and, although he fulfilled the functions normally attributed to a head of state, he was not usually referred to as such. The Front's real intentions were only revealed during the deliberations in the Provisional Council of National Unity, when the government tabled an electoral law, calling for the election of a two-chamber parliament and a president. By envisaging the creation of a 387-member strong Chamber of Deputies and a 199-member Senate, it appealed to the Romanians' sense of history. And at the same time, by calling for the election of a president, the Front hoped to kill off the issue of the monarchy once at for all. And thus, with most of the deputies not even realising what was happening, the Council adopted an electoral law which asked Romanians to vote for deputies, senators and a president, with little idea of their functions, responsibilities or powers.[17] Deputies who objected at the time were told that the electoral law was merely a temporary stop-gap, a necessary device in order to set Romania on its democratic course. In practice, the very same legislation was subsequently used in order to prove that Romania had already opted for a set of institutions. The government claimed that this was an unavoidable outcome, given the fact that country's revolution erased all previous constitutional arrangements. In fact, as Romanians learnt later, their 1965 constitution was only formally abrogated on 8 December 1991.

THE ELECTIONS OF MAY 1990

Having approved the electoral law, the Council faded from the political scene and Romania embarked on an electoral campaign. From the start, it was not a confrontation between equals: the Front claimed to be the 'emanation' of the revolution, while candidates from other parties were portrayed by the officially controlled media as either interlopers or, at best, old people desperate to gain power. The Liberals and the Peasants, which represented the Front's only significant opposition in 1990, could not have boycotted the elections even if they wanted to. By March 1990, the Front had created or supported so many alternative movements that any elections, even without the potentially most important parties, could have still been portrayed as democratic. Yet the travails of the opposition were just beginning. The electoral law prevented canvassing in factories during daytime, supposedly in order to avoid further losses to the economy. This did not prevent either Petre Roman or Ion Iliescu from doing precisely that.[18] The radio and television networks remained under complete state control, despite valiant efforts by groups of intellectuals to document the media's bias for the authorities.[19] The printed media joined the fray as well.

One of the revolution's greatest tangible achievements was the liberation of the press from state control. The personnel working on these papers remained the same, but management committees, elected by the workers, quickly changed editorial direction. It is obvious that the Front has no particular desire to encourage a flourishing free press either. On three occasions, an opposition paper, *Romania Libera*, had its existence directly threatened. In June 1990, police stood idly by as miners rampaged through the paper's offices. Later, the paper was threatened with legal action for 'misusing' the name on its masthead, which, the Prime Minister asserted, was a government-owned copyright. Finally, the paper was threatened with bankruptcy for alleging widespread government corruption. The paper's very existence, however, is an indication that the Romanian president has limited capacities of influencing the rest of the press.

Nonetheless, the Front appears not to have been too concerned about their relative freedom, and used the press effectively when it wanted to. Though the old files maintained by the Securitate are still inaccessible, this did not prevent the government from leaking their contents selectively. The government's main attention was on control of the television and, to a lesser extent, radio stations. Pro-government rallies were always reported during prime-time transmissions; opposition meetings were accorded limited showing during the late-night news bulletins. The opposition was accorded equal time in party political broadcasts. Yet, without access to anything but state-owned studios, no money and no expertise, the opposition's broadcasts usually consisted of a party spokesman, sitting ill-at-ease in a studio-provided couch, reading a closely typed and usually incomprehensible manifesto. These interminable party political broadcasts had no impact on an increasingly impatient population and actually worsened the opposition's predicament.[20] Television announcers were known to grimace when reading a statement opposing the government and frequently mocked opposition leaders in their transmissions.

This hatred campaign was combined with the Front's carefully-planned electioneering, which sought to promise Romanians a rosy future. They were assured a smooth transition to a market economy, with the minimum of unemployment and inflation, while protecting the country's valuable assets from unscrupulous foreign investors.[21] The slogan of 'We Shall Not Sell Our Country' proved extremely attractive. It was reinforced with populist appeals to envy: opposition leaders were accused of having eaten croissants in Paris cafés while most Romanians were starving. Yet behind this crude message the government's more subtle understanding of the country's situation was at work. Alone among all political parties, the Front never forgot that most Romanians were born after the establishment of communist rule. Although most regarded their economic system as bankrupt, they did not take kindly to politicians who, when calling for the radical and immediate overthrow of all former structures, were basically implying that the Romanians' very existence over four decades amounted to a complete failure. The Front offered them an easy escape, another exercise in collective amnesia. Given all its in-built advantages, it is surprising that the government still saw fit to 'doctor' voting figures on election day. Yet so strong was the Front's obsession with preventing the rise of Romania's historic parties that the new regime went even further. In the countryside peasants, usually confused about their choice,[22] were 'helped' in their decision by the president of the ballot station, who was usually a Front supporter or member. Furthermore the final tally indicated an interesting disparity: Romanians cast one million votes more than the total registered on the electoral roll. The opposition was not allowed to inspect the final returns. Thousands of appeals alleging malpractices were lodged with the Electoral Court. Not a single one of them was even discussed. Thus, the Front obtained its crushing majority and achieved complete dominance through ostensibly democratic means. Yet the May 1990 elections contained the seeds of Romania's future political deadlock.

AFTER THE BALLOT, BACK TO THE STICK

The outcome was the worst possible for Romania. Ion Iliescu was elected with an 85 per cent majority, only slightly less than that regularly manufactured for his predecessor. The country's Hungarian minority, however, avoided him *en masse*.[23] Iliescu's support was strongest among industrial workers and uneducated people, while the opposition's candidates performed best among the younger urban population, especially in the cities of Timisoara and Bucharest.[24] The Front captured roughly two thirds of the seats in both the Chamber of Deputies and the Senate. Since nobody was aware of any distinction between the two, the vote was almost identical for both,[25] thereby negating the very essence of a bi-cameral parliamentary system. The second largest representation in the Deputies' Assembly belonged to the ethnic Hungarians, a minority against whose 'dangers' the Front warned throughout the electoral campaign. The Liberals obtained only 6.41 per cent of the vote, and they were followed by a clutch of six further parties, none of them with more than 3 per cent of the seats. Not only was the opposition reduced to impotence. It was also deeply divided (at least two out of the eight potential opposition partners in parliament were the Front's allies, as subsequent events proved) and associated with the deeply mistrusted ethnic Hungarians. This outcome virtually guaranteed violence.

President Iliescu and Prime Minister Petre Roman were aware of the West's insistence on free elections as a precondition for extending much-needed economic aid. Elections having been held, the triumphant Front now expected a flood of aid and loan packages. None of the Front's luminaries understood that, even given optimum political conditions, Romania would have had an uphill struggle in attracting Western investment. The government frequently asserted that, alone in Eastern Europe, Romania did not have any outstanding foreign debts. By wiping out their debt, however, Romanians lost all leverage on their former creditors who, by 1989, were already free to consider any loan propositions without the burden of rescheduling previous repayments. And, since Eastern Europe offered plenty of other investment opportunities, they had little interest in becoming embroiled in Romania, a country ruled by a party which made the control of foreign capital a cardinal policy in its election. After exhausting their hard currency reserves in the pre-election binge, the Romanians passed their begging bowl around. Those elected on the promise that they would never abandon the country's assets to foreigners quickly discovered that there were no buyers, regardless of what Romania wanted to sell. Increasingly exasperated, the government looked for scapegoats. It accused the opposition of deterring Western investors; some of the Front's supporters hinted at even darker international plots.[26] A catastrophic drop in industrial production, followed by a huge inflation rate as the authorities strove to keep Romania's industries in business and spiralling retail prices, ultimately drove Premier Petre Roman from office

16 months after securing one of the largest parliamentary majorities in Eastern Europe's post-communist history. With hindsight, it is clear that, when faced with the post-electoral reality, the government could have taken some remedial action by placating the opposition. Instead, they opted for terror yet again.

A month before the elections were held, a group of students took over University Square in the centre of Bucharest. For a number of days the demonstration continued to grow with much elan: students and intellectuals spoke from the balconies of the University against a government which they charged with 'stealing' their revolution; intellectuals held 'literary circles' in the street below. Slowly, however, the sit-in degenerated. Black marketeers, petty criminals and plain-clothes security agents mingled freely. The city's sanitary authorities refused to perform their duties and a month after the demonstration started, the entire area was in deep squalor. With hindsight, it is clear that the students' leaders should have called a halt to their demonstration immediately after the May elections. To all intents and purposes, they failed in their task of galvanising a nation against the authorities and elicited little support among Bucharest's population.

On 13 June 1990, flying squads of heavily armed police moved in to disperse the crowds. Yet the demonstrators came back and the events thereafter can only be added to the long list of Romanian mysteries. According to the authorities, groups of students set fire to the police headquarters, attacked the television station and rioted in other parts of the capital. President Iliescu quickly accused the demonstrators of initiating 'an organised attempt, prepared for a long time, to overthrow by force and violence the government democratically elected on 20 May'.[27] Everything followed a now familiar pattern. Thousands of miners arrived in pre-arranged trains. Fed in specially created centres, they proceeded to beat up anyone who appeared an 'intellectual'. The University was attacked, headquarters of political parties were ransacked, *Romania Libera*'s journalists were prevented from publishing and shops (especially those privatised at the time) were looted. Throughout, the police did nothing. And needless to say, nobody was ever arrested or held to account for the death of six people and the wounding of 555 more.[28] A parliamentary committee of enquiry was duly appointed. With a delay of one year, it filed two reports: one absolving the authorities of any responsibility; the other pointing an accusing finger at the government. Yet the most eloquent evidence of June's events was presented by no other than President Iliescu, when he thanked the miners for their deeds. In any emotional rally, he congratulated them for their 'workers' solidarity' in opposing this 'fascist coup'. He also told them that the coup was engineered by 'foreign forces', which supported 'with dollars and drugs' an attempt to 'divert the Romanian revolution to the right and take over power'.[29] Iliescu was now enforcing his own revolution. Those unwilling to adhere to theories of 'democratic centralism' and still prepared to challenge him even after his overwhelming victory in the May elections had to be crushed.[30] Iliescu's victory was a ghoulish triumph. He achieved complete control, at the price of isolating his country for years to come.[31]

PARLIAMENTARY LIFE AND THE CONSTITUTION

Slowly, the opposition parties returned to their shattered offices determined to struggle as best they could in Romania's new parliament. The Front, enjoying a crushing majority, did as it pleased, but the opposition could at least enjoy a political platform. Parliament's primary task was the drafting of a new constitution, and the elaboration of legislation for fresh local and parliamentary elections immediately thereafter. In fact, the local elections were immediately postponed for one year,[32] and a short bill, introduced in direct contravention of the Deputies Assembly's own regulations[33] and actually applied before its final approval by parliament,[34] enabled the government to appoint prefects and mayors throughout the country without any popular consultation[35] and regardless of the ethnic make-up of each county.[36] Very soon, Ceaucescu's practice of instructing local deputies through the telephone was revived.[37]

In fact, it was obvious that parliament was not the institution from which all power flowed. On occasions too numerous to count, the government created new state bodies and asked parliament merely to legislate for their creation months thereafter. The secret police was officially revived under a different name on 23 March 1990. The decree reviving this reviled institution was never made public[38] and parliament only voted new legislation for this organisation a year later. The old Interior Ministry troops reappeared under the historic name of the Geandarmerie. More than 18 months after the event, parliament was presented with a bill regulating their powers. In an initial and rare display of prerogatives, deputies demanded the right to elaborate a law regulating the operation of government ministries and their spheres of competence. Yet, while the two chambers were debating the subject, the government ignored them and proceeded to create new ministries without the appropriate legislation.[39] The freshly appointed ministers (initially barred by the electoral law from being members of parliament) made few appearances in the legislature.[40] A year later, a change in the legislature's internal regulations, allowing ministers to retain their parliamentary seats was announced after, and not before, deputies were already made ministers while continuing to vote in parliament.[41] Throughout Prime Minister Roman's administration (which lasted 16 months) no cumulative state budget was tabled, no debate about the budgets of specific ministries was undertaken and parliamentarians had no idea of just how much the country was spending on defence. Meanwhile, President Iliescu created his own staff, grouped in separate departments closely shadowing the responsibilities of government ministries.[42] Significantly, most of those appointed to the presidential staff were old Securitate officers or communist party ideologues, and not one came from the opposition, despite the fact that the presidency was supposedly above all parties and ostensibly neutral.[43] In fact, Iliescu's intentions of playing a role in all issues, including economic decisions, was made clear very soon thereafter[44] and members of the Front initially did not even bother to pretend that the president was not, after his election, a member of their own party.[45] Although parliament approved Petre Roman's nomination as prime minister after the May 1990 elections, it was not even consulted when Roman was summarily dismissed by Iliescu in September 1991. Indeed, the legislature did nothing more than 'take note of the prime minister's resignation', despite Roman's persistent claims that he was, in fact, illegally dismissed by the president.[46]

The two chambers in a united session quickly agreed on the regulations governing the drafting of a new constitution.[47] A drafting committee was established, reflecting the parties' strength. However, while the protocols of the committee's deliberations remained secret, voting on each article was declared open, mainly in order to ensure that all the Front's deputies would toe the party line.[48] And right from the start, Ion Iliescu knew what his parliament would want: a republic with a strong presidency and a relatively weak legislature.[49]

The drafting committee presented its constitutional 'theses' in December 1990. From the start, it was clear that the constitution's crucial challenge was the distribution of power between the presidency and the legislature. Vasile Gionea who, as a member of Peasants Party served as the committee's vice-president, argued all along for a diminished presidential institution, which although not subservient would at least defer on most issues to parliament.[50] Indeed, precisely because of this, many opposition leaders who were not natural supporters of the King's return, argued for the restoration of the monarchy as the only guarantee against an encroachment on the powers of legislature. Yet popular support for the monarchy in a country which just emerged from decades of communism proved very feeble.[51] The Front's majority in the two chambers considered the issue closed and refused even to debate it, and the government remained determined to push through the constitution at whatever costs, especially since the Front's popularity was constantly falling.[52] Thus, although the elaboration of the constitutional provisions took quite some time, the actual voting was rapid and the final provisions were, in the words of a local observer 'marched' through the chambers. Out of a total of more than 1,100 tabled amendments, 145 were incorporated into the final text, but only 39 of these (or less than 4 per cent of the total) came from opposition parties.[53] Furthermore, since voting was by show of hands, the counting was often dubious. On a number of occasions, a particular article was rejected, only to be suddenly approved after a second count.[54] And to ensure that everything went smoothly, towards the end of the procedure new regulations were introduced which called for repeated votes on the same article, until it was passed.[55] Finally, the last vote on the entire text was made compulsory for every deputy (in order to defeat any filibustering attempt and by-pass regulations requiring a quorum). A noted ethnic Hungarian senator, who defied this obligation, forfeited his seat, in a procedure unprecedented in the annals of most parliaments. Yet despite these strong-arm tactics, Romania's constitution was ultimately approved by the Front and its satellite parties. The Hungarians party, the Liberals and the Peasants, as well as smaller formations voted overwhelmingly against the adoption of the constitution.[56]

Thus, against the wishes of the opposition and less than two years after toppling the most personalised dictatorship in Eastern Europe, Romania became, according to its new constitution, a presidential republic. The Front, aware of the apprehensions which this might raise, was careful to characterise the country's political system as 'semi-presidential'. Yet, to all intents and purposes, a combination of badly drafted provisions coupled with deliberate ambiguities have resulted in a potentially dangerous concentration of power in the hands of one man. Romania's president is directly elected for two terms not exceeding a total of eight years. Nevertheless, these terms could be extended by a special law 'in case of war or natural calamity'. It is the president – and not the parliament – who nominates a prime minister[57] and it is the president who dismisses ministers, at the recommendation of the premier. Furthermore, the president can chair Cabinet meetings and may 'consult' the government at 'times of great urgency', the character of which remains undefined. Under certain circumstances, the president can dissolve parliament no less than four times during each presidential term and may appeal above the heads of the legislators directly to the people in 'matters of national interest' which, again, are ill-defined. More importantly, the Front's majority has refused to write in Romania's constitution the principle of the separation of powers which, although not present in many other democratic constitutions, would have appeased the opposition's fears.[58] Indeed, by enshrining a Supreme Council for National Defence chaired by the president and tasked with organising the entire array of Romania's 'security' – a wider concept than merely defence – a fusion between different government departments, legislature and the head of state is already in existence. And to complete the picture, the constitution entrusted legal supervision not to a supreme court of immovable and impartial judges, but to a council of legal experts, appointed for a fixed and renewable period of time partly by president and parliament.[59]

Parliament has allowed the government additional powers which may thwart democratic guarantees. Thus, the government may rule by decrees and ordinances under specific delegation. It may also enforce 'emergency ordnances' by merely tabling them before the legislature, rather than obtaining their approval. And the institution of the prefect, as the government's directly appointed representative in each county, may negate local democracy. Concluding this constitutional document are provisions which make any amendments extremely difficult and forbid for posterity any change to the country's republican form of government.[60] Yet, in another indication of the Front's fear of the exiled King Michael, the government ultimately refused to present Romanians with the choice between a republic and a monarchy during the constitutional referendum, arguing that a simple 'yes' vote to the new constitution settled all these issues forever.[61]

It matters little that President Iliescu, in an attempt to calm opposition fears, has suggested that he has not yet used the powers which he had in accordance to the 1990 electoral law.[62] The main opposition parties accused him of seeking to establish a 'republican dictatorship'[63] and decided to boycott the referendum on the constitution.[64] The government ignored these complaints and rushed through the referendum. Much to the surprise of all parties (including the Front) the 'campaign' for the constitution started immediately. Within two days (one of which was a weekend) returning officers had to be appointed. Two days thereafter, parties had to nominate, if they wished, representatives in no less than 14,000 ballot stations[65] and had an additional 48 hours to query electoral rolls. The entire campaign was scheduled to last precisely six days.[66] A high abstention rate was predicted, especially given the season's harsh climate. Yet, once opposition parties called for a boycott of a referendum, the authorities did everything possible to ensure a respectable turnout. Senator Antonie Iorgovan, the man who piloted the constitution through parliament, warned that those who did not vote were, at best, 'idiots' and at worst 'traitors'.[67]

More importantly, the country learnt after the vote that the electoral roll, which stood at over 17 million in May 1990, was suddenly reduced to just over 15 million in 16 months. The attempt to boost the turnout figures by reducing the number of those eligible to vote was so haphazard and poorly coordinated that the total declared figure did not even tally with the number of the electorate as reported by each county.[68] According to the official figures, 77.3 per cent of the ballots cast were for the new constitution and 20.4 per cent against. The government claimed a complete victory. However, this was far from being the case. The turnout was 69.1 per cent according to the 'revamped' electoral roll and, therefore, it was evident that only 53.5 per cent of the electorate opted for Romania's new constitution.[69] Although abstentions cannot be equated with outright opposition, it is also clear that the constitution did not obtain the popular legitimacy which the authorities so craved. More importantly, the country's ethnic minorities – especially the Hungarians who voted *en masse* – overwhelmingly rejected the the constitution.[70]

ROMANIA'S ETHNIC MINORITIES

The December 1989 revolution found Romania's ethnic minorities in a unique situation, on the same barricades as the majority of the country. The authorities vowed to respect minority rights and the country's administration announced plans for a new national census, a crucial undertaking for any ethnic minority protection system.[71] From the start, minorities were allotted a specific number of seats in any future parliament and a minimum representation even if they failed to elect one deputy.[72] More importantly, the various 'councils' established by the communists with a claim to represent ethnic groups were dissolved, the government pledged to allow the establishment of a Hungarian consulate in Transylvania (an emotive issue between Romania and Hungary's communist regimes for years), and Bucharest promised to allow minorities to run schools exclusively in their own languages.[73] Yet two months after the revolution little was done, despite repeated protests.[74] Tension in Transylvania remained high. Demonstrations – some reaching 40,000 participants – became a common feature especially in ethnically balanced Transylvanian localities such as Tirgu Murei,[75] ultimately necessitating ever more frequent meetings between Hungarian and Romanian diplomats.[76] As the Front's administration in Bucharest was coming under increased pressure, the 'nationalist card' played by Ceaucescu with such dexterity was suddenly revived. Barely two months after the revolution, prime minister Roman faced

demonstrating soldiers and officers in the capital. They were demanding
a greater democracy in the army. Instead, the prime minister chose to
highlight his government's 'success' in 'refusing to give in to Hungarian
separatist demands'.[77] Nevertheless, the future character of Romanian-
Hungarian relations was set by the riots which erupted in Tirgu-Murei
on 16, 19 and 20 March 1990.[78] The honeymoon between Hungarians
and Romanians lasted not more than the wider promise of 'democracy'
in the country.

During the campaign leading to the May 1990 elections, nationalist
symbols were widely used by the Front in an effort to portray the
opposition as inherently anti-Romanian. Thus, opposition leaders were
either 'accused' of being Hungarian or Jewish, and Ion Raoiu, one of
Iliescu's contenders for the presidency, was presented with a Securitate
forgery purporting to prove that, while in British exile, he had 'agreed
to sell' Transylvania to the Hungarians. The government, ostensibly above
such chicaneries, did nothing to disprove allegations which were regularly
repeated in the press and on television.[79] Some ethnic Hungarians were
not above such tactics either. Thus, just before the elections, a document
purporting to come from the Vatra Romaneasca anti-Hungarian association
was published.[80] It contained a call to kill all Hungarians and it too
ultimately proved to be a forgery. Accusations between the country's
ethnic groups quickly acquired a pace which remains unbroken to this
day and which implicates both Hungary and Romania at an official level.
Yet the biggest victims are clearly the leaders of the Hungarian minority.
A year after the revolution, opinion polls indicated that Pastor Tikes,[81]
the man who sparked the revolt, is one of the most hated figures in the
country. And nothing is guaranteed to destroy a politician's reputation
more than allegations of association with 'the Hungarians'. Despite the
fact that Romania, the second largest East European state after Poland,
has always defeated Hungary in modern warfare, most Romanians still
believe that Hungary is their biggest danger.

For the Front, rekindling the anti-Hungarian campaign was more a matter
of necessity rather than choice. The Hungarians's demands threatened the
country's centralised control which the Front had every intention of preserving. In addition, the Hungarians displayed great organisational skills.
In the May 1990 elections and in the 1991 referendum on the constitution
they voted as their single party, the Hungarian Democratic Federation of
Romania (HDFR) told them to.[82] Indeed, they displayed a high degree of
sophistication. Thus, in May 1990 Hungarians split their votes, opting for
HDFR in parliament and for Radu Campeanu, the Liberals' leader, as their
presidential choice. The Front, which retained its control over the country

precisely by maintaining divisions among the opposition's ranks, could not tolerate such a challenge. Therefore, encouraging anti-Hungarian feelings was the surest way of preventing a coalition between the HDFR and other opposition parties. Furthermore, by assuming the nationalist mantle, Front leaders (especially prime minister Roman who was 'accused' of being a Jew)[83] could display their fervent nationalism.

Finally, few parties in Romania's history won power without controlling Transylvania's votes. According to the May 1990 elections, the Front captured only 43 per cent of the votes in Transylvania, compared with 79 per cent in Moldavia and over 80 per cent in Muntenia and Oltenia. Deliberately encouraging a 'Hungarian threat' therefore made perfect electoral sense for an increasingly embattled party and the Front started championing Romania's other unique contribution to East European post-communist history: a party devoted to the protection of ethnic Romanians in their own nation-state.

Externally, the existence of a vociferous group was presented as the only reason for the government's supposed inability to accede to the demands of its ethnic minorities. By acting as they did immediately after the revolution, the Front's leaders virtually condemned Romania to many years of ethnic strife. The Hungarian party is still controlled by older community leaders, many of whom gained publicity during Ceaucescu's rule. Most advocate a policy of steady pressure on Bucharest, through entirely legal means.[84] Yet they have little to show for their efforts and are increasinly challenged by younger Hungarians, frustrated by their impotence. Every one of the Hungarians' constitutional amendment proposals have been rejected, usually with contempt and parliamentary accusations of 'treason'. Hungarians are not identified as a specific ethnic group as they demanded[85] and Romania is characterised as 'a unitary, nation-state' despite the Hungarians' protests.[86]

Although Hungarians remain by far the most important group to be targetted by the authorities, Romania's other ethnic minorities have not gained a better consideration. The country's ethnic Germans spurned the government's offers of help and migrated *en masse* to Germany. Romania's 20,000 remaining and elderly Jews are constantly reviled. And the country's Gypsies are still regarded as more of a social rather than ethnic problem. Robbed, beaten and even murdered by Ceaucescu's secret police, they originally believed in Ion Iliescu's promises, contributing in no small amount to his personal triumph in May 1990. They were never rewarded: the March 1990 ethnic riots in Tîrgu Murei and the June 1990 miners' violence in Bucharest were ultimately ascribed in large part to the Gypsies. And when asked to comment on the large migration of

Jonathan Eyal

young people from Romania under his rule, president Ion Iliescu had no compunction in dismissing the matter as one involving 'only the Gypsies' and, therefore, of little consequence. Divided between clans and competing leaders, unable to articulate their demands in a coherent manner, associated with theft and laziness, the country's Gypsies remain Romania's most unloved minority.

NOTES

1. It remains unknown to this day.
2. See the Doinea Cornea interview in *Liberation* (Paris), 10 January 1990. See also *International Herald Tribune*, 10 January 1990 and her wider discussion in *Tribuna*, 18 January 1990.
3. Silviu Brucan, the Front's chief ideologue and strategist at the time demanded the death sentence on the Peasants leader Corneliu Coposu in the late 1940s.
4. *The Guardian*, 11 January 1990; *Daily News* (Budapest), 11 January 1990 and *Le Monde*, 12 January 1990.
5. *The Independent*, 11 January 1990.
6. *Adevarul*, 13 January 1990.
7. *Financial Times*, 17 January 1990.
8. *The Times*, 24 January 1990.
9. *Financial Times*, 24 January 1991; *Adevarul*, 13 January 1990 and *Adevarul*, 25 January 1990.
10. Ibid.
11. See, for instance, *Le Monde*, 29 January 1990.
12. *Le Figaro*, 30 January 1990. See also the testimony of miners involved in the action: *Romania Libera*, 14 February 1990.
13. *Romania Libera*, 25 January 1990.
14. For a fairly typical example of such machinations, see *Romania Libera*, 3 March 1990.
15. As was shrewdly pointed out by an observer at the time: *Libertatea*, 12 February 1990.
16. *Daily News* (Budapest) 13 February 1990.
17. *Romania Libera*, 14 February 1990.
18. *Romania Libera*, 2 March 1990.
19. For the demands of a 'civic forum' created in order to ensure the television's impartiality in the elections, see '22', 2 March 1990; *Baricada*, 3 March 1990 and *Dreptatea*, 5 March 1990. The efforts of this group bore no result.
20. Datculescu and Liepelt, *op. cit.*, p. 83. This was particularly so with the more educated and youger groups of voters who, before the electoral campaign was launched, tended to support the Liberal party by a slim majority: ibid., pp. 88–9.

21. *Platforma Program a Frontului Salvarii Naoionale din România*, Bucharest, 1990.
22. Out of 17 milllion votes cast, more than one million were considered void, usually because the name of more than one candidate was selected.
23. Comisia Naconala de Statistica, *Buletin de informare publica*, No. 5, May 1990.
24. Alexandru I Bejan, 'Prezentarea ui analiza comparativa a rezultatelor alegerilor de la 20 mai 1990', in Datculescu and Liepelt (eds), *op. cit.*, pp. 111–133, 117.
25. The Front obtained 66.31 per cent of the votes for the Chamber of Deputies, and 67.02 per cent for the Senate.
26. Versions popularly advanced interpreted US hostility to the government as an outcome of a Hungarian 'lobby' in Washington and the coolness of the European Community's Dutch presidency to the fact that the Netherlands' Bucharest ambassador was supposedly Jewish.
27. As quoted by *Foreign Broadcast Information Service*, 14 June 1990, pp. 41–2.
28. These are the government's figures: *Romania Libera*, 6 July 1990.
29. Bucharest Radio Domestic Service, 15 June 1990, as quoted in *Foreign Broadcast Information Service* 18 June 1990, pp. 67–70.
30. *Borba* (Belgrade), 11 August 1990.
31. See, for instance, the leader in *The Times*, 15 June 1990, which referred to his government as 'blood-thirsty'.
32. And were only actually held on 9 February 1992, almost two years after the parliamentary elections.
33. *Romania Libera*, 7 July 1990.
34. *Romania Libera*, 2 August 1990.
35. Mayors and prefects do not have to be even notified to parliament: *Tineretul Liber*, 18 July 1990; *Romania Libera*, 19 July 1990.
36. For the protests of the Hungarians in Covasna county against the appointment of an ethnic Romanian, see *Romania Libera*, 3 August 1990. See also Dan Ionescu, 'Government Moves to Recentralize Local Administration', in *Radio Liberty Report on Eastern Europe*, 7 September 1990, especially pp. 23–4.
37. Prime Minister Roman's first 'teleconference' is reported in *Dimineaoa*, 29 August 1990.
38. *Romania Libera*, 26 September 1991.
39. *Romania Libera*, 20 July 1990.
40. *Adevarul*, 22 July 1990.
41. *Adevarul*, 6 November 1991.
42. *Libertatea*, 23 July 1990.
43. For an analysis of the presidential department and their senior personnel, see Michael Shafir, 'Romania's New Institutions: The Presidency', in *Radio Liberty Report on Eastern Europe*, 7 September 1990, pp. 24–7.

44.   Such as his statements during a lengthy interview with Bucharest
      Radio's dokmestic service on 14 September 1990: *Foreign Broadcast
      Information Service* 17 September 1990, pp. 44–8 and his subse-
      quent involvement in halting Romania's land privatisation programme:
      Romania Libera, 6 November 1991 and, more directly, *Adevarul*, 16
      November 1991.
45.   See, for instance, the interview of Velicu Radina, then the Front's
      propaganda chief, with *Lumea Azi*, 7 February 1991, pp. 6–7. After
      prime minister Roman's dismissal, president Iliescu's close advisers
      claimed that one reason for the rising conflict between these two
      erstwhile allies was precisely Roman's attempt to 'separate' Iliescu
      from the Front: *Dimineaoa*, 20 November 1991.
46.   *Romania Libera*, 27 September 1991; *Azi*, 28 September 1991, which
      claims that Roman was dismissed by Iliescu and the Supreme National
      Defence Council, as well as Roman's own interview with Radio Bucha-
      rest, 29 September 1991, reproduced in *Foreign Broadcast Information
      Service*, 1 October 1991, pp. 29–34. Subsequent evidence suggests that
      Roman's dismissal was briefly 'discussed' in the Senate's Permanent
      Bureau, a closed circle of the chamber's president and his immediate
      subalterns: *Libertatea*, 7 November 1991 and *Cuvintul*, Nos. 52/53,
      December 1991–January 1992.
47.   For the arrangements, see *Monitorul Oficial al Romaniei*, Vol. II, No.
      90, 12 July 1990, pp. 1–3 and *ibid.*, Vol. II, No. 119, p. 1.
48.   *Adevarul*, 12 July 1990.
49.   See the president's statement more than 18 months before the consti-
      tution was finalised: *Romania Libera*, 31 July 1990.
50.   *Lumea Azi*, 4 April 1991, pp. 2–3 and *Renauterea Banaoeana*, 15 July
      1991. Gionea would subsequently forget his objection and support
      the constitutional arrangements wholeheartedly, despite the fact that
      none of his proposals were incorporated in the final text: *Baricada*,
      17 September 1991.
51.   According to the most reliable opinion poll conducted in early 1991,
      only 17 per cent supported the monarchy's restoration, against 82
      per cent which opted for a republic. Mihai Sturdza, 'Calls for the
      Restoration of the Monarchy Intensify', in *Radio Liberty Report on
      Eastern Europe*, 14 June 1991, pp. 17–22.
52.   *Le Monde*, 10 June 1991.
53.   *Azi*, 26 November 1991.
54.   For such an example, see, *Romania Libera*, 20 November 1991.
55.   *Romania Libera*, 20 November 1991.
56.   *Dreptatea*, 22 November 1991.
57.   Although the government as a whole must retain the support of
      parliament.
58.   For the dispute, see *Romania Libera*, 24 September 1991.
59.   Teofil Pop, the president of the Supreme Court of Justice and thus
      Romania's most senior judge at the time, attacked this provision in

the new constitution, but to no avail: *Romania Libera*, 16 November 1991.

60. For a discussion of this provision, see *Dreptatea*, 20 November 1991.
61. *Romania Libera*, 17 September 1991. Most of the opposition parties objected to the provisions which sought to enshrine a republic without a referendum specifically on the subject. See *Tineretul Liber*, 18 September 1991.
62. *Adevarul*, 17 November 1991.
63. *Romania Libera*, 26 November 1991.
64. For the attitude of the Peasants' Party, see *Dreptatea*, 26 November 1991; for the appeal of Doina Cornea to other opposition groups and the position of the Civic Alliance's party, *Romania Libera*, 27 November 1991.
65. *Romania Libera*, 28 November 1991.
66. *Adevarul*, 26 November 1991 and *Dimineaoa*, 27 November 1991.
67. *Dreptatea*, 28 November 1991.
68. *Adevarul*, 11 December 1991.
69. For detailed analysis of voting figures, see Michael Shafir, 'Romania: Constitution Approved in Referendum', *Radio Liberty Report on Eastern Europe*, Vol. 1, No. 2, 10 January 1992, pp. 50–55.
70. *Adevarul*, 10 December 1991.
71. Vasile Gheoau, 'Viitorul recensamint al populaoiei în Romania: citeva opinii', in *Revista Romana de Statistica*, February 1990, pp. 3–7 and *Monitorul Oficial al Romaniei*, Vol.II, No.45, decree 273, 15 March 1990.
72. *Adevarul*, 1 February 1990.
73. *Daily News* (Budapest) 1 February 1990.
74. For the rising suspicions among Hungarians, see Judith Pataki, 'Free Hungarians in a Free Romania: Dream or Reality?' in *Radio Liberty Report on Eastern Europe*, 23 February 1990, pp. 18–26.
75. *Daily News*, 13 February 1990; *Nepszabadszag*, 14 February 1990 and 27 February 1990.
76. *The Guardian* (London), 14 February 1990; *Romania Libera*, 25 February 1990 and 7 March 1990.
77. *Foreign Broadcast Information Service*, 20 February 1990, p. 62.
78. For the events, see *Romania Libera*, 22 March 1990.
79. See, for instance, the supposedly serious discussion on the 'treason' of Transylvania by Romanian emigres, in *Adevarul*, 8 April 1990.
80. *Mai Nap* (Budapest), 11 April 1990.
81. Meanwhile elevated to the rank of Bishop.
82. In the May 1990 parliamentary elections, the Hungarians' party captured 77.1 per cent and 85.2 per cent of the vote in Covasna and Harghita counties, respectively. These were also the counties in which the Front registered its worst results.
83. A charge revived by President Iliescu's supporters after Roman's dismissal. See *Dimineaoa*, 20 November 1991.

84. The Hungarian party decided in June 1990 to remain in parliament until
     the constitution was completed: *Epoca*, Vol. II, No. 6, 18–24 February
     1991, p. 4.
85. *Nepszbadszag*, 19 September 1990.
86. See, for instance, Domokos Geza's speech to the Constitutional Con-
     vention, reproduced in *Romaniai Magyar Szo* (Bucharest), 19 February
     1991.

8 Russia

Stephen Whitefield

> I beg you to observe with what industry the Muscovite government
> seeks to escape the despotism which weighs on the government even
> more than it does upon the peoples. Great bodies of troops have been
> disbanded; penalties for crimes have been lessened; tribunals have
> been established; some men have begun to be versed in the laws;
> the peoples have been instructed. But there are particular causes that
> will perhaps return it to the misfortune it had wanted to flee.
>
> Montesquieu, *Spirit of the Laws*, Book 5, Ch. 14.[1]

As its title suggests, the primary focus of this book is on the role of
institutions in the transformations under way in Russia and Eastern Europe.
Many observers have conceptualised these changes within the paradigm
of the transition from authoritarianism to democracy via the rebirth of
civil society. I will employ a slightly different and older terminology and
typology which puts the character of institutional change at the centre of
explanation and casts light – and doubt – on aspects of the transition which
have otherwise been missed.

The main questions raised by the transition are 'will institutions rule?'
and, if they do, 'what kind of institutions will they be?'. A continuum suggests itself, from personal and arbitrary rule at one end, to rule by rules at
the other – or from 'despotism' to 'constitutionalism' – where the former is
indicative of the absence of institutional bases of governance and the latter
is the co-incidence of formal institutional arrangements with the actual
distribution of power. As Elster, Przeworski, as well as Montesquieu, have
argued,[2] acceptance of rules is not the result of a 'constitutional culture'
imbued in people and institutions – is not, in other words, primarily a matter
of normative commitment – but occurs because the institutions have been
set up in the appropriate way to structure individual interests and behaviour.
Classically, 'constitutionalism' is established via the separation of powers
where each institution is constrained by and reliant on others and, therefore,
has an interest in obeying and enforcing the rules.

We should note, however, both limits to the claims of constitutionalism
and problems in its application. First, it is not the same as either 'the rule of
law' or 'moderate government'. This is evident in Montesquieu's phrase:'it

can happen that the constitution is free and the citizen not . . . ' and vice versa.[3] Moderation, as we will see, may result from factors other than the self-interested interplay of rational institutional actors, and judicial procedure may be observed even where the law is intolerant. Second, the formal constitution in and of itself will not produce adherence to rules if a real separation of institutions in correspondence with the constitution does not occur. It is in the details of actual institutional organisation and behaviour that the separation of powers is tested. Third, constitutionalism and the separation of powers are *institutionally* not sociologically founded. The constitutionalist's claim is that when arrangements are made properly, *regardless* of the state of social interests, institutions will out.[4] Clear conflict is possible, therefore, especially in periods of transition, between interests seeking to mould institutions and institutions seeking to mould interests. Put another way, where institutions mould interests they may be said to be relatively autonomous of those interests; where interests mould institutions, the latter may be said to be relatively captured. Success in achieving constitutional government can be measured by the extent to which interests pressure government via the formal constitutional process. A resolution of this conflict in favour of social interests, however, would fatally undermine a constitutional architecture.

Moderate government could still result where social interests achieve dominance over institutions but it would be founded on a much older, and more *sociological* principle than 'classless' constitutionalism. In the continuum from despotism to constitutionalism, therefore, there is a third term – or rather a whole murky area between the two poles – where institutions will still matter for a variety of reasons. Minimally, they may effectively *disguise* or legitimise the real exercise of power. Or more significantly, they may function as the organisational forum for bargaining among various social interests. Government of the latter kind, where the form and behaviour of institutions is not determined by formal rules regulating society but by the acceptance of the need to construct institutions and adapt rules to preserve *balance* among social groups – who are, of course, themselves deeply unbalanced in terms of power – was traditionally called 'mixed government'. As a type, it rivals constitutionalism as a credible alternative to despotism.[5] The main argument of this chapter is that it is 'mixed government' that is emerging in Russia. The subsidiary argument is that this makes the Russian state far more continuous with the Soviet state than might be thought. When asked, then, 'transition to what?', the misfortune of Russian government may be to be returned to 'mixed government' from which it had tried to flee, albeit one that may be more moderate and nearer the constitutional end of the continuum than previously.

THE SOVIET LEGACY

It is necessary to rake over the coals of the old system at least once more if only to extract the institutional components which continue to play a part in current developments. Arguments of the 1970s and 1980s about the appropriate characterisation for the Soviet system continue to have some importance largely, in my view, because the old system has still not been understood correctly. The debate between advocates of 'totalitarianism' and some modifed form of 'pluralism' was centrally connected with the problem of institutionalisation. On the one hand, 'totalitarianism' was definitionally a form of arbitrary personal rule. On the other, even its adherents admitted it was pursued via the whole panoply of institutions of the 'totalitarian' state: the party, the secret police, the cultural committees, and the economic apparatus. Much of the support for 'pluralism', however, was based upon evidence about the growth of the power of these institutions over leadership discretion; and this in turn, was used as support for arguments about the 'institutionalisation of Soviet politics'.[6]

In my view, however, the development of the Soviet system cannot be understood in terms of the slow growth of a basis for the 'rule of rules' in the institutions of the old order. The speed of institutional collapse amid the failure of rules are, minimally, difficult to explain on this model. However, on the basis of the continuum outlined, two key aspects of the old system which explain the apparent stability of much of Soviet politics, its periodic contortions, and the attempts since 1985 to shift to a 'constitutional' state can be uncovered.

First, it was not leadership but 'institutional' behaviour which became, as the Soviet system matured, the main source of *arbitrariness* in the sense that institutions frequently operated beyond the rules and procedures established by the leaders. Political systems with a highly developed institutional structure may be despotic, but this will seldom be the rulers' fault, at least over time, because of their need to discipline the agencies they created. The main contradiction of Soviet politics – and the greatest source of conflict and reform – was that the authority of the leaders was undermined by the independent power of the institutions they themselves had created.

Secondly, the 'institutional architecture' of the Soviet system was not quite as it appeared. Many of its components, in particular economic agencies whose arbitrary – unregulated – behaviour caused political leaders such problems, should not really be considered part of the state at all. They are better understood as distinctively Soviet *social interests* which exerted pressure on, and successfully dominated, the loose, poorly defined, and relatively captured set of governing bodies – the higher party organs,

Gosplan, and the inner apparatus of the Council of Ministers. The porosity of the Soviet state to the infiltration of social power can be measured by the difficulty one has in even defining its borders; economic agents not merely lobbied the state, they were given a place at the bureaux. The Soviet system was, in this sense, 'mixed government' in the fullest sense, and by structuring the institutionalisation of bargaining in the Brezhnev period to satisfy the balance of social power, considerable stability and relative moderation was achieved.

It was the combination of arbitrariness and the distinctive impact of social power on government which explains the motive for, and difficulties of, building constitutionalism in the Soviet Union. First, the weakness of the state against economic agents produced on-going conflict in the system. Faced with the independent power of their agencies, successive Soviet leaders, from Stalin onwards, sought to build authority, and it was in the battle to do so that the most immoderate and arbitrary actions in Soviet history took place. However, the 'traditional' methods of authority-building, organisational reform and attacks on personnel, time and again proved ineffective. By 1988, the leading politicians clearly understood the necessity of a radical shift towards the authority of rules and the creation of institutions – parliament, presidency, and judiciary – associated with the separation of powers if they were to effectively regulate social forces. *Perestroika* should be understood as an attempt at the creation of a constitutional state – albeit hesitantly – and as such had to be carried out *against* the existing institutions which were dominated by the country's economic agents.[7]

However, the '*classlessness*' of the separation of powers was fundamental to its appeal in the late Soviet period. What made constitutionalism desirable was not simply its westernness. It was also a response to the absolute illegitimacy (even in their own eyes) of all social groups, and of the balance of social power under Soviet rule. The results of 'mixed government' were evident in the country's disastrous economic performance. Control over dominant interests, particularly those of industry, demanded the independence of the state, the hardening of its boundaries, and the growth of its autonomy. Constitutionalism promised to provide all of these plus the remaking of social interests along 'civilised' lines. In this sense, constitutionalism may rightly be called a programme for the *reformation* of Soviet society.

Perestroika failed for the same reason it was launched; lack of political authority, weak state institutions, and a peculiar political sociology. The politicians who sought to build rule-based authority had little credibility with voters who had endured the arbitrariness in the behaviour of the institutions of the old system with which the leaders were associated. The new institutions of parliament and the executive emerged in the middle of a deep crisis of the state, and were largely reliant on the old institutions which they were attacking. Undercutting the power of the economic agents, which were perceived as the main obstacles to reform, only intensified the economic crisis and made society restless and then hostile. Rival institutions to the centre arose, less tainted by the old system, which could more plausibly claim to achieve the constitutional order that the centre was so palpably failing to build. *Perestroika*, not surprisingly then, ended in the farce of the August coup in which communist politicians were attacked by the hollow shell of their institutions. Power, like the owl of Minerva, had already flown elsewhere; the question to be addressed now is whether the new Russian state on which it landed would be any more successful in achieving the reformation given the legacy of Soviet society.

RUSSIAN POLITICS IN TRANSITION

The transfer of power to Russia did not, and could not, alter the fundamental questions left from the failure to reform the Soviet Union: how to build political authority and how to control social power. Constitutionalism and the autonomy of the state remained the only alternative to concluding compromising deals with the economic agents who had dominated the old order. The politicians on whom power devolved after August and the collapse of the Soviet Union in December 1991, however, had certain characteristics and advantages which Gorbachev and the other *perstroyshckiki* lacked. First, they were *even more* opposed to the power relations in Soviet society. For some of them, breaking the power of the military-industrial complex, for example, by refusing local subsidies or foreign aid, was even more important politically than the potential economic costs to society that would result from the battle.[8]

Second, the new politicians were *relatively less* tainted by association with the past. Yeltsin appointed government members from three main groups: from former party officials in Sverdlovsk where he had his power base; from specialists in the military-industrial complex; and from intellectuals and members of the democratic movement.[9] Much mud was thrown at the deputy prime minister, Burbulis because he had taught Marxism-Leninism, though this job was really a sign of being at a great distance from the dominant social forces. Far more revealing was the complaint by the vice-president, Rutskoy and the speaker of the parliament, of the lack of experience of those leading the reform in running the economy, a sure signal that the military-industrial complex was under-represented in the government. As Khasbulatov, the chairman of the Russian parliament, said, 'we need ministers who know real life, what real production is all about – is it not so? – and not armchair scientists'.[10] In terms of the connections of the core of the new team to the old economy, such inexperience surely signalled greater autonomy.

Third, the new state started off, if not *tabula rasa*, then at least far less institutionalised than the Soviet state had been. In some ways this caused problems; for example, it is far more difficult to obtain information about the work of the Russian parliament than its Soviet predecessor. But, as was argued above, the porous nature of Soviet institutions and their tight connections to economic agents made them largely inoperative instruments of control by the politicians. The Russian leadership was less encumbered of this problem.

Fourth, the coup had even further discredited both Soviet institutions and their economic supporters while the 'democrats' who had opposed it stood with at least some legitimacy derived from their recent election. A 'window of opportunity', therefore, was opened for politicians to build an institutional framework relatively autonomous of society that would be successful in structuring social inputs in accordance with a set of formal rules. The rest of this chapter tries to explain the dynamics of why the opportunity was not taken.

THE COMPROMISE ON REFORM

The most visible sign of the seriousness of the new team to act autonomously of dominant social interests, as Gorbachev had failed to do, was the decision to launch radical economic reform with a programme including the freeing of prices, cutting subsidies, and balancing the state budget.[11] Though these measures were not immediately accompanied by privatisation or anti-monopoly measures, and for this reason were criticised by some for actually *giving in* to economic agents of the old system, there can be no doubt that the package threatened to adversely affect a broad spectrum of social forces from the military-industrial complex to regional authorities to the average person who had been used to receiving subsidies in one form or other. Economically, the gamble of the reform against the array of social interests that might stand against it was that results would be produced quickly in terms of stabilised prices and growth in output particularly in the consumer sector and failure to achieve these would certainly increase pressure for a U-turn.

However, the programme also faced a further obstacle; if Gorbachev had failed in part because political reform had not been accompanied by economic reform, then the programme of the new Russian government encountered difficulties for exactly the opposite reason. Success in pushing through reforms that would adversely affect many social interests depended on building institutions that were capable of acting independently and forcing compliance to constitutional rules. However, institution-building or a real separation of powers failed to materialise. Given the inheritance of political weakness and the dominance of economic agents, failure to tackle political reform first was a serious flaw in the programme.

There were three main areas of institutional failure. First, the executive apparatus as a whole was not a coherent unit. Even before the coup, Russian people had voted by a large majority in a referendum for the creation of an executive president with considerable formal powers. Signs of executive drift, however, were evident in the days immediately after the coup when, while expectations of speedy action to take advantage of the 'window of opportunity' were high, Yeltsin took a holiday leaving his government, his advisors, and the state council behind to engage in public squabbling. The decision announced in a rousing speech to the Congress of People's Deputies in late October 1991 to launch radical reform was in part Yeltsin's attempt to make up for the earlier policy chaos.

However, the problems with the executive had deeper roots. At the same Congress at which Yeltsin announced his determination to pursue reform, he had been granted both the right to rule by decree in the economy subject to parliamentary over-ride, and an apparently unfettered right to decide on the structure and membership of the executive. In discussion, he promised to clear up some of the confusion which had emerged earlier between the various sub-structures of the executive by building clear, pyramidical lines of authority and responsibility. As he put it:

> I cannot imagine how one can implement a reform directed at democratisation and improvement of life in the future without having power. Vertical power. And we are creating this vertical power now, from the president and to executive power, to the very bottom. There should be responsibility. And if somebody does not deliver the goods, he must be answerable. This is the case in any democratic civilised state. But we say: well, power in fact means a dictator. Why? Power is by the law and demands are in accordance with the law. If someone is criminal, he should be made answerable in accordance with the law. I have signed a decree on combatting crime and corruption. Very tough measures will be taken now in this respect. But it does not mean that I am a dictator.[12]

To support his resolve, Yeltsin himself assumed the position of prime minister, though formal day to day responsibility for the government fell to the first deputy prime minister Burbulis. He also moved to impose his authority throughout the country by getting approval by the Congress of People's Deputies in November for a ban on elections for a year, for his right to appoint heads of local administrations, and for powers to allow higher bodies to rescind decisions taken by lower ones until the 1st December 1992. This was supposed to enshrine the principle of 'vertical control'.[13]

As we shall see, however, the problems of translating a desire for effective political authority into real power were shared by Gorbachev, Yeltsin, and other radicals.[14] A startling similarity with its communist predecessor, and symptom of the problem of authority, quickly became apparent in the structure of the new executive. In the old system, the problem of institutional capture of the part of the bureaucracy responsible for exercising operational control over industry had been tackled, not very successfully, by the creation of a shadow structure of departments of the Central Committee – the Secretariat. With typical irony, the new inner cabinet around Burbulis, Shakhray and Gaidar, fearful of the potential sabotage by personnel in the inherited ministries which had been boosted by the transfer of about 35 per cent of staff in the old Soviet apparatus, set up in precisely the offices in *Staraya Ploshch'ad* that the Secretariat had used before them.

The problem was that despite this political resolve to build institutional autonomy which was supported by the power granted Yeltsin to design an executive to match, clear lines of authority and organisational structure failed to appear. At first, Yeltsin made clear his preference for a streamlined administrative structure with a clear line of command. In mid-November, he proposed a new government to the Supreme Soviet in which the number of ministries was reduced from 46 to 23 and the State Council abolished. However, in typical Soviet style, the number of sub-units in the executive began to multiply with *ad hoc* committees sprouting to deal with matters that Yeltsin's declared economic policy apparently foreswore.

In a speech at the end of March 1992, for example, the economics minister Gaidar was forced to call for cuts in spending on the government apparatus, and a restriction in the growth of government departments such as one on defending the economic interests of the Russian federation. These, he said, had been created without powers or functions.[15] Anatoly Sobchak, the mayor of St. Petersburg, described the new Russian state as corrupt, without a viable administrative structure, and consisting in duplicate and parallel administrations.[16] Ivan Polozkov, former leader of the Russian Communist Party, commented that there were effectively three governments: presidential advisers, the president's apparatus, and the government itself. New ministries and departments, he said, were sprouting like mushrooms. Yeltsin was forced to agree that there were too many structures in the executive, and promised that they would be simplified. But in response, he clouded the issue further by appointing another first deputy premier for industry.[17]

Within the government, the notion of 'collective responsibility' was quite foreign, as different agency heads announced policies at odds with the government's objectives. In particular, the potentially powerful Ministry of Industry, which had inherited perhaps the largest proportion of structures, personnel, and connections from the old system, espoused policies which were at variance with the whole anti-industrial strategy that the government, seeking to reform rather than convert society and the state, was committed to. Like many Soviet leaders before him, despite declarations that he would soon introduce clearer and simpler structure, Yeltsin has not tackled the problem. What seems to have happened, as we will see, is that the battle to build autonomous executive had been compromised. Those who may have wished for an executive capable of reforming society by authoritarian means, therefore, are as likely to be disappointed by Yeltsin as they were by Gorbachev.[18]

The second area of institutional failure lay in the fact that the behaviour of parliament and its relations with the executive worked against the consolidation of institutional power. Parliament was, of course, far more susceptible to and infiltrated by powerful interest groups and social pressures, as a number of commentators commented. It was also, as one of the candidates for the chairmanship of the Supreme Soviet, Konstantinov, noted, under-resourced and dependent on the executive for information.

At the same time, it was also the arena that the radicals, both nationally and in some localities, had made most progress towards capturing. However, as Gavril Popov found – no doubt reflecting on his own experience as mayor of Moscow faced by a hostile council of erstwhile supporters – the 'democrats' themselves were divided on coming to power between those favouring systemic reform via support for the new economic structures and actors, and those favouring reform via an attack on the privileged in the old order. This cleavage was reflected, in Popov's view, in two distinct tendencies among the democrats, the entrepreneurs and the populists, the former demanding strong executive power, while the latter favoured the parliaments.[19]

The difference in strategy spilled over into institutional competition and a tendency towards overlapping jurisdiction and parallel structures. The lines of authority between executive and legislative bodies were frequently blurred. The situation was exacerbated by the economic reform programme which parliament attacked on Rutskoy-type grounds as being ill-prepared by inexperienced leaders, and then threatened to undermine by organising its own apparatus to replace the government if changes were not made. Despite his formal ability to rule by decree, in practice Yeltsin found that parliament frequently exercised its over-ride. For example, according to Sergei Shakhray, a deputy prime minister in Yeltsin's government, of fifteen draft laws submitted by the president only five were supported in part. 'That is, all the powers given to the president by the Congress have been blocked by the Supreme Soviet.'[20]

Even the president's right to determine the structure of the government was under threat from parliament. In mid-January 1992 Khasbulatov threatened: 'Parliament has no intention of allowing a situation in which government policy may form the basis for the establishment of dictatorship. Parliament therefore has the right to put forward before the president of Russia the question of a change of government or to tackle the question independently.'[21] The crisis came to a head in April when parliament appeared to assert its authority to appoint and dismiss ministers.

The 'rule of rules' depends upon separation of powers between institutions, and the channelling of demands by social groups along the formal lines of authority. Relations between parliament and the executive, however, were essentially unstructured and confrontational, and while the executive was incapable of authoritarian action to resolve the crisis,[22] parliamentary leaders frequently appealed to a populist constituency whose interests in the economic crisis lay in forcing the government to back away from their reformationist policy by softening the blow of reform. What parliamentarians failed to explicitly recognise was that in the Russian context, paradoxically again, the blow could only be softened by diminishing populist attacks on those who operated the structures of the inherited economy.

The third area in which failure to achieve institutional reform resulted in a weakening of the autonomy of the state was the inability of the politicians to agree a new constitution. In part, this was a consequence of factors just mentioned. The draft constitution prepared for the Congress of People's Deputies in April 1992 by a Supreme Soviet committee which Yeltsin chaired was essentially a programme for a parliamentary republic. Not only would parliament have retained the right of override, but it would have taken the power to appoint and dismiss the government and determine its structure. Furthermore, control over the Central Bank, which had been the source of on-going conflict between parliament and the executive, was left in the hands of the former, though Yeltsin insisted that actual policy was being determined by him.

Not suprisingly, therefore, in the run-up to the Congress Yeltsin repudiated the draft and threatened a referendum on the constitution – much as de Gaulle had done – if he did not get his way. The government itself, following an attack on its economic programme at the Congress, threatened to resign *en bloc*. In such confrontational circumstances, the Congress ended in a fudge whereby the old constitution of the Soviet period remained in place and Yeltsin promised to present a law on the government within six months.

Federal relations constituted the second problematic area for constitutional reform. As was made clear in the discussion of the Soviet inheritance, political authority in Russia was limited in its coverage – and not very deep anywhere. The first draft of the new constitution which had been presented in October 1991 had been rejected because it promoted a system of German-style *Lander* which would have adversely affected the status and interests of the former 'autonomous republics' which constituted a major part of the federal structure. The second draft presented in March was much more conservative regarding reform of republican rights, but its federal section was outdated almost as soon as it was published by a federal treaty agreed by 18 of the 20 former autonomous republics which conferred substantially more powers upon the localities. The Federal Treaty was then subject to intense criticism for giving away far too much central power and for not specifying where power lay in the event of a disagreement.[23]

The third area of weakness in the process of creating a constitutional state relates to all the others mentioned above. A system of rules requires an adjudicator, and encouraging the expression of social interests via the constitutional process requires not only autonomous institutions but social access to rule adjudication. A Constitutional Court, of a sort, had been established in the Soviet Union in 1989, though its jurisdiction was limited to federal law – republican relations were too politically fraught – and access was restricted to political figures or recognised social movements. Only the Constitutional Court had the right of judicial review.

The Russian parliament in mid-1991 took similar measures and appointed the court in October.[24] The court soon demonstrated its independence by ruling against a decree of Yeltsin establishing a ministry handling both state security and internal affairs. Though its decision was at first opposed by Shakhray on the grounds that the court had overstepped its jurisdiction by ruling on a 'political matter', the president himself accepted it a few days later.[25] Despite this evidence for a measure of judicial autonomy, however, the federal treaty and the failure to ratify the constitution both undermined the authority and accessibility of rules.

First, the federal treaty clouded the issue of what may be within the centre's jurisdiction, including matters of civil rights. It is not clear what disputes mechanism is in place in the event of disagreement between a republic and the centre. Second, the draft constitution had contained clauses which, for the first time in modern Russian history both afforded citizens direct access to legal defence of their constitutionally given rights, and empowered all courts to adjudicate on them. While it is not clear whether Russian jurists would have been willing to accept the political load such reforms would have placed on them, the willingness of citizens to pursue their interests via constitutional channels would surely have been strengthened.

The argument I am making is that the failures just detailed to build institutional autonomy or the 'rule of rules' meant that the institutions which did emerge were vulnerable to social pressure, especially when economic reform produced difficulties for many sections of society. The effect was to make the formal rules, even if these had been agreed, a less important guide to institutional behaviour and the pattern of social pressure than the nexus of informal relations and bargains struck between branches of government and powerful interest groups. Once the institutional fudge was made, the scope of policy restricted any aim at the reformation of society on 'constitutional' principles and favoured the balancing of social forces which threatened to destabilise the polity. Society once again had to be relegitimised even if the old regime was not; and institutions and personnel which resembled those of the past were either recreated or given more power. 'Mixed government', as I have called it, once again came to be the most accurate way to characterise the Russian state.

There are a number of facts which support this claim. First, the government was forced to abandon its programme for balancing the budget, limited the freeing of prices, and continued to supply subsidies to enterprises. In mid-December 1991, the first deputy prime minister, Burbulis, had declared an intention to introduce a deficit-free budget, to stop financing loss-making enterprises, and to reduce defence procurement by 50 per cent. By mid-January 1992 Gaidar had conceded that deficits would continue in the first quarter, in part because Yeltsin had made unplanned spending promises while on tour of Russia. By April, it was evident that the level of debt of industry, reported to total 500 billion roubles, was forcing the government to relax its policies and seek an alternative strategy. After agreeing that extra credits should be given to priority industries, Yeltsin announced that the ministries of the economy, finance, and industry would work out a schedule for payment, and Gaidar confirmed that more money would go into converting the military-industrial sector.[26]

Though the retreat was clearly a consequence of the difficulties of achieving successful economic reform, from a political point of view the manner in which the retreat occurred is of greater importance. Government departments seem to have negotiated a series of *ad hoc* deals providing special factor funding to those capable of applying pressure, especially regional authorities whose votes matter in parliament, and large industrial plants. The military-industrial complex, for many reformationists the biggest threat of all to a decisive break with the past, seem to have received special recognition via the sort of 'conversion programme' that radicals denounced while Gorbachev was in power. Not surprisingly, social programmes, where pressure is least organised, suffered most.

Second, at odds with a wish to build a stable framework of law, members of the executive, and Yeltsin in particular, bowed to pressure from the public and embarked on a populist course of inventing rules on the spur of the moment to head off immediate unrest. Yeltsin's decrees became increasingly specific. In early January 1991, for example, at a meeting with the labour collective of the Ulyanovsk Industrial Complex, Yeltsin dealt directly with 26 operational questions in the plant. In Nizhny Novgorod, he ordered the local governor close the town's milk department after hearing that it costs more for milk in state shops than in the private market. At a meeting in St Petersburg, he promised a decree turning the Baltic Shipping Line into a joint-stock company with 51 per cent of shares to the work collective, and he then announced a ban on the monopoly by the St Petersburg trade organisation.[27] In some ways, as *Izvestiya* noted, this was a reversion to communist type. 'Serious politicians make no discoveries at either plant cafeteria or a market – these are all games for party economic-administrative activists.'[28] But, it was also right to point out such 'discoveries' were possible because of the absence of an institutional framework for holding firm against populist pressures.[29]

The third indication of a retreat from 'constitutionalist' ambitions came with the promotion of three figures with clear connections to the old dominant industrial interests to senior posts in the government: Shumeyko, who had been an industrial manager before becoming deputy chairman of the Supreme Soviet; Khizha, who had been a defence plant manager; and Cheronmyrdin, who had been a Soviet gas industry minister. Though this move appeased the criticism mentioned above about the government's lack of hand-on experience in the economy, it was less a personal than institutional compromise in two ways. The promotion of Shumeyko who had been a deputy speaker in the parliament signalled a further softening in the confrontational attitude between legislative and executive branches which had been underway since the Congress in April. Shumekyo, in particular, had called in December 1991 for cooperation between parliament and Yeltsin on all economic questions, including control of the central bank, and had asked journalists and deputies to stop trying to drive a wedge between parliament and the executive.

However, their promotion also indicated a shift in the institutional shape of the executive itself, and of its relations with economic and social interests. Shumeyko himself, had offered a detailed description of the failures of the current institutional framework in a speech in January 1992 where he also expressed his own view that the revival of Soviet-style economic management bodies, with all that entailed for the capture of state institutions, was the best available alternative for the government.

> Many deputies of the SS and, on the whole, specialists in com-
> missions and committees are coming to the conclusion that thanks
> to the latest government decisions a super-monopolised, multi-link
> administrative and managerial monster, which in a number of aspects
> is looking more rigid than the old system, is being formed in the gov-
> ernment . . . . There is such a view. I must say that it is not quite so.
> For example, departments of the Ministry of Industry are independent,
> they are run by very skilful specialists; they could be regarded as being
> of the same rank as the old industrial ministries . . . . Since the gov-
> ernment cannot show a devil-may-care attitude to its property, to state
> enterprises, one should immediately revive such a system of running
> state industry . . . . True, in our view, at the same time the government
> should give a clear annual task to these ministries for privatising a defi-
> nite number of enterprises within each branch . . . [But] a decision on
> obligatory preservation of at least 50 per cent of ties of last year's level
> should be adopted for state enterprises. Given the existing economic ties
> between state enterprises, command methods are permissible since this
> is state property . . . . We see this drop in production and we must not
> remain indifferent to it.[30]

The shift in economic policy and institutional relations which has just been described entailed a turn from building an autonomous state to one which sought to come to terms with the forms of power and economic realities left from the Soviet Union. There are a number of important consequences for the future shape of the political system which follow from this revival of 'mixed government' in Russia.

First, the pattern of interest group formation and the relationship of interest groups to government is altered. 'Sociological' governance demands that the importance of interest groups in policy be prioritised with special importance attached to the most powerful groups in the economy. There are already signs that business associations and, to a lesser extent, trade unions are being granted privileged status within the corridors of power as had been the case under Gorbachev. The major business association, the Russian Union of Industrialists and Entrepreneurs, exhibits a peculiar Soviet inheritance which will affect the outcome of policies it helps negotiate; it encompasses state, cooperative and private enterprise and supports worker as well as management rights.[31] Large associations of state enterprises which are associated with the union also favour the maintenance of social policy instituted via enterprises. Incorporating such an organisation, therefore, entails a fundamental social conservatism in which old patterns of association will be preserved, including patterning the interests of ordinary people more to their status as workers than citizens or consumers. Social interests acquire, in these circumstances, more cohesion than diversity with workers, managers and administrators sharing coincident interests which further strengthens their hold over policy.[32] Pluralism in social terms will probably suffer as a result of this bunching.

A second, and related point, concerns the form of party competition and the importance of parties in the policy process. Tendencies to social cohesion will, of course, undercut the formation of parties along the different points that diverse social groups occupy in western European societies. Parties may well form on regional or ethnic lines, as suggested above, or on the basis of issues – breaking with the past, running the economy, defending the nation – which they may claim, rationally or not, to be more trustworthy or competent to deal with. Some evidence suggests that the dimensions on which Russian parties compete are just those.[33] A party that successfully associates itself with the co-incident interests of many social groups – and there are those who argue that 'Renewal' which has emerged out of the dominant business association is doing just that – may be effective in monopolising support for current economic policy. At the same time, fragmentation at the regional and republican level is more likely to lead to the formation of parliamentary groups representing only their own parochial position than cohesive parties aggregating diverse interests.

Though the fractional affiliation of deputies to the Supreme Soviet is not regarded as a reliable guide to their voting behaviour, it does tend to support the argument just offered. Of 754 deputies listing their affiliation, 162 are part of the 'Russian Unity' coalition, 55 are supporters of 'Sovereignty and Equality' a regionalist grouping, 138 are affiliated to either Rutskoy's 'Free Russia' party or 'Renewal' both of which support conversion-type economic policies mentioned above. If we include supporters of the conservative 'Agrarian Union' which is also an affiliate of Russian Unity, then the number of supporters of parties or fractions that have are oriented on the development of social pluralism may be numbered at 237 at most. However, among many of these, the dominant issue will remain the pursuit of justice against those who benefited from communist rule.

At the same time, however, institutional and social factors will tell against parties rather than pressure groups assuming importance in policy formation. For one thing, the presidency and the executive will be central to the *ad hoc* bargaining typical of the system of governance, and the president is capable of identifying issues without requiring party support. The absence of party discipline on president or government is also, as *Izvestiya* put it, a further source of issue-based and populist politics. Though Yeltsin said that he saw parties as a powerful link to the people in the transition period, and planned monthly meetings with them, their influence on policy has been negligible.

> Unfortunately we lack a multi-party system and cannot, as is done throughout the world by voting for this or that party programme in elections, demand its unconditional fulfilment. The people who are at the top, while not obeying a party programme or their own party discipline, in effect represent nobody but themselves.[34]

In addition, as the Soviet Communist Party itself demonstrated, where social interests are co-incident important decisions are either taken inside the parties or in the nexus between the party and the apparatus rather than between parties competing to aggregate disparate social groups.

Third, ironically parliament is likely to be the victim of its own success in shifting policy back in a populist direction. One of the aims of *perestroika*, at least after 1988, had been to transfer power from a captured executive to an authoritative and relatively autonomous parliament. In the post-Soviet period, the failed reformationist ambitions of Gorbachev were taken up by Yeltsin and the other radicals who were then attacked by the legislature. By defending society from the worst effects of reform and inhibiting the reformation of social interests, however, parliament could only throw itself back on governance by subsidy which is worked out in private by negotiation among the powerful. This makes parliament increasingly irrelevant.

Finally, as a result of the porosity of the executive mentioned above and the acceptance of the distribution of social power, it will be difficult for the state to build authority over economic and other actors. As before, society, in its peculiar form inherited from the Soviet period, will continue to dominate institutions of the state. It will be doubly ironic, therefore, if the executive, faced with their domination by social interests at some time in the future return to parliament, the sanctity of law, and the independence of the judiciary as a way of building its own authority. *Perestroika*, in other words, has not been completed; as before in Soviet politics, we should expect it to happen again in Russia.

NOTES

1. Montesquieu, *Spirit of the Laws*, Cambridge, 1989, pp. 60–61.
2. See J. Elster, 'Constitutionalism in Eastern Europe: An Introduction' in *The University of Chicago Law Review*, Vol. 58, 1991, pp. 447–82; and A. Przeworski, *Democracy and the Market*, Cambridge, 1991.
3. Montesquieu, *Spirit of the Laws*, p. 187.
4. See T. Pangle, *Montesquieu's Philosophy of Liberalism*, London, 1973.
5. For insightful history and commentary on the relationship between constitutional and mixed government see M. Vile, *Constitutionalism and the Separation of Powers*, Oxford, 1967.
6. Contributions to the debate on 'totalitarianism' versus 'corporatism' are too numerous to mention in detail. The classic statement of 'totalitarianism' was made by C. Friedrich and Z. Brzezinski, *Totalitarian Dictatorship and Autocracy*, 2nd Edition, Cambridge, Mass., 1965. The 'institutionalist pluralist' case is put, extremely, by J. Hough in *The Soviet Union and Social Science Theory*, Cambridge, Mass., 1977. The best commentary on this literature can be found in S. Solomon (ed.), *Pluralism in the Soviet Union*.
7. For a detailed discussion of the relationship between political authority and economic power in the Soviet system see my forthcoming book, *Industrial Power and the Soviet State*, Oxford, 1993.
8. Larissa Piyasheva, for example, who ran privatisation in Moscow, opposed western credit to industry long after the Soviet Union had collapsed. See *The Guardian*, 30 July 1992, p. 8.
9. See A. Rahr, 'El'tsin Sets Up New System For Governing Russia' in *Radio Liberty Report on the USSR*, No. 34, 1991, pp. 9–12.
10. *Summary of World Broadcasts*, BBC, 20 January 1992.
11. See Yeltsin's speech to the Congress of People's Deputies in *Summary of World Broadcasts*, BBC, 30 October 1991.
12. *Summary of World Broadcasts*, BBC, 22 November 1991.
13. *Summary of World Broadcasts*, BBC, 4 November 1991.

14.   For a discussion of the problems faced by democrats in local govern-
       ment see M. McAuley, 'The Regional Perspective: Electoral Politics,
       Economic Stalemate, and Elite Realignment' in *Soviet Economy*,
       forthcoming. Despite his strong language, Yeltsin met with his regional
       representatives rarely. They complained that they lacked the power of
       the old regional party secretaries and that their work was made difficult
       by the lack of a legal basis for their authority. See *Summary of World
       Broadcasts*, BBC, 28 November 1991.

15.   *Summary of World Broadcasts*, BBC, 31 March 1992. On 21 January
       1992 Yeltsin established a Russian Ministry of Nuclear Energy to
       coordinate nuclear enterprises that are acquiring some autonomy in
       their production tasks, though weapons technology will be under total
       ministerial control. He appointed the former Soviet minister of the
       nuclear industry to head it. On the same day, a Russian Ministry
       of Science was established incorporating the State Committee for
       Science and Technology and other Soviet bodies. There was also a
       State Committee for Conversion created at the same time.

16.   *Summary of World Broadcasts*, BBC, 5 March 1992.

17.   *Summary of World Broadcasts*, BBC, 13 April 1992.

18.   See, for example, A. Migranyan, 'Gorbachev's leadership: a Soviet
       view', *Soviet Economy*, No. 2, 1990, pp. 155–60.

19.   *Summary of World Broadcasts*, BBC, 11 October, 1991.

20.   *Summary of World Broadcasts*, BBC, 8 April, 1992.

21.   *Summary of World Broadcasts*, BBC, 16 January 1992.

22.   As parliamentary leaders ought to have recognised following the
       débâcle when a state of emergency was introduced in Chechen-
       Ingushetia in November 1991. After a humiliating retreat by internal
       troops, parliament itself overrode Yeltsin's decree.

23.   The division of powers worked out by the federation treaty allowed the
       republics far greater control than the draft constitution had envisaged
       over local resources, government structures, foreign relations, states of
       emergency, and residual matters not mentioned specifically in the treaty
       as belonging to the centre. In areas under the joint jurisdiction of the
       centre and the republics specified in the treaty, federal law required
       legislation by the republics to become effective.

24.   See *Radio Liberty Report on the USSR*, No. 51/52, 1991, pp. 13–16.

25.   One Supreme Soviet deputy suggested instituting impeachment pro-
       ceedings against Shakhray for interference in the independence of the
       courts. Shakhray continued to defend his position.

26.   *Summary of World Broadcasts*, BBC, 9 April 1992.

27.   *Summary of World Broadcasts*, BBC, 17 January 1992.

28.   *Ibid.*

29.   *Ibid.*

30.   *Summary of World Broadcasts*, BBC, 17 January 1992.

31.   See S. Peregudov, I. Semenenko, and A. Zudin, *Business Associations
       in the USSR – And After: Their Growth and Political Role*, Paper

for IPSA Congress, Buenos Aires, July 1991, Revised and Extended January 1992.

32. See the *Financial Times*, June 12 1992.
33. See V. F. Petrenko and O. V. Mitina, 'Semanticheskoe prostranstvo politicheskikh partiy' in *Psikhologicheskiy zhurnal*, Vol. 12, No. 6, 1991, pp. 55–77.
34. *Summary of World Broadcasts*, BBC, 17 January 1992.

9 Yugoslavia

David Dyker

INTRODUCTION

It is indeed ironic, after the dramatic and tragic events of 1991–92, to seek to talk about a new institutional framework in Yugoslavia. But while the end of the civil war is still not in sight, and the only certain thing is that Yugoslavia no longer exists, the civil war will not go on for ever. At some point in the future, the Yugoslav area will begin to 'settle down' as a group of independent states sharing a given economic space. Each of these states will have an institutional framework of sorts, and it would be improbable indeed if these frameworks did not show some resemblance to one another, and did not owe something to the institutional history of Yugoslavia. It is on these grounds that we focus, in this chapter, on the institutions of Titoism, the breakdown of those institutions in the 1980s and early 1990s, and the emergence of provisional institutional structures in the various successor states from 1991 onwards.

Just as Yugoslavia's pre-1990 history was completely different from that of any other East European communist country, so the developments that followed the beginnings of democratisation in the early 1990s were quite *sui generis*. Before that watershed, as after it, Yugoslav politics were dominated by relations and tensions between the various nationalities of the federation, to an extent unparalleled even in the Soviet Union/CIS. In Titoist Yugoslavia institutions only had meaning in terms of the articulation of nationality standpoints. During its brief life post-Titoist Yugoslavia oscillated between a centrifugal tendency which threatened to (and eventually did) destroy Yugoslavia altogether, and an attempt to construct a new institutional framework within which nationality relations could be mediated. It is against that background that we must seek to understand the curious ambivalence of many Yugoslav institutions.

TITOIST COMMUNISM – A HISTORIC COMPROMISE

As in China and Albania, communists came to power in Yugoslavia on the basis of communist leadership of a predominantly peasant resistance

162

*Table 9.1   The Nations of Yugoslavia, by Language
and Traditional Religion*

	Traditional religion	Language
Serbs	Serbian orthodox	Serbo-Croat
Croatians	Roman Catholic	Serbo-Croat
Slovenes	Roman Catholic	Slovene
Ethnic Muslims	Muslim	Albanian
Montenegrins	Serbian orthodox	Serbo-Croat
Macedonians	Serbian-Macedonian orthodox	Macedonian
Albanians	Muslim	Albanian
Hungarians	Roman Catholic-Protestant	Hungarian

movement against fascist occupiers. But it was the national heterogeneity of Yugoslavia which gave the revolution in that country an extra dimension. Royal Yugoslavia's brief and ill-starred existence from 1918 to 1941 had been chequered with nationality conflicts. The principal of these had been between the Serbs, the most numerous group and the only one (tiny Montenegro apart) with a modern tradition of independent statehood, and the Croats, a nation at a higher level of economic development than Serbia, but which had enjoyed only very limited autonomy within the Habsburg Empire prior to its collapse. During the Second World War inter-nationality conflict reached genocidal proportions, with the Croatian fascist *Ustase* committing appalling atrocities against Serbs and Serbo-Croat-speaking Muslims, and Serbian organisations like the *Chetniks* replying in kind. The communist-led Partisans were predominantly Serbian in make-up, but they did take their active membership from all the nationalities of Yugoslavia except the Albanians of Kosovo. Their leader, Josip Broz Tito, was a Croat of mixed Croatian and Slovenian descent. While the Partisans were certainly not immune from the evils of ethnic sectarianism, they were able to maintain focus on the fight against the Germans and Italians as the main goal, and thus to develop a genuinely Yugoslav image.

The articulation of nationality standpoints was, until the early 1950s, placed firmly out of bounds. The map of Yugoslavia was redrawn in such a way as to recognise, but at the same time neutralise, traditional ethnic differences. The Serbian republic of the 1946 constitution was very much a 'lesser' rather than a 'Greater' Serbia. Macedonia, part of Serbia before the War, was constituted as a separate republic. The areas of Vojvodina

Table 9.2   *Population of Yugoslavia by Main National Group in 1981*

	Percentage of total	Number (in millions)
Yugoslavia	100.0	22.4
Serbs	36.2	8.1
Croats	19.6	4.4
Ethnic Muslims	9.0	2.0
Slovenes	8.0	1.8
Albanians	7.6	1.7
Macedonians	5.8	1.3
Montenegrins	2.7	0.6
Hungarians	1.8	0.4

and Kosovo, with their large minorities of, respectively, Hungarians and Albanians, were given the status of autonomous regions within Serbia. But the Serbian minority areas within Croatia were given no such status, while Bosnia and Hercegovina, with its mixed Serbian, Croatian and Ethnic Muslim population, was constituted as a separate republic. The Serbs, as they had been in the Partisan movement, remained dominant in the apparatus of the new state – in the army, the police and the civil service. [1] But everything was done to 'cut Serbia down to size', in order to avoid a return to the inter-regional disequilibria which had so devastated the old Yugoslavia.

After the break with Moscow in 1948–49, the Yugoslav leadership sought to construct a distinctive version of socialism based on:

1. The abolition of central planning and the creation of a form of market economy based on workers' self-management in industry and private enterprise in agriculture.
2. The transformation of Yugoslavia from a Soviet-style quasi-federation into a genuine federation.
3. The retention of the one-party system, but the abandonment of the 'leading role' of the Communist Party (renamed the League of Communists, LCY).

In the initial phase of market socialism, 1953–65, the federal Yugoslav authorities retained a large degree of control over crucial economic variables like investment and foreign trade, which they used to implement a fairly conventional Soviet-style industrialisation programme. On the political side, the abandonment of the 'leading role' proved tricky, and the period 1956–58 witnessed a definite movement back to classical Leninism. But by the early sixties one could discern a clear-cut trend towards greater reliance on the market mechanism at enterprise level, paralleled by a shift in the nexus of political power – and of control over resources – from the centre to the republics and communes. The 1965 economic reform sought, *inter alia*, to take the bulk of investment funding out of the state capitalist sector and nest it at the level of enterprises and, most importantly, commercial banks.

The trouble with the banking reform of 1965 was that while it effectively put an end to the dominance of the federal government in matters of investment finance, it did not remove politics from banking, and the 'new', supposedly commercial banks of the post-1965 period found themselves vulnerable to pressures from republican and local political élites. That was enough to start Yugoslavia on the road to the regional autarkism which so blighted the economy in the 1970s. But the story took a twist which presented Yugoslavia with its biggest crisis since 1948. The late 1960s saw the development of a powerful Croatian cultural autonomy movement which coalesced with a trend in Croatian public opinion that interpreted the banking developments of the late 1960s, not as an assertion of Croatian control over Croatian money, but rather as an assertion of *Serbian* control over Croatian money, as the Belgrade-based central investment funds turned themselves into quasi-commercial organisations. By the early 1970s opinion in Croatia on these matters had become so inflamed as to threaten the very existence of Yugoslavia, with Croatian *LCY* leaders in the forefront of the nationalist movement. Finally, at the end of 1971, Tito himself decided to intervene. There ensued a massive purge of the Croatian party (other republican parties were also purged of 'liberal' elements), and a general political clampdown which marked the end of a period when Yugoslavia had been edging towards a more pluralistic political system at all levels.

Tito's formula for neutralising this new outburst of nationality tension was to permit, even encourage, a movement towards even greater independence for the republics and autonomous provinces of Yugoslavia. At the same time, however, Tito looked to the *LCY* to reassert something of its Leninist leading role in society, albeit not in a Soviet-apparatus interfering style, and in particular to provide the political cement that would ensure that republics enjoying a wide degree of autonomy would ultimately pull in the same direction. Specifically, republican and local party cadres were given the task of positively vetting candidates for all key posts in their region. This effectively created a decentralised version of the Soviet *nomenklatura* system. The presumption was that the prerogative would be used 'in the national interest'.

The formula proved to be a disastrous failure. Far from providing the cement to hold Yugoslavia together, regional party cadres were themselves more guilty than anyone in relation to the process of continuous fragmentation that proceeded apace during the 1970s and early 1980s. The power over appointments was extensively used, but it was used to build up local patronage systems, not to provide a responsible general staff for Yugoslav socialism. Federal government, and indeed the Yugoslavia-wide organisation of the *LCY*, was reduced to the level of bickering committees, paralysed for much of the time by the need to reach unanimity between the regions on any important issue. On the death of Tito in 1980, the individual presidency was replaced by a Collective Presidency, with one member from each republic and autonomous region elected by regional *LCY* delegates, and the chairmanship of the Presidency – the titular head of state – rotating.

Pernicious enough in purely political terms, this trend was especially damaging in the economic sphere. Amidst the uncertainties of the post-oil shock world, Yugoslavia needed, more than anything else, a strong economic-policy-making centre. Yet by the late 1970s, for example, the National Bank of Yugoslavia had completely lost control of the money supply and the balance of payments. This loss of control was one of the root causes of two of Yugoslavia's great disasters of the succeeding decade – the External Debt Crisis of 1982–83, and the escalation of inflation into hyper-inflation in the late 1980s. Thus while Tito's historic compromise with nationalism had worked well enough as a way of releasing pressure in the short run, it had simply compounded the problem in the longer run.

THE BEGINNINGS OF POLITICAL CRISIS

The wave of democratisation that hit Yugoslavia in 1990 took its immediate origin from the groundswell of democratisation that had started to build up within the Soviet sphere of influence in Eastern Europe in late 1989. But here, as elsewhere, the underlying trends in Yugoslavia were essentially autonomous. As early as 1986 public opinion surveys conducted in Yugoslavia were revealing a dramatic fall in public support for, and public confidence in the *LCY*, particularly in Slovenia but also in Serbia.[2] It was against this background that Slobodan Milosevic made an explosive entry onto the centre-stage of Yugoslav politics in 1988, when he captured the leadership of the Serbian *LCY* on a platform of 'solving' the Kosovo problem which consisted in the increasing Serbian belief that there was an Albanian conspiracy to push out the Serbian minority by intimidation and harassment, as a prelude to the establishment of Kosovo as an Albanian republic, possibly outside Yugoslavia altogether.

On the basis of this platform, Milosevic engineered a spectacular revival in the fortunes of the *LCY* in Serbia. But while he was able in this way to generate substantial political reconsolidation within Serbia, Milosevic's effect on Yugoslavia as a whole was to deepen the trend towards fragmentation. Slobodan Milosevic's 'solution' to the Kosovo problem was to deprive the province of the autonomous status it had been granted in the late 1960s. In reintegrating Kosovo back into Serbia proper, however, Milosevic had, for the sake of consistency, to do the same thing to the other autonomous province of Serbia, Vojvodina. This produced a bitter, and essentially gratuitous clash between Milosevic and the Vojvodina leadership. The latter were crushed, as Milosevic adeptly manipulated the nationalist emotions of the masses, but the victory was an ambivalent one for the Serbian leader. For both Serbian majority and Hungarian minority of the relatively prosperous Vojvodina region had tended to line up with the north-western republics on many issues during the last years of the Titoist system. Slovenes and Croats alike were now understandably alarmed by the prospect that what had been done to Vojvodina might be done to them. The sense of alarm seemed to receive further justification by a sequence of events which started in late 1989. Incensed by Slovenia's support for the Albanian Kosovars, Milosevic, now president of Serbia, announced his intention of organising a series of Serbian demonstrations in Slovenia itself. The Slovenian government banned the demonstrations. In retaliation, the Serbian government proclaimed a boycott of Slovenian goods.

There is a slightly farcical tone to these developments, yet they provide a key to the understanding of the political events of 1990. The very way in which Milosevic had succeeded in reviving the fortunes of the *LCY* in Serbia was almost bound to kill off communism once and for all as a political force in Slovenia and Croatia. At a time when old-style Yugoslav communism was already losing credibility in the north-western republics, a new brand had arisen which in Zagreb and Ljubljana seemed indistinguishable from the Greater-Serbian hegemonism of the pre-war period. There was simply no way this could have any appeal at all in Croatia and Slovenia, certainly amongst the Croatian and Slovenian populations.

THE ECONOMIC CRISIS AND THE MARKOVIC PLAN

In the midst of all these political fireworks, the Yugoslav economy continued to decline, and by late 1989 the rate of inflation had reached 2,500 per cent. Federal prime minister Ante Markovic decided that the time was ripe to launch a new and decisive initiative, based on Polish-style 'shock therapy' aimed at resolving the deep-seated structural problems which had been partly to blame for the debt crisis, and which remained essentially unaddressed.

In accordance with the principles of the quasi-confederalism of the 1974 constitution, the federal prime ministership, like the presidency, had rotated amongst representatives of the republics and provinces in the post-Tito period. Proposed by the Collective Presidency, the appointment of the premier was confirmed by a National Assembly itself made up of delegates from republican assemblies, rather than directly elected MPs. In that context the head of the federal government was almost condemned to ineffectuality. Buggins' turn had come to Branko Mikulic of Bosnia, an energetic and able man, in 1986, but in December 1988 Mikulic resigned in the face of widespread loss of confidence in his government. Mikulic's resignation broke the pattern of rotation, and provided a real chance of significant evolution in the institution of the premiership. There was every reason to believe that Ante Markovic, the Croatian technocrat who took over the federal premiership in early 1989, would be a different kind of prime minister. In the event, he remained largely invisible over the first ten months or so of his tenure – perhaps conveniently so – on a political landscape dominated by the populist colossus of Slobodan Milosevic. Quite apart from its economic content, however, the launching of the Markovic Plan on 1 January 1990, as an integrated policy package to be imposed on all the regions of Yugoslavia, was implicitly revolutionary in political and institutional terms (see below). Just as much as the populism of Milosevic, the new technocracy of Markovic signalled the end of Titoism as a system.

The main elements in the Markovic Plan were as follows:

1.   The currency was reformed, with a new dinar replacing the old at a rate of 1 to 10,000, and pegged to the deutschmark at a rate of 7 to 1.
2.   The new dinar was to be partially convertible, in that Yugoslav citizens would now be able freely to convert dinars into foreign currency.
3.   Control over the money supply was to be reconcentrated in the hands of the National Bank, and this was to be the cornerstone of the fight against inflation.
4.   Imports were to be liberalised.
5.   Regulations on joint ventures, and on access for foreign capital to Yugoslavia in general, were to be liberalised.

6. Agencies for Restructuring and Development were to be set up at republican level to provide a financial basis for the restructuring of the economy, and an instrument to see through a privatisation programme projected to increase the share of the private sector within the Yugoslav economy to 35 per cent by 1995.

It is not the purpose of this chapter to provide an exhaustive assessment of the extent of implementation of the Markovic Plan up to the outbreak of civil war in mid-1991. But the Plan allocated key roles to two institutions – one old, one new – namely the National Bank and the Agency for Restructuring and Development, which would in one way or another survive the collapse of Yugosalvia as such. Let us now look at these in greater detail.

THE NATIONAL BANK

Before the banking reforms of 1965 the National Bank of Yugoslavia had continued to exhibit two key features of the Soviet State Bank/Monobank system on which it had been modelled. Firstly, it had operated as a commercial bank as well as a central bank. Secondly, it had pursued a policy of selectivity in its credit activities, a policy aimed to back up the priorities of the state development plan. After 1965 the National Bank drew nearer to the standard Western model of a central bank, in that it ceased altogether to lend directly to clients – it became exclusively a bankers' and government's bank. But the tradition of selectivity in credit policy survived, and was complicated in the post-1965 period by the creation of republican national banks with definite rights of currency emission. It was the interaction between those institutional features and the peculiar political environment of the 1970s and early 1980s that produced a pattern characterised by the institutionalisation of soft budget constraints – to the extent that governments, federal, republican and provincial, and even local, enjoyed what amounted to a license to print money. In that context the role of the National Bank of Yugoslavia as a guardian of the soundness of the dinar was reduced to an empty charade.

The keystone of Ante Markovic's Stabilisation Plan was the attempt to break utterly with this peculiar Yugoslav tradition of central banking. The 'new' National Bank was modelled down to the last detail on the German *Bundesbank*. It was meant to be politically independent, so as to be able to pursue a policy of monetary stability without fear or favour. It was meant to stick exclusively to macro-economic priorities, with the implication of no more selective credits. The republican national banks retained some rights of primary emission, but were permitted to exercise these only with the prior approval of the Board of Governors of the National Bank of Yugoslavia. The main tactic of the new central banking philosophy, as laid out in the Markovic plan, was to be the one favoured by Nigel Lawson during his tenure of the British Chancellorship of the Exchequer – 'shadowing the deutschmark'. By tying the dinar to the German currency at a fixed parity, Markovic ensured that any slippage of monetary control in Yugoslavia leading to accelerating inflation would automatically tend to produce a balance of trade deficit, which would force the National Bank to take corrective action. In this way the Yugoslav National Bank could go beyond imitation of the *Bundesbank* to a direct linkage between Yugoslav monetary policy and German monetary policy.

THE AGENCIES FOR RECONSTRUCTION AND DEVELOPMENT

Again, the model is overwhelmingly a German one, with the Agencies set up very much on the pattern of the German *Treuhandanstalt*, the special authority which has been entrusted with the job of overseeing the restructuring and privatisation of the economy of the former GDR. In the Yugoslav case there was to be an Agency for each republic. The Agencies were to operate essentially as public enterprises, offering consultancy services to firms. They would have no monopoly over the purveyance of such services, and it was, indeed, explicitly foreseen that big firms, for which privatisation was bound to be a highly complex affair, should be able to set up their own restructuring agencies. The proceeds of privatisation, in cases where whole enterprises were simply sold off, should go, not to the Agencies, but to republican (Regional) Development Funds. These were 'old' institutions, but the advent of privatisation totally transformed their function. Development Funds were explicitly empowered to lend the proceeds of privatisation back to the the firms privatised. It should be noted, however, that this was not the only pattern of privatisation which the legislation of 1990 permitted. It was also foreseen that enterprises might be privatised through the selling of shares to employees and former employees. This would maintain the self-managing flavour of the Yugoslav system.

No federal Agency for Reconstruction and Development was set up. But Markovic's government did set up a federal Agency for the Restructuring of the Banking System. The creation of this agency reflected a realisation on the part of the government that it was not enough to seek to remodel the central bank and restructure industry – that neither of these goals would in fact be attainable unless the linking dimension of the commercial banking system were placed on a sound and profitable footing.

1990 – THE YEAR OF DEMOCRATISATION

In April 1990 the republics of Slovenia and Croatia held parliamentary elections which were Yugoslavia's first free elections since the War. The election in Slovenia left the *LCY* as the biggest single party – but with only 17 per cent of the total vote. The numerous right-of-centre nationalist parties were then able to come together to form a governing coalition under the name of Demos. The new Slovenian parliament elected Milan Kucan, a former communist, president of the republic. In Croatia the election produced a landslide victory in terms of seats (though with just 42 per cent of the vote) for a new nationalist formation called the Croatian Democratic Union (*HDZ*), led by Franjo Tudjman, an ex-communist and ex-army general who had broken with Tito in the 1970s, and paid for his dissidence with a spell in prison. The *LCY* were virtually annihilated as a political force, with the Party of Democratic Change, a grouping of 'liberal' ex-communists, coming second with around 15 per cent of the seats contested.

The pattern of these results inevitably produced a reaction in Serbia – among leaders and masses alike – which identified democratisation with anti-Serbian nationalism, and the Milosevic line throughout the summer of 1990, fully supported by the Montenegrin leadership, remained firmly Leninist in relation to the issue of democratic elections. But a number of new factors came into play over the course of that summer which finally induced a change in Milosevic's policy. The *LCY* had virtually ceased to exist at Yugoslav level after the fiasco of the 14th Congress of the League, convened in January–February 1990, which had broken up in disarray. With what was left of the communist movement in Slovenia and Croatia unwilling to join a new pan-Yugoslav Union of the Left, Milosevic was almost forced into setting up his own Serbian party. This he did under the rubric of the Socialist Party of Serbia, following the pattern of nomenclature changes which most of the East European communist parties had followed, including those like the Bulgarian that remained a major force in national politics. While the change of name was in a sense cosmetic, it did represent an admission that the terminology of Leninism was now a political liability. In that context there was mounting pressure on Milosevic to find a new basis of legitimacy.

The picture was further complicated by federal prime minister Ante Markovic's announcement around the middle of the year that he intended to form a new political party, with the express purpose of seeking electoral support for the restructuring policies of the government. The formation of the League of Reform Forces underlined the extent of political vacuum created by the break-up of the *LCY*, and placed the weight of the federal go vernment – originally placed in power by the *LCY* – behind the movement for democratic elections.

But Milosevic, threatened by signs that the Serbian public were turning against him, was still in no hurry to go to the polls. The authorities in Bosnia and Hercegovina and Macedonia pressed ahead, however, and called elections to their republican parliaments for November 1990. There was a degree of expectation that these elections might provide some counterweight to the overwhelmingly nationalist trend which the Slovenian and Croatian elections had produced. The attractions of some kind of Yugoslavism in Bosnia and Hercegovina, with its mixed population and memories of war-time sectarian atrocities, might have been expected to remain strong. In Macedonia, small, land-locked and poor, threatened equally by Greater-Serbian and Greater-Bulgarian nationalism, a highly ethnocentric political profile might have seemed equally dangerous. In the event, the first round of the Macedonian elections did give both the *LCY* and the Union of Reform Forces substantial proportions of the total vote. But in the second round the Macedonian National Party (*VMRO-DMPNO*) swept the board, producing a final result similar to those recorded in Slovenia and Croatia. In Bosnia voting went largely along ethnic lines, giving a plurality, but not a majority of seats to the Ethnic Muslim Party of Democratic Action (*SDA*), with the Serbian Democratic Party and the *HDZ* taking the bulk of, respectively, Serbian and Croatian votes. The election over, however, the major parliamentary groups took a conciliatory approach to each other, permitting formation of a 'grand coalition' government under the presidency of *SDA* leader, former dissident Alija Izetbegovic.

As the rigours of the new monetary regime threatened to make savage inroads into Serbia's obsolescent and heavily subsidised industrial struc- ture, elections to the Serbian parliament were finally held in December 1990. They were preceded by an extraordinary event which has come to be known as the 'Great Bank Robbery'. The Serbian government prevailed upon the national bank of Serbia to rediscount 18 bn dinars ($1.7 bn) worth of bank loans, thus effectively creating new, 'high-powered' money to the tune of some 10 per cent of the total Yugoslav stock of money at that time, and inflicting deep damage on Markovic's programme of monetary stability. The Great Bank Robbery enabled Milosevic to pay salaries and pensions to millions of state employees, retirees, invalids, etc for the first time for months. That, combined with a highly effective if sometimes coercive mobilisation of the media in favour of the Milosevic cause, ensured that the Socialist Party of Serbia took as much as three-quarters of the seats in the elections (with around 50 per cent of the popular vote), while the opposition Serbian National Renewal Movement (right-wing, nationalist, anti-communist) and the Democratic Party (liberal-centrist, quite distinct from the Serbian Democratic Party) did much worse than expected, winning about 5 per cent of the seats contested each. In Montenegro the *LCY* fought the election under its old name, though on a platform which allied it closely with Milosevic's Serbian socialists, and won a landslide victory.

What, it may be asked, was happening to the federal parliament all this time? According to the Yugoslav constitution, there should have been elections to the federal *Skupstina* before the end of 1990. In the event, they were never held. If they had been, they would have been largely meaningless. For with, for example, Slovenian delegates boycotting the *Skupstina* for much of 1990, the highest representative institution in the land largely ceased to function in that year. Such 'concertation' as did take place between the republics in this critical period was increasingly concentrated in the eight-member collective Presidency.

DEMOCRATISATION AND THE ARMY

The latter part of 1990 produced yet another trend in the newly pluralised stream of Yugoslav politics. The Yugoslav army had always played a central role in the Titoist system. It had developed directly from the wartime Partisan movement, and had therefore a particularly close link with the party which had led that movement. Right up until the 1980s the great majority of both *LCY* and army leaders had been Partisan leaders, and were therefore bound together in a particularly tightly-knit 'old boys' club'. As we saw earlier, the strength of the Partisan tradition ensured also that the bulk of the officer corps of the army remained ethnically Serbian, which in turn meant that traces of pre-war Greater-Serbian hegemonist attitudes also survived. It was the combination of traditional ethnocentric hegemonism and Leninist-internationalist ideology that provided the officer corps with the psychological basis – and in the latter case the justification – for seeing itself as the trustee of the principle of 'brotherhood and unity' among Yugoslav republics. In 1988, with the one-party system still intact but the authority of the *LCY* declining dramatically in Slovenia, it was revealed that the army had a contingency plan for taking control in the northern republic if party authority collapsed altogether. The plan was never put into action, but the very knowledge that it existed provided an important input into the Slovenian, and indeed Yugoslav, political situation at that time. The military made no attempt to influence directly the outcome of the elections of 1990, but as explicit separatism came more and more to the fore, particularly in the case of Slovenia, so the high command felt it necessary to reiterate its commitment to the continued existence of Yugoslavia. Defence minister Veljko Kadijevic had emerged by the end of the year as a tough but relatively sophisticated character with a clear vision of how the army might play an active role, not just in salvaging, but indeed in rebuilding Yugoslavia.

It is significant that Kadijevic was also prominent among the founders in December 1990 of another new political movement – the League of Communists – Movement for Yugoslavia. At one level this represented simply an attempt to recreate a national communist movement, and to use that movement as a focal point for the regrouping of the various socialist/communist forces still active in different parts of Yugoslavia – significantly Milosevic' wife was also a high-profile activist in the new communist movement. At another, more subtle level, it represented a reassertion of socialism/communism as the ideology which gave the Yugoslav army the legitimate right to intervene to defend the integrity of Yugoslavia. On both these counts, it seemed to represent a deepening rapprochement between the hegemonistic communism of the army and the socialist populism of Slobodan Milosevic.

THE POLITICAL CRISES OF FEBRUARY–MAY 1991

The early months of 1991 witnessed a dramatic evolution in the relations between the various institutions described above, as Yugoslavia moved rapidly towards total break-up. In December 1990 a referendum on 'national independence' in Slovenia produced a massive 'yes' vote. However, since there was no clear ruling on what exactly national independence should mean, the government of the republic decided that there should be a grace period of six months before any concrete steps were taken. The army was, no doubt, drawing its own conclusions. When the first direct clash between the Yugoslav army and a local national government came, in February 1991, it involved Croatia, not Slovenia. The crisis issue was the army's charge that Martin Spegelj, defence minister of Croatia, had

*Table 9.3   The Political Parties of Yugoslavia on the
Eve of the Outbreak of Civil War*

League of Communists – Movement for Yugoslavia: President Dragan Atanasovski
Union of Reform Forces: President Ante Markovic
Demos (Slovenia): President Joze Pucnik
Croatian Democratic Union: President Franjo Tudjman
Socialist Party of Serbia: secretary Mihajlo Markovic
Serbian National Renewal Movement: President Vuk Draskovic
Party of Democratic Action (Bosnia): President Alija Izetbegovic
Macedonian National Party: President Ljupce Gorgijevski
Serbian Democratic Party (Bosnia and Croatia): President Milan Babic
Democratic Party (Serbia): President Dragoljub Micunovic

---

plotted armed insurrection with the goal of setting up a totally independent Croatian state. The army wanted to arrest Spegelj in order to interrogate him on this charge. It was supported in this by the Serbian chairman of the Presidency, titular president of the country, Borisav Jovic. The Croatian government refused to surrender him, and President Tudjman sent Croatian police in to guard Spegelj. The result was a nail-biting stand-off between Yugoslav army and Croatian police which was only ended at the beginning of March when the Presidency finally ordered the army to withdraw, with the Croatian leadership agreeing that Spegelj should be brought to trial – in Zagreb.

By then the crisis spotlight was shifting to another stage altogether. In setting up his victory in the December election, President Milosevic had scored a great tactical victory but there was no long-term strategy. As the National Bank, furiously defending its new institutional role, took measures to ensure that there would be no more 'Great Bank Robberies', the backlog of unpaid salaries in Serbia's beleaguered economy, cruelly hit by the cuts in trade with the Soviet Union and the collapse of trade with Iraq, was building up again. Meanwhile the Serbian population was beginning to chafe at the tight media controls which Milosevic had imposed. The opposition called for an anti-government demonstration to be held in Belgrade on Saturday 9 March. The demonstration was big, but did not threaten to overthrow the state. Milosevic responded by calling in the Yugoslav army, which dispersed the demonstration using live bullets. Two people were killed. The rapprochement between the army and Milosevic seemed to be complete.

The equilibrium was, however, to be an unstable one. The brutality of the government action on 9 March was a political gift of major proportions to the Serbian opposition. It enabled Vuk Draskovic, left for dead after his crushing defeat in the December election, to make a dramatic comeback in circumstances which were ideally suited to his charismatic style. It also began a hesitant, in the event temporary, process of disengagement of the military from Milosevic as striking as the process of rapprochement which had preceded it. Chief of Staff Blagoje Adzic, along with a number of other military leaders, demanded that the Presidency impose martial law on the whole of Yugoslavia. Adzic was supported by the Serbian members of the Presidency, and when the majority vote in the Presidency went against against martial law, the Serbian members, led by President Jovic, walked out and left the Presidency inquorate. But defence minister Kadijevic, apparently the most influential military man in Yugoslavia, did not support the call for martial law. The army high command, with some disgruntlement, accepted the ruling of the Presidency that there should be no martial law, thus nullifying Jovic's ploy to invalidate the decision by withdrawing the Serbian members of the Presidency. Meanwhile the Serbian parliament instructed Jovic and the other Serbian members to rejoin the Presidency.

The plot thickened further towards the end of March, when a Croatian police convoy was ambushed by Serbian guerillas in a part of the Serbian minority area of Croatia (Krajina), leaving one policeman dead and many injured. The Presidency met in emergency session and agreed, without dissent from the Slovenian and Croatian members, to send in the Yugoslav army to keep the two sides apart, even as the Krajina Serb leadership declared the unification of the region with Serbia. It is not difficult to perceive the hand of Slobodan Milosevic behind an explosion of Krajina Serb militancy which may be seen to have forced the hand of the Presidency and the military. At the same time it was the Serbian Democratic Party under Milan Babic, not the Serbian Socialist Party, that commanded the loyalty of the *precani* ('over the border') Serbs of the old Military Frontier region of Croatia, and there were already indications that many Krajina Serbs felt that Milosevic was not giving them enough support. Like the British Army in relation to the Roman Catholics in Northern Ireland, the Yugoslav army in the event found it extraordinarily difficult to convince the Croats that it was in Krajina for any other reason than to support the *precani* Serbs and the Milosevic line. In early May the crisis reached new heights when Croatian anti-army demonstrators in the Dalmatian port of Split killed a soldier.

Mid-May 1991 added a new twist to the downward spiral of Yugoslav political life. In accordance with the principle of rotation, Croat Stipe Mesic should have succeeded Serb Borisav Jovic as chairman of the Collective

Presidency. But Serbia and Montenegro blocked the transfer, alleging that Mesic merely wanted to use the Presidency to break up Yugoslavia, and Mesic was in fact never effectively to succeed to the chairmanship, leaving Jovic the doubtful distinction of having been the last titular president of Yugoslavia. Significantly, the army supported the Serbian position over Mesic's chairmanship. Meanwhile the people of Croatia had voted overwhelmingly for a 'sovereign state' in a referendum along the same lines as the earlier Slovenian one.

SLIPPING INTO CIVIL WAR

It was the official declaration of Slovenian independence in June 1991, at the end of six-month grace period following the referendum, that marked the beginning of the end for Yugoslavia. Ironically, the attempt by the Yugoslav army to head off Slovenian independence in June and July at the same time marked the beginning of the end for the Yugoslav army as a credible trustee of the principle of 'brotherhood and unity'. The attempt was clumsy and militarily incompetent, and the army finally retreated with a badly bloodied nose. But the military's loss of face over Slovenia introduced a new volatility into the situation. As clashes between Croatian authorities and Serbian irregulars in the Serbian minority areas of Croatia became daily more frequent and more intense, the Yugoslav army came increasingly to take sides openly with the Serbs. By the autumn of 1991 a fierce and bloody war was being waged in both Krajina and Eastern Slavonia, with the Yugoslav army centrally involved in the destruction of whole Croatian towns and villages, and the killing of large numbers of Croatian civilians. At the critical point, the more subtle, more political approach of Defence Minister Kadijevic (reportedly in poor health at the time) seemed to be overwhelmed by the crude Serbian revanchism of Chief of Staff Adizic.

The progress of the war, and particularly of the battle around Vukovar, critically weakened both old and new institutions. Of course it destroyed the Federal Presidency, with Slovenian and Croatian representatives simply ceasing to participate. In the end, the army, too, gained little from its partisan intervention. Having thrown away its Yugoslav credentials, it found itself less and less able to maintain morale among its troops, even those of Serbian nationality. By early 1992, 80 per cent of conscripts called up *in Serbia* were failing to report. Meanwhile it was being increasingly upstaged, in military terms and as defender of Serbs, by sub-fascist groups like the *Chetniks* (a name used by the non-communist Serbian resistance during the Second World War). These groups operated independently of the army, and made it impossible for the army to deliver on the countless cease-fires agreed through the closing months of 1991.

The outbreak of war destroyed the National Bank as effectively as it destroyed the Yugoslav army. Of course the only way to pay for the war was through a succession of 'Great Bank Robberies'. By October 1991 every region of Yugoslavia already effectively had its own currency – through the rediscounting of commercial bank loans by republican national banks and the overstamping of banknotes. The National Bank of Yugoslavia no longer had any effective control over primary emission. Over the first eight months of the year federal budget revenue actually collected was standing at 41.1 bn dinars, as against a planned level of 79.9 bn dinars. From the beginning of September, not a single republic was delivering revenue from turnover tax and customs duties to the federation. It was estimated in October 1991 that increases in primary emission for 1991 would reach 160–220 bn dinars, against a planned level of 44 bn dinars. Within this estimated total, 70 – 130 bn dinars would go on support of the federal budget.[3] Inevitably, the rate of inflation, briefly reduced by the Markovic Plan to less than zero, had climbed again to 402 per cent, on an annualised basis, by September 1991.[4]

But it was not only the institutions of the old Yugoslavia that were undermined by the war. For while Milosevic found himself in increasing danger of being outflanked by front-line sub-fascist groups at the political level, President Tudjman of Croatia was subjected to extreme pressure from Croatian sub-fascist groups who could claim, with some justification, that they were doing all the fighting at Vukovar, and that Tudjman had done nothing to defend Croatia. At time of writing the possibility that, under the continued pressure of civil war, the democratic, if sectarian populism of Croatia and Serbia might not give way fairly quickly to something altogether more sinister could not be discounted.

CONCLUSION – THE INSTITUTIONALISATION OF THE SUCCESSOR STATES

As hopes that full-scale civil war in Bosnia might be averted are finally dashed, it is increasingly clear that we should not expect complete institutional 'normalisation' in the Yugoslav area at the general political level, even in the medium-to-long term, except in Slovenia, and possibly Macedonia. The most likely scenario at time of writing was one dominated by a re-born Greater Serbia, occupying large areas of Croatia and Bosnia,

Table 9.4   The Presidents of the Yugoslav Successor States

Serbia: Slobodan Milosevic
Croatia: Franjo Tudjman
Slovenia: Milan Kucan
Montenegro: Momir Bulatovic
Bosnia & Hercegovina: Alija Izetbegovic
Macedonia: Kiro Gligorov

with substantial minorities of Croats and Ethnic Muslims to add to existing Albanian and Hungarian minorities, and in permanent economic depression in conditions of international ostracism. On such a scenario, democracy would be unlikely to survive in Serbia, even if there is no dramatic lurch towards overt fascism in the short term. For quite different reasons, the institutions of democracy in a rump Croatia, controlling not much more than half its traditional national territory, would be equally at risk, again irrespective of any immediate threat from the extreme right. If Bosnia survives as an independent state, it will be on the basis of an effective partition of the republic between its three main communities which would preclude parliamentary democracy as we understand it in Western Europe. Indeed in all these cases there is a considerable probability of reversion to something like the old, non-totalitarian one-party system, as a third-best way of arriving at, or imposing, some kind of minimal consensus.

But no successor state will be able to duck the essential economic policy issues addressed briefly by Ante Markovic. Each will have to run its budget, and its monetary policy, each will have to have a policy on restructuring and privatisation, and that goes as much for 'stable' Slovenia as for 'unstable' Croatia. So now let us look, in turn, at these two crucial institutional dimensions – central banking and economic policy management, to see whether we can discern the likely future path of institutional evolution in the successor states.

The December 1990 assault by Slobodan Milosevic on the National Bank of Yugoslavia, and implicitly on the whole of Ante Markovic's economic policy package, was no quirk, no personal idiosyncracy of an eccentric demagogue. Rather it was a symptom of the fundamental incompatibility of a central bank modelled on the *Bundesbank* and traditional communist politics, even under a different name, and with democratic credentials. Does that mean that the Serbian central bank of the future will be hard pressed to maintain any institutional autonomy, and may end up printing the money the politicians want to spend, like Yugoslav central banks in the past? Certainly the prospects at April 1992 for a Serbian *Bundesbank* did not look very bright. Over the first quarter of 1992, the National Bank of Yugoslavia, still the issuing 'authority' in residual Yugoslavia, was called upon to finance as much as 92 per cent of the 'federal' budget (primarily the military budget) from primary emissions. The figure is indeed hardly surprising, given that none of the remaining (at that time) Yugoslav republics, *not even Serbia herself*, were handing over due tax revenues to the federal authorities.[5]

The situation is remarkably similar in Croatia, now effectively constituting a 'Croatian dinar zone'. 'Here too nothing has really changed, with monetary sovereignty still seen as primarily a function of the centralist ambitions of the state, despite fierce opposition from the Central Bank of Croatia.'[6] In Slovenia, now a *tolar* zone, the situation is rather more stable, with, of course, military expenditures not distorting the expenditure side of the budget in the way they do in Croatia and Serbia. Overall, however, it is difficult to dispute the conclusion that 'however things work out, primary emission to cover the budget (budgets) will remain the main problem *in the long term*' (emphasis added).[7]

The point emerges equally clearly if we look at the evolution of the role of republican Agencies for Restructuring and Development and Development Funds. As a general rule, before and after the final break-up of Yugoslavia, the Agencies have tended to operate much more as instruments of a new state capitalism than as instruments of privatisation. It is hardly surprising that in Serbia Milosevic, still, perhaps, a communist at heart, has tended to assert direct state control over areas of the 'self-managing' sector. Much more striking is the way that the Tudjman government in Croatia has placed the emphasis on overt *nationalisation* rather than privatisation. Public utilities and major elements in the energy complex like the big oil company INA have already been brought into *Croatian* public ownership.[8] So-called 'holding companies' have been created in the engineering industry which effectively bring a number of the leading Croatian enterprises in that sector under state management. In both Serbia and Croatia privatisation plans posit that enterprises that have not been sold off by a certain date will automatically become the property of the state.[9] In the Serbian case, where all the proceeds of privatisation go in any case to the Development Fund, enterprises have little incentive to privatise themselves[10] – but the state wins either way. In Slovenia the plan is to distribute the bulk of shares in 'privatised' industry to holding companies and pension funds. Distinguished Slovenian economist Ivan Ribnikar has pilloried the plan as a mask for state interference and even nationalisation,[11] and demanded that as a safeguard against this, the state funds should be forbidden to interfere in management except in cases of receivership or bankruptcy.[12]

It is not difficult to make sense of this apparently paradoxical approach to the restructuring of ownership patterns in the economy. All the republican governments of Yugoslavia are now dominated by populists of one kind or another, and populist leaders cannot risk economic shock therapy which might generate overnight unemployment at levels of 30 per cent and above. That is as true for Milan Kucan in Slovenia as it is for Tudjman in Croatia and Milosevic in Serbia. But while this explains the slow pace of progress on privatisation, it hardly explains the positive appetite for nationalisation. We must, it seems, seek the origins of that appetite in a kind of economic tribalism which perceives ownership, not as a basis for enterprise by individuals and companies, but rather as the basis for the survival and consolidation of the nation. The important thing, therefore, is that INA, for example, should be secured as part of the Croatian patrimony, just as, for Serbian nationalists in the context of the civil war, it is so crucial to secure Krajina (the main Serbian minority area within Croatia) as part of the Greater Serbian patrimony. (More cynically, we may perceive a parallel between the campaign by the new élites to gain control of the local money supply – 'monetary sovereignty' – and the campaign to gain direct control over the production structure.) Perhaps we should not find this surprising in a part of the world where tribes are still seeking to become nation states. But against the background of the emergence of a new passion for protectionism,[13] the trend towards economic tribalism must raise the most serious questions as to whether the political economy of the Yugoslav region can be stabilised in the foreseeable future.

By the time this book is published, the civil war in Yugoslavia may mercifully be over. It will leave behind it a clutch of successor-states, the majority of which will be unable to develop the full panoply of governmental and parliamentary institutions that we take for granted in the West. Against a background of critical economic restructuring requirements, intensified by the destruction and disruption of the war, most of the successor-states will likely find it equally difficult to develop the kinds of institutions of national economic management that they so desperately need. It will take a long time indeed to fill the institutional vacuum that communism created.

NOTES

I am deeply indebted to Mr Christopher Cviic of *The Economist* and the
Royal Institute of International Affairs, whose help was indispensable to me
in writing this chapter.

1. D. A. Dyker, 'Yugoslavia: unity out of diversity?', in A. Brown and
    J. Gray (eds), *Political Culture and Political Change in Communist
    States*, London, 1977.
2. J. Seroka, 'The interdependence of institutional revitalization and intra-
    Party reform in Yugoslavia', *Soviet Studies*, 40 (1), 1988, pp. 84–5;
    J. Grizelj, 'Koliko ste zadovoljni radom SIV-a', *NIN*, 17 June 1987,
    p. 10.
3. V. Grlickov, 'Ostavljen od svih', *Ekonomska Politika*, 14 October
    1991, pp. 10–12.
4. 'Na uzletistu', *Ekonomska Politika*, 14 October 1991, pp. 36–7.
5. V. Grlickov, 'Neobuzdana emisija', *Ekonomska Politika*, 16 March
    1992, pp. 10–12.
6. 'Dva lica suverenosti', *Ekonomska Politika*, 30 March 1992, pp. 23–4.
7. Grlickov, 'Neobuzdana . . . ' (see fn 7), p. 10.
8. V. Djordjevic, 'Put u drzavni socializam', *Ekonomska Politika*, 25
    February 1991, pp. 15–17; T. Dumezic, 'Nezakonita nacionalizacija',
    Ekonomska Politika, 25 February 1991, pp. 14–15; V. Kovac, 'Hrvatski
    zakon', *Ekonomska Politika*, 11 February 1991, p. 14.
9. D. Kalodjera, 'Nedopustiva avantura', *Ekonomska Politika*, 15 April
    1991, pp. 12–13; L. Madzar, 'Malaksali meandri privatizacije',
    Ekonomska Politika, 23 September 1991, pp. 25–6; S. Bogdanovic
    and M. Lakicevic, 'Drzava odumire jacajuci', *Ekonomska Politika*, 15
    April 1991, pp. 10–11.
10. V. Grlickov, 'Zamke svojinskih promena', *Ekonomska Politika*, 14
    October 1991, pp. 20–1.
11. V. Grlickov, 'Maska za drzavu', *Ekonomska Politika*, 23 September
    1991, pp. 23–5.
12. Grlickov, 'Zamke . . . ' (see fn 12).
13. 'Recept za nezaposlenost', *Ekonomska Politika*, 1 July 1991, p. 7.

10 The Road from Post Communism

George Schopflin

This chapter evaluates the chances of establishing properly functioning democratic systems in Central and Eastern Europe. The argument makes a number of assumptions. First, regimes of the pre-communist period were authoritarian, but not totalitarian, that is to say that while power was heavily concentrated in the hands of the ruling élite, some elements of pluralism and social autonomy could and did exist. Furthermore, while the systems were authoritarian, they were hidden behind a facade of democracy, signifying that their legitimating ideologies were likewise not totalitarian. Second, the communist period pressed these societies through a very particular kind of one-sided modernisation. Modernity was defined in highly static and purely economic terms, emphasising heavy industry with a relatively low technology content. Once the system was established, – i.e. when 'the foundations of socialism' were laid – the communist rulers felt that no major change would ever be needed again. Third, communist rule was a kind of 'desertification'. It promoted the atomisation of society and swept away ideas, values, institutions, solidarities and people, preserving only a few of these, often in a distorted form, from the previous state of affairs, so that not much of the pre-communist past remains.[1]

The task of constructing new systems in the aftermath of the properly named 'revolutions' of 1989 will obviously be a prolonged undertaking. The situation is, as a result very fluid and it would be precipitate to suggest that the systems have reached even their interim shapes, let alone their final ones. However, the central problem, of post-communism appears to be the gap between democratic form and real substance. Democracy demands a set of values from both rulers and ruled that involve self-limitation, compromise, bargaining and the like that post-communist states and societies cannot be expected to acquire overnight, for they can only result from many years of practice. In this chapter, the main emphasis will be on the Central European countries (Poland, Czechoslovakia and Hungary), though there will be occasional references to the Balkan states (Romania, Bulgaria and Yugoslavia).

CONSTITUTIONAL FORMS

The constitutional forms that have been or are in the process of being adopted are firmly anchored in the traditions of liberal democracy. After living through four decades of having liberal democracy dismissed as class oppression, the post-communists are now hastening to introduce systems based on the separation of powers, the rule of law, multi-party democracy, market economy and so on. However, as has been repeatedly remarked, the destruction of a social and political system is far easier than the construction of a new one. In particular, the post-communist reformers face a major dilemma. In introducing the institutions of Western democracy, they are bringing in forms that do not match socio-political realities. Hence, their aim is gradually to transform those realities until the mismatch diminishes.

This does raise the problem of how far these polities are to be guided by élites, enlightened or otherwise, and how far they are to respond to what the citizens demand now. Indeed, as will be argued later, there are currents in the post-communist world that are not in every respect friendly to representative democracy, but look to the immediate implementation of their desires as the definition of a democratic order. Above all, throughout the area there are social strata which believe that democracy means that they should enjoy a Western standard of living at once – those who voted for Tyminski in the presidential elections in Poland exemplify this.

In developed polities, individuals are guided in their aspirations by a mix of material and non-material interests. The latter, like morality or identity – what is accepted as right and wrong in a community or who are to be defined as its members – are essential in establishing the broad constitutional framework within which the political contest takes place.[2] Material interests are to do with the acquisition of goods and resources, consumption – both individual and collective – and how these are to be allocated and redistributed. Both groups and individuals see themselves as possessed of cross-cutting and overlapping interests, as producers and consumers, as employers and employees, as being committed to the environment and to job creation and so on.

Thus in Western democracies, where the constitutional framework has been largely settled, the political game is overwhelmingly about who receives what, how far-reaching taxation is, how much the state redistributes or how much control the individual has over his or her resources. Both groups and individuals define their interests along this line stretching from individual to collective allocation and redistribution. In Western terms, left-wing parties are those that support higher collective allocation; right-wing parties emphasise individual rights, although this picture is muddied by a strong strand of right-wing paternalism.

The types of parties that have come into being in the post-communist world are very different from those found in the West and do not divide along a political spectrum resembling that in the West.[3] On the whole, the most characteristic political formation in Eastern and Central Europe is the conglomerate party or political movement that includes a wide variety of different or even contradictory political currents and which are held together by considerations like tradition or morality, rather than material interests. The representation of economic interests remains weak, predictably given that the identification of interests by social groups is similarly weak. Although these conglomerate parties are widely defined as 'left-wing' and 'right-wing', left and right in Central and Eastern Europe have rather different connotations from what obtains in the West. In this sense, the quality of politics, the terms of the political contest are different and so are popular responses to policies. Public opinion tends to assess these by reference to moral or national criteria as much as by its economic interests, because these economic interests were thoroughly homogenised and atomised under communist rule.[4]

The essence of the problem is that the modernisation of these societies under communism was partial and distorted and the complexity and mutability characteristic of Western societies was blocked by communist power. Soviet-type systems sought to maximise the monopoly of the party and for this reason did what it could to atomise society, to destroy the institutions, bonds of solidarity and loyalty that hold a society together as a society, rather than as a group of disparate individuals, by giving their actions and interactions content and meaning. Romania under Ceausescu was an extreme case in the 1990s.[5] This very largely impeded attempts by society to adapt to the changes brought about by communism, e.g. the one-sided modernisation of industry. Consequently and ironically, the Soviet-type system preserved a variety of pre-modern values and ideas, which are out of tune with the true shape of these societies, but which engender a variety of beliefs and values which may be at variance with social realities. The nascent party system mirrors this.

Thus the split in Solidarity in Poland was as much about the different styles of government favoured by Walesa as against Mazowiecki as it was about the the ostensible cause of the split, the speed of the changes. Mazowiecki favoured a considered, cautious style, appealing to reason and argument in an attempt to promote a closer identification between the Polish population and its economic interests. The populism espoused by Walesa was a classic appeal to non-material values of morality through his attacks on *nomenklatura* privatisation and an offer of an easy solution to problems that simply do not have easy solutions.

The reverberations of the statement by the Hungarian foreign minister in the autumn of 1991, that the governing coalition represented the most authentic European values in parliament, was another illustration of much the same phenomenon. Ultimately, this was a rhetorical declaration without much relevance, but it was taken with deadly seriousness by the opposition, which chose to make a major issue out of it, because it felt, as a result, that the government was denying it a European, ie., a democratic identity. Examples could be found in all the post-communist states. What is missing from the debates in these polities is any sense of the urgency of economic reform, the introduction of economic and material issues into the political argument, notably those of privatisation and the modernisation of the legal system to make investment smoother.

Another aspect of this difficulty is that the impossibility of modernisation under communism has had the result that both left and right are woefully unprepared for rule. The left has, in any case, suffered a massive defeat with the collapse of communism and its place has been taken, in Hungary for example, by parties professing liberalism. More serious is the dilemma of the right. Because there was no opportunity to modernise conservatism under communist rule, the conservative traditions to which right-wing or 'moderate' parties harken back are those appropriate to a pre-modern polity and society, that of the 1930s. These referred to the gentry values of the time, emphasising nationhood, honour and morality, assuming that society was relatively homogeneous and undifferentiated. The values of commerce and finance, of buying and selling, were regarded as dishonourable and alien, and indeed, associated with the Jewish community. Parallel with this, liberal individualism was similarly regarded as an alien category. The trouble is that in the meanwhile, major changes have taken place in these societies and the ideas of the 1930s are barely appropriate to the situation.

The wasteland left by communism, therefore, consists of ideas and values that make the smooth functioning of democracy problematical. Concepts of honour, glory, morality, which may or may not be attached to perceptions of nationhood, have little role to play in daily politics in a functioning democracy, though they do indeed have a role in consti- tutional politics, the definition and redefinition of the broad framework of values and institutions within which the allocation of resources takes place. But once this has been settled, then politics is about compromise, bargaining, impersonal interactions all mediated by a large number of institutions.

PERSONALITIES AND INSTITUTIONS

The role of personalities as against institutions also militates against the smooth functioning of democracy. One of the central legacies of the Soviet-type system was the atomisation of society into individuals and the consequent destruction of the basic bonds of community through distrust. In particular, the relationship between the individual and the state was badly distorted in this way. Not surprisingly, the state has come to be regarded as remote and abstract, beyond the will and control of the individual, and the institutions of the state as not much more than facades. The elimination of communist systems has not, in itself, changed this.

As a result, there is a far greater inclination to believe in persons rather than institutions and to accept the former as the true focus of political attitudes. It may be that the individual holding office has a status enhanced by that office, but for many the authenticity of the relationship is the personal one. This leaves institutions locked in a cycle of relative weakness, because they find it difficult to acquire their own legitimacy in competition with the real or supposed charisma of personalities.

What seems to have happened in the early months of post-communism is that as the communists faded away or were expelled from power, societies found themselves without a political focus with which they could feel comfortable. New parties were the relatively remote constructs of the intellectuals and the symbols of the nation were no strong guides in the circumstances. Almost hypnotically, people turned to personalities, virtually without regard to their political programmes, as a repository for societies hopes and desires. In particular, because persons were felt to be more reliable, more authentic and thus more likely to embody what the individual wanted, personalities were invested with what amounted to a supra-political status.

The-pattern has been replicated throughout the area. The November–December 1990 presidential elections in Poland have confirmed the ascendancy of Walesa, almost without regard to his strategy or ideas. In a sense, the quarter of the vote that went to Tyminski confirmed this. Here was another personality, with the simple message 'I'm rich, vote for me and you too will be rich', providing evidence of the same attitude, that personalities were more significant than institutions.

Vaclav Havel had enormous moral authority which propelled him to the *Hrad* in a very short space of time. Once there, he added to his authority and built up his charisma by a series of initiatives, but also through his personal charm and abilities as a communicator, so that he was effectively above criticism. In Hungary, until the end of November 1989, popular aspirations were vested in Imre Pozsgay and it was only by a tiny margin of 6000 votes that, in effect, his candidacy for the presidency was torpedoed in a referendum. There then ensued a period where no personality dominated the political scene. But after the general elections, the population entrusted itself to the care of Jozsef Antall, the prime minister, who as a result has established an ascendancy over politics that goes well beyond his office. Indeed, political observers in Hungary are now concerned not that there is an overmighty president, one of the fears about Pozsgay's candidacy, but that there is an overmighty prime minister, whose removal is virtually impossible. The enormous vote amassed by Iliescu in Romania speaks for itself and so does Slobodan Milosevic's success in the December 1990 elections in Serbia. Milosevic, indeed, should be seen as the archetypal demagogue, who uses nationalist slogans and populist simplification to project himself. Arguably, Helmut Kohl played an analogous role in the former GDR.

The difficulty with investing persons with so much authority is that it tends to weaken the effective functioning of institutions, it allows individuals to be above criticism, to pursue personalised rather than popularly sanctioned policies and ultimately to ensure that representation is personal rather than grounded in the system. On the positive side, especially in the short term, however, charismatic or semi-charismatic figures can be useful as a way of channelling accumulated frustrations and uncertainties in immature political communities. The problem arises when these persons are called upon to leave the political scene. In general they are reluctant to do so and their successors will invariably be weaker, leaving a gap in the system.

CIVIL SOCIETY

The state of civil society is the most thorny and most problematical aspect of the post-communist condition. For the best part of a decade, this has been one of the more fashionable concepts in the context of Central and Eastern Europe; indeed, as a political rallying cry, the 'rebirth of civil society' was highly effective in bringing about the demise of communism. Its revival was antithetical to a system that required social atomisation as a necessary condition for survival and reproduction and did virtually everything in its power to prevent the types of social-political-economic interactions that could promote individual and group autonomy. Civil society, therefore, is to be seen as the articulation of its interests by society independently of the totalising state.

This has had a number of consequences, the most striking of which has been that, in a paradoxical way, the definition of civil society was easier and clearer as long as it could measure itself against totalising power, while the process became increasingly more complex, as is appropriate, once that power had disappeared. Thus self-definitions and the articulation of interests must undergo a painful process of identification and re-identification in societies which in some cases have no traditions of this or only weak traditions. In any case, very few people now have direct experience of the inter-war or immediate post-war period, when civil societies of a sort did exist. Besides, Central and East European societies have changed thoroughly over the last 40 years as a result of the Stalinist modernisation, and the pre-communist experience is hardly an effective guide to the contemporary period.

Nevertheless, in one vital respect, the pre-communist period must be examined. Despite everything claimed by communist propagandists and their Western supporters, the polities of Central and Eastern Europe were ruled by authoritarian and not by totalising legitimating ideologies. The old élites relied on a mixture of traditional and charismatic legitimation and they never sought to encompass all the spheres of social activity. Nor did they profess any overarching ideology, except nationalism, and nationalism left some space for social initiatives. This made it possible for a range of activities, like opposition newspapers, non-state education, nascent trade unions and opposition political parties to exist, albeit often under pressure from an expanding state.

The significance of all this for the communist period was that for at least sections of society, the totalising ideology and practices of the communist state were alien and worked against the grain of the cultural tradition. That tradition itself may have been destroyed and distorted, but the sense that the Soviet-type system was imposed and unassimilable prevented it from becoming rooted. Thus in this form, the cultural tradition existed as an off-stage set of alternative ideas to which reference could be made. This became even more important after the communist systems of the Central and Eastern Europe were exposed to the images and culture of the West, where – so it was thought – Central and Eastern Europe's own traditions were being continued with far greater success.

In this comparison, the role of Austria, Finland, Greece and eventually Spain were especially noteworthy, because these were in no way countries that had been a part of the developed West; on the contrary, they were seen as backward as the Central and Eastern European countries themselves had been before communism. The failure of the hyper-etatist state to fulfil its side of the bargain by creating a superior civilisation level undoubtedly contributed to a sense that society could and should organise itself.

During the communist period itself one can distinguish two different types of social-political expression that should be seen as the articulation of civil society. In the first place, there were the major upheavals causing and caused by moments of weakened party control – East Germany in 1953, Poland and Hungary in 1956, Czechoslovakia in 1968 and Poland in 1980–81 are the most obvious instances. The characteristic of all these expressions of social aspirations was that they were predicated on an assumption of homogeneity and that they were, to an extent, energised by nationalism.

The bulk of those who made up the working class were either directly first generation off the land or were not that far removed from peasant values, above all because they not been integrated into any alternative value system that emphasised complexity, interrelatedness and the counterproductive nature of simple solutions. In this sense, the myth of society acquired considerable strength as a source of resistance to the state; it is far from having been dispelled under post-communism.

Any scrutiny of the programmes of these upheavals will readily show that they were based on the assumption of a minimum of differentiation and complexity, that there were in reality only two actors, the 'evil' state and the 'good' society, this being the unavoidable consequence of taking action against a totalising power. There is more than a relic here of peasant value systems, with their suspicion of complexity and their corresponding approval of simplicity.

The other flexing of muscles of civil society in the communist period came with the various forms of pluralism that evolved particularly in the final period of Soviet-type decay, in the 1980s, when the state was still strong enough to prevent society from controlling and limiting political power and the totalising ideology, but it withdrew from certain areas, whereby society gained space for degrees of self-organisation.

Although the state probably intended this as a concession that could later be retracted, a concession exercised over a period of time gradually acquires the force of custom and comes to be perceived as a right by those concerned. This could and did start a process of rooting pluralisms in society, except unfortunately the maintenance of the totalising ideology and the exercise of arbitrary power had a negative impact on the security with which these 'customary rights' could be practised. The effect of this discretionary regime was to weaken the autonomous exercise of power by society and to create a mind-set that looked to short term solutions. Individuals developed a form of negative dependence on the state – even where positive dependence did not exist – whereby, even as they were involving themselves in the secondary economy or printing *samizdat* or going on pilgrimages, they were forever looking over their shoulders and calculating the political significance of what they were doing.

The halting emergence of pluralism can equally be seen as a quest for representation in whatever sphere the system permitted – legal, religious, economic, political, aesthetic, etc. Representations of one sphere through the medium of another, however, are bound to be imperfect and to distort both to some extent. Thus the fact that Roman Catholicism became one of the principal expressions of the aspirations of Polish society in the 1980s meant that both religion and the political aspirations expressed through it were given an awkward, intermediated expression. Neither the political nor the religious aims could be genuinely articulated. While the Roman Catholic church may have declared itself satisfied at achieving what appeared to be the 'recatholicisation' of Polish society, with a rise in adult baptisms, church attendance, vocations etc., it was the density of Roman Catholicism that was ultimately diluted, in as much as the Roman Catholic church was not and could not be a political institution.

The construction of an alternative cultural sphere under the aegis of the church may at first sight be less susceptible to analysis of this kind, except for the proposition that not everything that is in the aesthetic sphere can or should be politicised, not every expression of opposition to the system was necessarily political, though it was frequently so interpreted. The legacy of the Polish experience of the 1980s was somewhat ambiguous for the construction of liberal democracy, because the over-politicisation of a large part of the space available to Polish society meant that it could not be depoliticised once the totalising power disappeared.

In Hungary, the situation was a shade easier, though this was a matter of chance rather than policy. In the context of social autonomy, the Kadar regime stumbled on a very particular stabilising device, the secondary economy, which did in fact do something to encourage economic initiatives, albeit with the severe limitation that this activity could not extend beyond the framework of the family and that in order for individuals to maintain their standard of living, they would be obliged to exploit themselves.

This signified that in reality they were offered much less of a freedom of choice than appeared originally, in that Hungarians really had no option but to participate in a controlled secondary economy, the legal limits and tolerance of which were blurred. Nevertheless, the secondary economy has given a very considerable number of people the experience of operating under something resembling market conditions, making the idea of a market and economic independence less alien. The secondary economy also produced a stratum of entrepreneurs, who could, in fact, constitute a bourgeoisie if they were given the encouragement in the form of know-how, capital, and access to technology.

In Czechoslovakia, the carving out of any major social space was much more difficult, because the regime had renewed itself after 1968 through a variety of devices and was able to construct limited but authentic social bases for itself. It satisfied Slovak nationalism by retaining the federal structure, it exercised patronage over the half million jobs of those who were purged as supporters of the Prague spring to promote a generation of working class activists, it offered the population a range of economic concessions and it used the threat of Soviet invasion far more directly than elsewhere in the region. Consequently, the amount of space that could be established was smaller and reached out in different directions.

Space was opened then in the private sphere, in the possibility of individuals living relatively atomised lives untouched by the regime, to some extent through religion, through the use of state resources for private ends and the creation of an alternative culture, of which the activities of the Jazz Section were the best known example, but extended way beyond it.[6]

Civil society also received a major boost from the determination of an initially small group of intellectuals to launch themselves independently into the political sphere and to establish what became the democratic opposition. The impact of the democratic opposition varied substantially in all the countries of Central and Eastern Europe depending on local conditions. In Poland, it was successful in encouraging the birth of Solidarity and in helping to maintain a large section of Polish society in a state of politicised readiness throughout the 1980s. There was an explosion of *samizdat* and underground organisation and much of Polish society was touched by the political experience that resulted. This has left its mark on post-communist Poland and made it possible for the transfer of power to pass fairly smoothly from the communists to the post-communist order.

In Hungary, the democratic opposition was overwhelmingly concerned with the creation of an alternative public opinion in the intelligentsia; there was little attempt to mobilise the wider public, although towards the end there was some interaction between the democratic opposition and the secondary economy. The legacy of this was that the transfer of power was largely restricted to élite negotiations and the emergence of political cleavages that have their origins as much in the history of the opposition as in social realities and interests.

The Czechoslovak experience was different again, in that the democratic opposition was under severe pressure throughout its existence, it had limited contact with the bulk of the population, but its resolute stand earned it much moral capital. In consequence, it had no difficulty in placing itself at the head of the revolutionary movement and to take over from the communists at the end of 1989. The East German opposition was weakened throughout its existence by its insistence that it supported the 'socialist' character of the East German state and it was very slow in coming to the conclusion that the problems it was addressing derived from the nature of the system, which had to be rejected. The result was that when the Soviet-type system collapsed, the opposition was badly placed to assume any leadership and was effectively swept away.

THE ROLE OF INTELLECTUALS

A key role is being played and will be played in the construction of democracy by intellectuals.[7] In many ways, this was predictable given the traditionally important position that intellectuals and intellectual ideas have held in Central and Eastern Europe. When in 1955 Adam Wazyk, the communist poet, published his 'Poem for Adults', a bitter critique of Polish Stalinism, this was widely seen as a major attack on the system and contributed to the upheaval of 1956.[8] However, the full ramifications of a revolution in which intellectuals have been so salient as in the overthrow of communism requires particular attention.[9]

A key element in the end of communism was the loss of self-legitimation on the part of the ruling élite. In part, this came about because intellectuals withdrew what had until then been passive or tacit support to the system. The old élite was ill placed to defend itself against newly formulated critiques in which the intellectuals made an active commitment to Western democracy as the sole, acceptable political system. In Central Europe, in this case including Croatia and Slovenia, this model was generally applicable. In Bulgaria, the loss of élite self-legitimation was not so far-reaching, so that the shape and content of the Bulgarian political system remained unsettled. In Romania, intellectuals were essentially excluded from the transformation, which came about as a result of a party putsch veiled as a popular revolution. In Serbia, nationalist intellectuals were given free rein by the nationalist wing of the party.

Events since 1989 have helped clarify the relationship between intellectuals and society, though none of them are particularly encouraging. The events of June 1990 in Bucharest, when the Jiu valley miners were encouraged to 'restore order' in the Romanian capital, were the most extreme. Although some of the miners now claim that they were misled and tricked into beating up anyone who looked like an intellectual, this misses the point. The issue was that they could be 'misled', they could be easily mobilised and to come to regard anyone who dissents as a threat to democracy. In other words, from their point view, democracy is to be understood as a highly homogeneous concept with no room for alternative views – hardly a definition of democracy that will commend itself. The situation in Romania is, of course, particularly acute, because the intellectuals have no moral capital from having opposed the Ceausescu regime and are seen as parasites. Nor is the Iliescu regime concerned; it can dispense with intellectual legitimation for democracy, because it is not really interested in introducing a system that is, in fact, democratic.

In Poland, the massive vote against Mazowiecki in the first round of the presidential elections was clearly motivated by a kind of anti-intellectualism, an impatience with complex solutions and a particular style of governing that the bulk of the population disliked. The split in Solidarity into a populist and an intellectualist wing resulted in the defeat of the latter and the rise of a populist alternative, which is likely to have far-reaching consequences both for the style and the substance of Polish politics. Notably, Polish opinion was dismayed at the length of time that economic recovery was taking and incensed that many of the beneficiaries of the changes appeared to be members of the old élite through *nomenklatura* privatisation, ie., the establishment of private enterprises by members of the former communist élite, who had the best contacts, know-how and access to capital to achieve this.

The taxi drivers' blockade in Hungary, where taxi drivers protesting against a sudden 65 per cent increase in fuel prices were immediately backed by much of the population, likewise falls into this category, in that it represented a turning away from the issues raised by the government coalition and the opposition, which were abstract and intellectual rather than practical and empirical. Still, in the Hungarian case the outcome was nothing like as devastating, in that after three days' negotiations the two sides reached a compromise. However, it should certainly have served as a warning that the themes of the intellectual-dominated public discourse are of limited interest to the bulk of the population.

SOCIAL HOMOGENEITY

A particularly intractable problem with serious consequences for a wide range of issues is that of blocked social mobility and homogenisation –

resulting in a rigidly demarcated and largely immobile social system – imposed by communism on these societies. The argument is straight-forward and has been frequently put forward.[10] Soviet-type systems went through a single experience of large-scale upward mobility with the seizure of power and the resulting one-off promotion of a generation of individuals of working class and peasant backgrounds on the basis of political loyalty. This was parallelled by the demotion of the old élite; alternatively, the old élite was destroyed during the war and its place would in any case have been taken by persons promoted from a lower social status.

In all, this constituted the new class of political appointees and the new intelligentsia which filled positions in the new bureaucracies. However, upward mobility effectively ceased on a large scale with this one single act, with exceptions noted below, and thereafter there was an increasing trend towards the hereditary transmission of class status. The exceptions were connected with political change. Thus in Czechoslovakia in the 1970s, as noted above, a second promotion of low status individuals took place. In East Germany, the positions of the 3 million who left for the West likewise had to be filled which meant that to some extent social mobility in the GDR was never quite as clogged as it was elsewhere. In Poland, with every leadership change large numbers of individuals were newly promoted into the bureaucracy. But the phenomenon that was noteworthy about this last change was that many of those appointed were not so much from worker or peasant backgrounds but a younger generation of professionals.

The problem for Soviet-type systems was that upward mobility had become restricted to too few channels. Political loyalty was always a possibility, but comparatively few people could, in reality, take advantage of it in normal circumstances by joining the party. Further, the instruments of coercion provided another channel, though at a high cost in terms of social ostracism. Education, the most obvious channel, was blocked in another way. In the deal made with the 'new class' in the 1960s, the rulers accepted that the children of the intelligentsia could maintain their parents' status and tolerated the erosion of systems of preferential access for others through 'class points' at university admission. The classic channel of upward mobility through economic achievement simply did not exist, except towards the end of the system in Hungary and Yugoslavia, where the secondary economy offered individuals the economic freedom to give their children the extra coaching needed to pass university entrance requirements, but this was probably rare. Economic status – wealth – on its own was simply incompatible with the established norms of the system and the occasional campaigns equating entrepreneurs with corruption served to underline the ambiguity involved.

The outcome of all this was, for the most part, that the natural leaders of the working class were not creamed off, but remained workers, thereby giving rise to frustrated aspirations.[11] The difficulty in this connection is that the status of 'worker' is a contradictory one. On the one hand, workers were the nominal ruling class and this message was reinforced in a variety of symbolic ways; on the other, they were as far from power as possible, except in moments of party enfeeblement. Thus in a backhanded way, they were encouraged to think themselves as special, to see themselves as separate, even while the system continuously frustrated their aspirations. Only in Poland was a section of the working class able to maintain itself with some semblance of an organisation and a clear consciousness of being separate from the state in status and values as the result of their mobilisation through Solidarity.

A further complication here was the very type of working class created by communism.[12] Communism proved to be, inter alia, a method for building up a 19th century industry, with super-large enterprises using relatively straightforward technology. The ideal worker was always the male manual worker using simple technology as portrayed under Stalinism; this did not change symbolically in any major way later.[13] In this sense, the working class that emerged from communism was relatively homogenised, confused and economically increasingly threatened by the collapse of these economies. It disliked differentiation, whether in material or in status terms and was characterised by a kind of negative egalitarianism. Equally, it was, with some exceptions, strongly anti-intellectual, impatient with the complex solutions offered by the new governments and politically inexperienced, making it vulnerable to demagogic manipulation.[14]

A particularly difficult problem has arisen in connection with the antagonism exhibited by the Soviet-type system to social integration. With the elimination of mobility, the satisfaction of individual and group aspirations and the acquisition of other, wider value systems were blocked too. There was nowhere for talented individuals in the working class to go, but to remain within the class. The potential result, which became actual in Poland, was that the working class acquired a dynamism, an internal coherence, a set of values and a strong identity which either set apart from other social groups or it would seek to integrate the rest of society into itself.

Various kinds of integration can be conceptualised. Integration into the intelligentsia, the one reference group which the communist system did permit, was too difficult and was in any case impeded, as argued, by the narrowing of educational opportunity. Under post-communism, if integration into a democratic system of values were to prove unsuccessful, only nationhood could offer the wider set of goals that could provide the intellectual instruments for the working class to construct the culture by which it could encompass politics and economics, except that nationhood is ultimately incapable of providing this because this is not its function.

Again, it was absence of economic integration that explained this gulf between intellectuals and workers and, when the former sought to establish democratic systems, political communication became notably difficult. The failed relationship between the Mazowiecki government, the nearest to a government of philosopher-kings that Europe has witnessed since the war, and the highly politicised consciousness of Polish workers is a clear illustration of this problem. The near impossibility of Poland's existing entrepreneurs performing this integrative function is shown by the bitter hostility towards the emergence of a bourgeoisie based on the *nomenklatura*. Despite evidence that the *nomenklatura* and those who previously constituted the state-dependent private sector are virtually alone in having the know-how, the technology and the capital to launch a private enterprise based economy, for many Poles this is quite unacceptable. Members of the former ruling élite cannot become the new ruling élite, exchanging political for economic power, which in turn would again give rise to political power or at least influence. Yet the extraordinary vote for Tyminski in the presidential elections suggests that there is no hostility to wealth as such. The contradiction here implies that there is a good deal of confusion in much of Polish opinion. The confusion seems to be made up of wish-fulfilment, impatience, intolerance and strong unwillingness to accept that the reconstruction of Poland will involve years of complex effort as a result of which there will be major winners and losers.

An added complication in this connection is the existence of relatively large youthful age cohorts in Poland, for which Solidarity and martial law were the dominant, constitutive experiences and from which they drew a set of values deeply antagonistic to existing institutions. These cohorts have been large enough to attain a critical mass in the generation of values, to reject socialisation into official value systems and it will be difficult to integrate them into alternative ways of viewing the world.

One observer, writing of the Czech working class, has described it as being egalitarian in the sense that it accepts meritocratic achievement only verbally and regards too great a social difference as amoral; that it believes all work as having the same value but actually arrogates a higher status to manual labour than to intellectual; that it is anti-intellectual and anti-elitist; that it overestimates the value of manual labour; that it attaches a high value to welfarism and social security; that it believes in the *etatistic* provider state; that social life is almost exclusively determined by economic rather than cultural considerations; and that it prefers economic rights to civil rights.[15] Analogous currents may be found elsewhere in the post-communist world, notably Romania.

In Hungary, it could be that this problem of a self-contained working class, resistant to integration, is not so acute. If so, then this must be ascribed in the first place to the secondary economy that evolved during the Kadar years and which offered some experience of the market to the great majority of the population. This helped to re-establish social hierarchies that society felt could be scaled and to provide a degree of openness of opportunity that is missing elsewhere in Central and Eastern Europe.

It is evident from the foregoing that integration into a single, more or less cohesive political community is best achieved around economics, the satisfaction of material aspirations, and upward mobility. This, in turn, demands opportunities for money making and an acceptance of a social status to accompany economic success. Only economic integration can satisfy the aspirations of the bulk of society and these have irreversibly accepted Western levels of consumption as desirable. Alternatives, like integration via political, ideological, or cultural aspirations will simply not work.

From this perspective, despite the underlying hostility of the intellectuals to the nascent bourgeoisie, it is in their eventual interest to ensure that an entrepreneurial class does come into being in order to effect the necessary integration. Failure to achieve this could result in a scenario in which rather negative introverted working class ideologies dominate politics and these will be maximally anti-intellectual, given that intellectuals threaten the homogenised, simplistic construction of reality by which these working classes understand the world around them. Thus only a polity with a strong bourgeoisie can provide the economic and political space within which intellectuals can exercise their critical function.

Besides, there is the problem of technological change. In the West, the kind of manual working class that is emerging in the post-communist world has been disappearing as a result of the technological revolution. The transformation of Western social and economic patterns needed was far from easy, but it was made possible by the implicit promise that the shedding of outdated manual skills would be rewarded by material gains on the part of the working class. A defensive, protectionist, and internally cohesive working class will not be willing to make this adjustment readily, posing the danger of major Luddite resistance. To this working class base, there would undoubtedly follow support from a section of intellectuals who would create an ideology to legitimate it. The consequence could be that the technological gap between Western Europe on the one hand and Central and Eastern Europe on the other would widen continuously.

The experience of the West is clear that economic integration, whatever its shortcomings, is the most effective motor of social stability, because it has proved to be surprisingly even-handed in offering life chances from which the majority, though not everyone, can benefit. If the post-communist countries fail to establish channels of economic integration, they may well be faced with class politics that will severely weaken their democratic prospects.

CONCLUSION

The tasks of creating democracy out of communism are daunting. In this complex of difficulties, there is one further problem that demands a brief mention. The current approach by post-communist governments is a rather *etatist* one. The idea that the state can construct a modern society and political community, however, is fraught with dangers. After all, this was the project attempted in the nineteenth and twentieth centuries before communism. On the whole, the record of the state in calling civil society into existence is not a good one, for in order to achieve this, the state would have to accept degrees of self-limitation that seem implausible. The state seldom likes to limit its power; on the contrary the record of the modern state has been in the opposite direction. Yet without clear and intensifying self-limitation that extends to all spheres, the chances of establishing stable democracies are slim.

NOTES

1. Elemer Hankiss, *East European Alternatives*, Oxford, 1990.
2. Ralf Dahrendorf, *Reflections on the Revolution in Europe*, London, 1990.
3. I have analysed this problem in greater detail in my article 'Why communism collapsed: the end of communism in Eastern Europe', *International Affairs*, No. 1, 1990, pp. 3–16.
4. See the argument in Jadwiga Staniszkis, 'Forms of Reasoning as Ideology', *Telos*, No. 66, 1985–86, pp. 67–80.
5. Trond Gilberg, *Nationalism and Communism in Romania: the Rise and Fall of Ceausescu's Personal Dictatorship*, Boulder, CO, 1990.
6. H. Gordon Skilling, *Samizdat and an Independent Society in Central and Eastern Europe*, London, 1990, provides an account.

7.   Aleksander Gella, *Development of Class Structure in Eastern Europe: Poland and her Southern Neighbours*, Albany: New York, 1989.

8.   Flora Lewis, *The Polish Volcano: A Case-History of Hope*, London, 1959.

9.   I have explored some of these themes in greater detail in 'The Chances of Democracy in Central and Eastern Europe', in Peter Voltened (ed.), *Uncertain Futures: Eastern Europe and Democracy*, New York, 1990, pp. 19–34.

10. Walter D. Connor, *Socialism, Politics and Equality: Hierarchy and Change in Eastern Europe and the USSR*, New York, 1979.

11. Bill Lomax, 'The Rise and Fall of the Hungarian Working Class', in C. M. Hanned (ed.), *Market Economy and Civil Society in Hungary*, London, 1990, pp. 45–60.

12. Jacques Rupnik, 'The Roots of Czech Stalinism', in Raphael Samuel and Gareth Stedman Jones (eds), *Culture, Ideology and Politics*, London, 1982, pp. 302–19. Rupnik argues that the characteristics of the Czech working class were reinforced by the Soviet-type system.

13. Gombar Csaba, *A politika parttalan vilaga*, Budapest, 1986.

14. Miroslav Petrusek, 'A posztkommunizmus mint szociopolitikai fogalom es problema', in Vaclav Belohradsky, Peter Kende and Jacques Rupnik eds., *Politikai kultura es allam Magyarorszagon es Cseh-Szlovakiaban*, Turin, 1991, pp. 87–105, discusses the Czech case.

15. *Ibid.*

Index